Carved in Stone

The History of Stone Mountain

by

David B. Freeman

Mercer University Press
Macon, Georgia

ISBN 0-86554-547-2 MUP/H418

The paper used in this publication meets the minimum requirements of American National Standard for Information Sciences—Permanence of Paper for Printed Library Materials, ANSI Z39.48-1984.

Library of Congress Cataloging-in-Publication Data

Freeman, David B., 1968-
Carved in Stone: The History of Stone Mountain / by David B. Freeman
x + 200 + 50 (photographs) pp. 6 x 9" (15 x 22 cm.)
Includes bibliographical references and index.
ISBN 0-86554-547-2 (alk. paper)
1. Stone Mountain Memorial (Ga.) --History. 2. Stone Mountain Memorial State Park (Ga.) --History. I. Title.
F292.S85F74 1997
975.8'225--dc21 97-14201
CIP

Contents

Illustrations and Photographs

Illustrations

Photographs

(Section 2 appears after page 156.)

Photographs are by courtesy of the Stone Mountain Collections, Special Collections, Robert W. Woodruff Library, Emory University; the Stone Mountain Memorial Association; Elias D. Nour; and George D. N. Coletti, DMD.

Preface

Stone Mountain has been for generations an object of great pride and interest to the residents of DeKalb County, Georgia. There has been, however, a surprising lack of credible, scholarly research on the subject. This present volume is an effort to fill that void and provide a reliable account of human activity at the mountain. I did not set out to write a book on Stone Mountain, but like many others I became intrigued by the complexity of events surrounding the carving of the Confederate Memorial. Once committed, I undertook to separate the truth from fiction and sort out contradictory accounts of the mountain's history. I believe I have managed to set the record straight.

This book has been written for the ordinary, intelligent reader who may not know much about Stone Mountain, but would like to learn. Those who are already familiar with the mountain's story will also benefit from the quantity of new information that I have brought to light. There have undoubtedly been some omissions of events, but in time I hope this will be rectified.

I gratefully received assistance from numerous people during the preparation of this book. The staffs of the DeKalb Historical Society, the Atlanta History Center, the Robert W. Woodruff Library at Emory University in Atlanta, and the Gilbert Library at the Georgia Institute of Technology were most helpful in my research. It has also been necessary to impose upon many individuals for specialized knowledge. The gracious hospitality with which my questions were endured was one of the most rewarding aspects of this undertaking. I would like to extend my thanks to John Worth of the Fernbank Museum of Natural History for sharing some of his research on Spanish explorations of Georgia, to Roy Faulkner for his valuable input on the memorial carving, and to Stone Mountain residents George Coletti, Hugh Jordan, Leon New, and Mary Payne for sharing their memories of the mountain.

Of course, no work on the mountain would be complete without the courteous assistance of the staff at Stone Mountain Park who made their records available, answered endless questions, and accommodated my every need. I would particularly like to thank Jerry Deagan for his encouragement to follow through with this project.

David B. Freeman
Tucker, Georgia

Stone Mountain: An Introduction

Often referred to as The Eighth Wonder of the World, Stone Mountain is the largest exposed mass of granite in the world. Located in eastern DeKalb County, sixteen miles east of Atlanta, Georgia, this phenomenon of nature rises to an elevation of 1,683 feet. Like some giant, grey humpbacked whale surfacing from a sea of green foliage, Stone Mountain dominates the landscape. The nearest neighboring mountain is more than thirty miles away. The west side of the mountain rises gradually from ground level and affords the only ready access to the summit. Up this side runs a footpath, nine-tenths of a mile in length, that has been worn into the surface of the mountain from the passage of men and beasts over the course of centuries.

Along the southern and eastern flanks the slope is steeper, particularly higher up along the sides. The north face is a perpendicular cliff rising to the height of a fifty-story building before curving steeply to the summit. Here, far above the ground, ride the gigantic carved figures of the three Confederate heroes.

The mostly bald domed surface is littered with large boulders and islands of stunted trees, shrubs and flowers growing in isolated spots where soil has collected in cracks and between rocks. Some of these plants are so rare that they grow nowhere else. One grove of stunted cedars positioned prominently high on the northeastern slope is called Buzzard's Roost. Some of the trees, although only a foot in diameter, are estimated to be 800 years old. The steel grey color of the weathered granite is streaked by the growth of mosses and lichens where rainwater cascades down from the top.

This awe-inspiring monadnock, or an isolated mountain, is approximately 8,300 feet in length along its east-west axis, and 3,500 feet wide at its maximum width. The circumference at the base is roughly 3.8 miles, enclosing an area of approximately 560 acres. It rises 780 feet above the surrounding terrain, providing the visitor with a commanding 360 degree view of the countryside for a distance of some thirty miles. There are a few other granite formations similar to Stone Mountain a few miles south of the big rock, but these outcroppings are much smaller.

Stone Mountain was once the site of extensive quarrying activity, and engineers have estimated the volume of exposed granite at 7,543,570,950 cubic feet. At 168 pounds per cubic foot, the weight of the mountain above ground level is more than 633 million tons. If the mountain were cut up, the stone would fill 12,660,000 standard size railroad gondolas, which coupled together would make a train long enough to circle the earth nearly three times around the equator. These estimates include only the granite that is visible; no one knows for sure how much more lies below ground.

The conspicuousness of Stone Mountain in both its appearance and its isolation has made it an important landmark for centuries. It has been a gathering place for Native Americans, a signpost in the wilderness for early settlers, and is today as prominent in the consciousness of area residents as it is on the skyline. Over the years, the mountain has been utilized in many ways by the inhabitants of the land. Centuries ago the summit served as a place of ceremony for the pre-Columbian tribes nearby. More recently, it has been exploited as a tourist attraction and for its very content as building material. For nearly two hundred years it has been the economic mainstay of its surrounding community. It has also been a place of leisure for nature lovers, an inspiration for poets and dreamers, and a trysting place for lovers captivated by the mountain's moonlit beauty.

The mountain also has a sinister side. It has been the bane of untold numbers of climbers beguiled by its deceptive and treacherous slopes. Some of these deaths have not been accidental. The 700-foot drop of the north face has attracted its share of suicides. Stone Mountain also has a way, as if bearing some ancient curse, of creating discord among those who attempt to capitalize on it. Without question, the greatest area of controversy has been the creation of the Confederate memorial and building of a 3,200 acre state park. This project, which took more than fifty years to complete, although long since an accomplished fact, still stirs considerable debate.

The creation of this Confederate memorial, the world's largest work of sculpted art, brought the mountain to the notice of the nation and the world. In 1915 the United Daughters of the Confederacy leased the land and commissioned Gutzon Borglum, later the sculptor of Mount Rushmore, to carve the Lost Cause memorial on the mountain where the Ku Klux Klan had been resurrected by William J. Simmons. Proceeding intermittently over six decades, the project was once again revived during the South's massive resistance to racial integration. In 1958, capitalizing on this impulse, Georgia legislature funded the completion of the project for use as a tourist attraction. Opening in 1970 as a theme park, Stone Mountain now draws some five million visitors a year, exceeded only by the Disney theme parks in Orlando, Florida.

The story of the mountain's continuing relationship with its human neighbors is a long and interesting one. The more recent effort to carve the monument is a saga that spans two generations. But out of it emerged an object that is doubly unique--both a natural and a man-made wonder. What happens next in this story only time will tell.

Chapter One

Native American Domain

The origins of Stone Mountain are believed to date back some 200 million years. It almost certainly was formed by volcanic action, created by an underground vent of magma that bubbled up, but did not break through the surface. Over the eons, as the molten mass cooled, the softer surrounding rock and soil wore away to expose the hardened granite dome. This process continues today, with an inch or two of the mountain being newly uncovered with each passing millennium.

The mountain has a sheet structure similar to that of an onion. The thickness of the sheets ranges from one inch to twelve or more feet, with the upper layers being thinnest and growing thicker further down until they finally die out. The joints between the layers can be readily seen in the abandoned quarries on the southern and eastern slopes where they have been exposed to a depth of forty feet.

Over time the forces of nature have left minor marks on the mountain. These are limited to shallow weather pits carved by rain and wind, and saucer-size dimples blasted by lightning bolts that have created a cratered appearance on the summit similar to that on the moon. The mountain has actually changed more in the past 150 years than in all of its prior existence, due primarily to the arrival of human beings and their industrial age.

For example, on top of the mountain at one time stood what must have been one of the most unusual geological formations in the world. A tremendous flat oval-shaped boulder roughly two hundred feet in diameter and between five and ten feet thick contained two fissures, one oriented north/south and the other east/west, which crossed in the center at right angles. These fissures began at the edges of the boulder as mere cracks, expanding to four feet wide and five feet deep at their intersection. Over this juncture was another flat boulder about twenty feet in diameter. This marvelous natural compass was called the Devil's Crossroads and was a favorite place for picnickers. Unfortunately, it was cut up and carried away by quarrymen in 1896 for its high quality stone.

Between 8,000 and 10,000 years ago human beings were first attracted to the vicinity of Stone Mountain by the abundance of game and ample water supplies.[1] Archaeological investigations have turned up tantalizing evidence of ancient human habitation, principally by a group of nomadic peoples known to archaeologists as Paleo-Indians. Among the artifacts found near the mountain are soapstone bowls, which predate the development of pottery. The Paleo-Indians made bowls, pots, ceremonial pipes, and other utensils out of stone. Soapstone was favored because it retains heat well for cooking and warming, and it has a high talc content, which makes it soft and easy to carve. The talc also gives it a "soapy" feel, hence the name.

Soapstone Ridge, a 25-square-mile area in southwest DeKalb County, was the site of several Paleo-Indian stone quarries between 4000 BCE and 1000 BCE. Native Americans used cutting tools made from hard rock, like basalt, to carve out chunks of soapstone and then shape it and hollow it out. Although they began to replace soapstone bowls with pottery by the beginning of the Woodland Period (1000 BCE), they continued to use soapstone for the manufacture of pipes, ornaments and ceremonial objects.

These early Paleo-Indians did not live near the mountain year-round; their hunter-gatherer lifestyle prevented them from staying in one place too long. As these people developed a knowledge of agriculture they were able to settle down and establish more permanent villages. Scores of prehistoric Indian sites have been found in the flood plains of DeKalb County's rivers and creeks.

During construction of the dam at Stone Mountain Park in 1962, Roy S. Dickens, of Georgia State University, conducted an archaeological excavation of a Native American site on Stone Mountain Creek that would be covered by water when the lake filled. He wrote that the two-acre site showed habitation during the Woodstock phase of the Mississippian period, a time of small, stable villages associated with agricultural pursuits. Later, as villages increased in size and populations became concentrated along the larger river systems, the Stone Mountain site was virtually abandoned. Dickens also found numerous smaller sites of the Archaic (8000-1000 BCE) and Woodland (1000 BC-900 CE) periods. Located on hilltops, these campsites were only large enough to have been occupied by hunting parties.

---

[1]Charles Hudson, *The Southeastern Indians* (Knoxville: University of Tennessee Press, 1976), 44.

Much more could have been learned from this site, but most of it was destroyed by bulldozers before excavation could begin.

In June 1822 the Rev. Francis R. Goulding happened upon what native peoples had long since noticed--a wall of loose rocks that circled the top of the mountain. This wall represented a significant relic from prehistoric days. Twelve years old at the time of the expedition, Goulding traveled with his father, a merchant from Darien, Georgia, their slave boy Scipio, and a Cherokee guide named Kaneeka. Writing many years later, Goulding described the wall as

> about breast high, built of loose, fragmentary stone, and evidently meant for a military fortification . . . the only place of entrance was by a natural doorway under a large rock, so narrow and so low that only one man could enter at a time, by crawling on his hands and knees.[2]

The Gouldings questioned their guide as to the origins of the wall, but Kaneeka could only tell them that the wall was there when his people first came to the area and that they knew no more of it than did the white men.

Like Goulding, many early visitors to the mountain speculated that the wall was meant to be a rude fortress of some sort. William C. Richards published a theory in 1842 in his book *Georgia Illustrated* that the wall may have been constructed by Hernando de Soto's expedition in 1549 for protection against the Indians. This supposition is implausible for several reasons, but many people accepted it nonetheless. Nineteenth century bias would not allow most people to consider that primitive Indians could be responsible for such a remarkable feat. Serious archeological study over the years has shown that the native peoples were indeed builders of the Stone Mountain wall and others like it. Fort Mountain, near Chatsworth, and Lookout Mountain, near Mentone, are two other sites in Georgia with similar walls.

Most experts believe that such wall enclosures were built during the Middle Woodland period (100 BCE-500 CE) when agriculture and food storage methods were well established. This enabled people to live a more settled existence and to devote their energies to large-scale building projects which perhaps would have taken generations to complete. No one

---

[2]Rev. Francis R. Goulding, *Sal-O-Quah; or Boy-Life Among the Cherokees* (New York: Dodd, Mead and Co., 1870), 123.

really knows for certain the purpose these sites served, but early speculation held that these sites were defensive structures. This now seems highly unlikely, since the time and labor necessary to construct such walls would suggest that their builders were not under threat of imminent attack. Also their location high atop peaks far removed from food and water resources would have been militarily untenable.

Evidence gathered to date supports the view that these enclosures were used for religious or ceremonial purposes, with the wall marking the boundary of a sacred area. The scarcity of artifacts within the area indicates very light usage, perhaps only once a year. The entrance that must be negotiated on hands and knees may have enforced a ritual act of supplication and humility or have been symbolic of the womb.

The exact uses of these ancient ceremonial rings and the beliefs associated with them remain a matter of speculation. Unfortunately, the full story of the enclosure at Stone Mountain will probably never be fully known. The wall continued to deteriorate during the 1800s as visitors took great delight in rolling the rocks down the sides of the mountain. The remains of the wall were completely destroyed in 1916 when Gutzon Borglum, the first designer of the Confederate memorial, had the last stones cast down to ensure that some mischievous vandal did not hurl them down on top of his workers.

The Woodland phase of Indian existence ended around 900 CE when the Mississippian culture invaded Georgia from the northwest. This may have been a literal invasion of new people coming in and absorbing the old ones, or merely the transfer of ideas from one group to another through trade or other such contacts. In any case, the Indian culture of the Georgia area underwent considerable change in a fairly short period of time.

At the height of their achievement, the Mississippian peoples were noted for their large, palisaded villages situated on river flood plains, extensive agricultural activity, construction of large earthen mounds for temple platforms, and for their relatively complex social/political structure. In Mississippian society, great chiefs held almost absolute power over wide areas. These chiefdoms were composed of several small villages subordinate to one of a number of larger villages that owed allegiance to the principal town of the chiefdom, often having a population of several thousand people. Etowah and Ocmulgee were the seats of power of two well-known chiefdoms in Georgia. The majority of these people were Muskogean speakers and ancestors of the later Creek Indians.

The widespread Mississippian culture naturally spawned a number of regional variations. In Georgia and parts of Tennessee, the Carolinas, and Alabama, the "Lamar" phase began around 1350. Lamar is the name applied to later southern Mississippian cultures that produced a certain type of pottery and these cultures were the first with which European explorers came into contact.

Ponce de Leon initiated the first Spanish exploration of the southeastern coast in 1513, and eight more expeditions followed over the next two decades. Hernando de Soto mounted his famous expedition in 1539 and for four years wandered all over the southeast without ever passing close to Stone Mountain. At some point historians mistakenly began to view Captain Juan Pardo as the first European to gaze upon Stone Mountain, basing their conclusion on misinterpretation of the documents regarding Pardo's 1567 travels.

Pardo was sent into the interior with 125 soldiers by the Governor of the Santa Elena colony (near present-day Charleston, SC) to ease the colony's food shortage. The ostensible reason for the expedition was to bring the Indians under the dominion of Spain and to find a route to the Spanish silver mines in Mexico. Governor Pedro Menendez de Avilés probably knew that this was an impossible task, and it is not surprising that Pardo failed. Pardo did write, however, of finding crystal mines at "Los Diamantes," a veritable mountain of diamonds located on a plain. The fame of Los Diamantes spread throughout Spanish Florida and even to Spain as members of Pardo's force repeated tales of a "crystal mountain, bare of trees, consisting entirely of diamonds." It was said to "shine so brightly during the day that one could not look at it, and so had to approach at night."[3]

This fanciful description of Los Diamantes led some to assume that the Spaniards were referring to Stone Mountain. This is just wishful thinking, for Pardo's force never came within two hundred miles of the great monadnock. Most archaeologists today believe that Los Diamantes is actually Carpenter's Knob in western North Carolina, and the "purple diamonds" collected by the Spaniards were probably corundum, a gem that is found there and is next in hardness to diamond. Despite his efforts to raise another expedition, Pardo never returned to his mountain of diamonds, as apparently most people did not believe the wildly exaggerated tales.

---

[3]Ibid., 189-193.

It currently appears that the Spanish *entrada*, or the expedition opening the way into the interior, that came closest to Stone Mountain was led by Franciscan missionary Pedro de Chozas. This small party, consisting of two friars, thirty Christianized Indians, and a soldier, penetrated the interior in 1597. The group stayed for a few days in the province of Tama (the Indian chiefdoms were called provinces by the Spanish) before moving on to the province of Ocute. Here they were warned to turn back or they would be killed by the Indians in the next province. While the party advanced no further than Ocute, Gaspar de Salas, the lone soldier of the expedition, made note of another region even deeper into the interior. The Indians described to Salas a mountain "very high, shining when the sun set like a fire" that was four days travel from Ocute. This could possibly be a reference to Stone Mountain.

The exact location of Ocute is not certain, but it is believed to have been near the confluence of the Oconee and Little Rivers, perhaps in the vicinity of present-day Eatonton, Georgia. The sixty-mile distance to Stone Mountain could easily have been covered in four days. Even though many details of the early contact period remain uncertain, it is clear that no Spanish explorers came within sight of Stone Mountain. The first Europeans to see the mountain were probably English traders and slave raiders who came into the area in the late seventeenth century.

Spanish settlements were military garrisons requiring thorough documentation. Expeditions were generally large and generated an equally large quantity of records. Even small expeditions left a paper trail. Individual traders seeking to enter the interior, and there were few among the Spanish, needed permission for the colonial governor and were required to pay taxes on their profits. Any attempts to evade official channels would have eventually come to the attention of the governor through reports from the Indians. The Spaniards' meticulous record-keeping render the routes of these expeditions fairly well known, making an unknown or unrecorded entrada very unlikely. The English colonies, on the other hand, were civilian rather than military, and entry into the interior was far less regulated and poorly documented. It is much more likely that intrepid English explorers were the first Europeans to lay eyes on Stone Mountain.

The Spanish entradas of the sixteenth century had a devastating effect on the Mississippian chiefdoms of Georgia. Explorers unwittingly spread diseases that took a heavy toll on the native inhabitants who had no resistance to the foreign viruses. When de Soto made his extensive expedition, he found several villages that had suffered recent epidemics with losses of hundreds of lives. Later explorers revisited some of these chiefdoms and noted a continual decline in population. When an epidemic struck, some of the inhabitants fled to other villages and carried the disease with them. As the population dwindled, many villages consolidated until, in some extreme cases, only remnants of the principal towns remained. Several waves of epidemics during the 1500s appear to have reduced the native population by as much as ninety percent.[4]

This rapid depopulation essentially destroyed the Lamar culture at its height. As the leaders at the top of the hierarchy fell to disease, the operations of government were hindered, causing the chiefdoms to break down into smaller, less centralized units. The loss of labor force brought mound building to a halt and the interruption of agriculture produced widespread famine. The deaths of village elders and specialized craftsmen resulted in a general loss of skills and ancestral traditions. Whole sections of the state were deserted as the survivors abandoned their former homes to reorganize themselves into new social entities. These migrations are probably responsible for the occurrence of Lamar pottery found at Stone Mountain. There is no evidence of a permanent Lamar settlement, but different bands may have temporarily settled there to flee an epidemic before moving on to merge with another group.

Europeans made little direct contact with the interior tribes during the 1600s as Spain had largely given up on large-scale colonization and, aside from isolated traders, the English did not enter the area until the founding of Charles Town in 1670. With the establishment of southern English colonies, the Indian slave trade intensified and thousands of Southeastern Indians were captured and taken as slaves to the northern English colonies and to Caribbean plantations. French exploration and settlement up the Mississippi River and Spanish missions along the coast surrounded the Indians with an ever-tightening circle of European influence.

Added to this in the northern colonies were the Iroquois Wars, which were basically a series of conflicts in the late seventeenth century between the French and English, fought by proxy through the Indians. The Iroquois and their allies were backed by the English and fought the Hurons and their allies, who were supported by the French. The Iroquois eventually prevailed, overrunning and pushing out many of the neighboring tribes.

---

[4]Marvin T. Smith, *Archaeology of Aboriginal Culture Change in the Interior Southeast* (Gainesville: University of Florida Press, 1987), 58.

Some of these displaced tribes, armed with French-made guns, migrated south and came into conflict with the established tribes who suffered a distinct disadvantage because they had no firearms.[5]

In response to these external pressures, many of the indigenous tribes, remnants of once-great chiefdoms, began making alliances with one another for mutual protection against the Europeans. This process is thought to have begun shortly before 1700 and eventually became known as the Creek Confederation. The Confederation grew to include thirty-seven tribes in Georgia and Alabama, most of whom called themselves Muskogees after the name of their linguistic family.[6]

In place of the great chiefs commanding the allegiance of numerous towns and villages, the towns of the Creeks were autonomous units. A council of elders chose a leader called a "mico" to serve as spokesmen for the town. The powers of the mico were largely persuasive rather than coercive, and a mico's actual authority varied with his ability. He received visitors and represented his town in negotiations with other towns or the Muskogee National Council, always consulting with his town council before making important decisions. The mico could be put out of office if the town's affairs went badly.

The old Cherokee chiefdoms, like the others, suffered greatly as a result of Spanish incursions. Cherokee society of the 1500s is known today as Qualla, another subculture of Mississippian, and was concentrated in the Tennessee/North Carolina area. According to Roy Dickens's studies, since the Qualla Cherokee chiefdoms were less hierarchically organized than the Lamar Muskogees, their social order may not have collapsed as completely as the others. Archaeologists have shown that there was a general migration of the Cherokee settlements toward the southwest into northern Georgia and an abandonment of the northern tier of Cherokee settlements. This was probably part of some social reorganization as the result of epidemics. Linguistic analysis of historic period place names shows that

---

[5]Spanish trade policy at this time forbade selling guns to the Indians. This changed later in the eighteenth century.

[6]In recent years the appropriate nomenclature for Native American, or Indian, peoples has become a matter of sometimes intense debate. Though perhaps the most common name used by Euro-Americans, the designation "Creek" was never used by these peoples themselves. Most of the peoples called Creek spoke Muskogean dialects and normally employed the term "Muskogee" for themselves. In light of the different terms among Euro- and Native Americans, I will use them both interchangeably. See Joel W. Martin, *Sacred Revolt: The Muskogees' Struggle for a New World* (Boston: Beacon Press, 1991), 6-13.

numerous southern Cherokee settlements had Muskogean-derived names, indicating that before European contact north Georgia had been occupied by Muskogee chiefdoms.[7]

The Cherokees of the 1700s reflected less political organization than the Muskogees. They had fifty to sixty towns scattered throughout four separate regions, which were based on linguistic differences. Each town remained largely independent and generally acted in its own interests with little regard for the others, even if it was detrimental to the whole. The towns rarely acted in concert, unless some crisis forced them to do so. The independent nature of the Cherokee towns made it easy for the English colonists to play one against another for their own advantage. The Cherokees did not become politically united until the turn of the nineteenth century when they founded a state organization to resist removal from their lands.

Between the Creeks and the Cherokees lay a large buffer area in which no one lived. These zones were a tradition extending back to the time of the Mississippian chiefdoms. To the Indians, anyone not of their tribe was a competitor, and therefore an enemy. The buffer zones were one way of dealing with the competition between tribes for hunting territory, agricultural land, wild food resources, and raw materials. Areas closest to the settlement were safest for planting, hunting, and other activities. The farther one went into the zone the greater the danger of attack from an opposing village. Such skirmishes probably occurred infrequently as most people would avoid straying too far from their own territory unless their business was important.

The Creeks and the Cherokees often clashed with each other and with other tribes around them. War was important to the social structure because status was connected to bravery in battle. War parties were frequent, but deaths were few. Two or three casualties would be sufficient to induce a retreat. Most of the skirmishes occurred in the buffer zone between competing hunting parties from different tribes or in occasional retaliatory raid on the other's home territory. Like medieval tournaments in Europe, warfare among the Indians was a contest--a game, by which honor was attained. Much of the bad blood that did exist between the tribes often resulted from their manipulation by the different colonial powers.

---

[7]Hudson, *Pardo Expeditions*, 105.

Times of conflict intermingled with periods of peace and cooperation between the tribes. In one instance the Creeks offered to form an alliance with the Cherokees against the colonists. Even though the latter could not come to an agreement among themselves on the matter (that independent nature again), the episode does show a willingness to put aside differences. In another case, during the American Revolution frontiersmen pursued a war against the Cherokees, causing many of them to take refuge in Creek villages. Obviously, the concepts of "enemy" and "friend" were subject to change and tribal hatreds did not run very deep.

The subject of buffer zones and warfare becomes relevant to Stone Mountain when one realizes that the mountain is located in the middle of what was once a buffer area between the Creeks and Cherokees. It is possible that rival war parties clashed in the shadow of the mountain.

Just as the mountain was important to the Woodland Indians as a ceremonial or religious site, so it was important to the modern Indians as a meeting place. Its prominence on the horizon and its location at the junction of two major trails in neutral territory made it a natural place for parties to gather. One of these trails was the Ita-wa Trail, which ran northward to settlements on the Etowah River and southward toward Augusta. Recognized as the eastern boundary between the Creeks and Cherokees, the name of the trail was eventually corrupted to "Hightower" by white traders. The present-day border between DeKalb and Gwinnett Counties follows this trail. Intersecting the Hightower Trail was the Echota Trail, more commonly known as the Sandtown Trail, which ran westward along a low ridge to the village of Sandtown on the Chattahoochee River. Sandtown was located about ten miles west of what later became Atlanta and was one of the principal Indian villages in the area. The tracks of the Georgia Railroad roughly parallel the old Sandtown Trail.[8]

After the founding of the Georgia colony in 1733, the number of English traders and explorers visiting the interior increased greatly. They usually followed the Indian trails and would certainly have passed within sight of the gleaming granite mountain. If, however, anyone ever recorded their impressions of it, the account has not survived. The earliest known description of the mountain was written by a British officer and published

---

[8]Carl T. Hudgins, "DeKalb County Indian Trails," *Collections of the DeKalb Historical Society*, 1952, 8-12.

in London in 1788.[9] The officer's name, unfortunately, was not given, so his identity may never be known for certain. Most likely he saw the mountain around 1777, during the American Revolution, when the British attempted to incite the Creek Indians against the rebellious colonists.[10]

Stone Mountain's first role in modern history came on 9 June 1790, when President Washington sent Colonel Marinus Willett to confer with the micos of the Creek Confederacy regarding a treaty. Since 1783, the State of Georgia had sought to induce the Creeks to surrender all of their territory east of the Oconee River--a strip of land sixty miles wide and two hundred miles long. The Creeks had a new leader, however, who refused to deal with Georgia. The son of a Scottish trader and the daughter of a Muskogee mico, Alexander McGillivray enhanced his natural leadership ability with education and business experience in Savannah before the war. When his loyalist father returned to Britain, the younger McGillivray went to live with his mother's people, among whom he quickly became a figure of influence.

His personal tastes were primarily those of his white father. He lived in a plantation house, owned slaves, and did not know the Muskogean dialect. Nonetheless, his talent, training, knowledge of whites, his Indian lineage (always traced among Indians through the mother), and his bitter hatred of Georgia made him a leader in the Creeks' struggle against the state. His sway over the Creeks was such that the British, Spanish, and Americans all sought his favor.

Since the Muskogee Nation was only a loose confederation, a general meeting of representatives from all the towns was necessary to make decisions affecting the entire nation. Towns without a representative present at such a meeting tended to repudiate any decision that they did not approve. Such was the case in 1783 when the State of Georgia induced a small band of Lower Creeks to sign away the Oconee lands. The other Creeks, led by McGillivray, denied the validity of the treaty and sought assistance from the Spanish in Florida to resist the settler's advances.

---

[9]The description is mentioned in an 1830 article from the *Macon Telegraph*, 3 April 1830.

[10]This policy was not very successful. The Indians got arms from the British to fight, and from the Colonists to stay neutral. Few Creeks actively joined the British because the British did not want indiscriminate raiding, which would hurt Loyalists. There was enough fighting, however, to sour relations between Georgia and the Creeks after the war.

Frontier fighting often threatened to erupt into all-out war between the Creeks and Georgia, but this never materialized. Creek aggression was always directly proportional to the amount of military supplies obtainable from the Spanish. McGillivray never got the level of support he wanted from Spain, but he believed that the United States government was too weak or was unwilling to back Georgia--that is until George Washington became President.

Wanting to assure Georgia's loyalty to the new government, Washington agreed to arrange for a new treaty to get a cession of the Oconee lands from the Creeks. He sent Marinus Willett down to the Creek country as his personal representative to invite McGillivray and other Creek leaders to New York, the U.S. capital at the time, for negotiations. Willett first met with McGillivray at the latter's home to gain his interest and support. Once persuaded, McGillivray took Willett on a tour of the Creek Nation and convinced each of the micos to consent to peace talks. Stone Mountain was agreed upon as the place for the leaders to meet to begin the trip to New York. Later, the colonel wrote about his visit to the mountain in his *Narration of the Military Acts of Col. Marinus Willett*:

> Here we found the Cowetas and Curates to the number of eleven waiting for us. While I was at Stony Mountain, I ascended the summit. It is one solid rock of circular form about one mile across. Many strange tales are told by the Indians of the mountain. I have now passed all Indian settlements and shall only observe that the inhabitants of these countries appear very happy.

Twelve more micos arrived for the meeting, making the total number twenty-three, not including a number of warriors. Willett led the party on their six-week long wagon journey to New York, where they received a lavish welcome and were entertained while negotiations proceeded.

To gain McGillivray's support for a treaty, the United States paid him for his property in Savannah that had been confiscated during the Revolution and made him a brigadier general in the army--the same rank he had also held in the Spanish army--with a pension of $1,200 a year. He then agreed to accept payment of $100,000 in gold for the Oconee lands, along with a guarantee that no more land would be demanded of the Creeks. The Treaty of New York was signed in August, 1790. When McGillivray returned home, he reported his actions to the Spanish authorities in

Florida, who offered to pay him $1,200 a year to continue harassing the Georgia frontier.[11]

Intended to appease both sides, in reality the Treaty of New York satisfied neither. Some of the Muskogees were angry with McGillivray for giving away their land, while his political rivals used the treaty to undermine his support in the tribe. Recognizing that they could not hold on to the Oconee lands any longer, McGillivray pushed for the best deal he could get for the tribe. He was nevertheless accused of selling his people out for personal gain. He later journeyed to Florida where he became ill and died in 1793. Like the Muskogees, Georgians were also bitter over the treaty. Despite receiving the Oconee section, the state was greedy for more land further west, land that was now off-limits.

Fighting continued intermittently along the frontier. President Washington made another effort to settle the Creek troubles in 1796 by sending Colonel Benjamin Hawkins to be the U.S. Agent for Indian Affairs to the Creeks. The 42-year-old Hawkins was the ideal candidate for the job. His honesty, forthrightness, and genuine concern for the Indians soon won their respect and trust. They held him in such high regard, in fact, that they placed many of their national affairs under his management. Of his work with the Creeks he later wrote:

> . . . We begin to understand each other; we have black drink and talks during the day, and dancing at night. . . . They bring their private and public claims; I attend to them, and I am happy to find that by my exertions the benevolent views of the government have already taken so deep root that I may defy the malice of the enemies of it. . . .[12]

From the Agency on the west bank of the Flint River, Hawkins provided guidance and counsel to the Creeks for twenty years. He encouraged them to abandon hunting pelts for the whites and take up farming and husbandry for their living. He taught them the crafts of weaving cloth and blacksmithing, and generally improved their domestic lives. He also managed to keep a delicate peace between the Creeks and the State of Georgia.

---

[11]John Walton Caughey, *McGillivray of the Creeks* (Norman: University of Oklahoma Press, 1938), 44.

[12]*Letters of Benjamin Hawkins 1796-1806*, Georgia Historical Society, 1916, reprinted 1982.

Hawkins possessed a keen mind and meticulously studied the Muskogean language and culture. From his invaluable letters and essays historians have learned the Muskogee name for Stone Mountain. In describing the Flint River, he wrote, "It heads near [the] Ocmulgee [River], and near *Thennethlofkee*, the southernmost mountain on the left side of the Chattahoochee." Hawkins' transliteration of the mountain's name is not quite accurate, however. The proper pronunciation is *Thuh-nih-thof-kee* (spelled "Rvne Rofke" in the Muskogean language) and means, quite appropriately, "Bald Mountain."[13]

The full story of Indian/white relations of the early nineteenth century is rather complicated. A brief sketch will suffice to put matters surrounding Stone Mountain into context. In 1802 the Federal government and the State of Georgia signed an agreement whereby Georgia would give up her claim to the territory west of the Chattahoochee River and the Federal government would see to the removal of all Indians from the state as quickly as it could be done on peaceable terms. Within two years the state gained control of the territory between the Ocmulgee and Oconee Rivers, but that was the last land cession for awhile.

The beginning of the end of Creek resistance came during the War of 1812 when the Upper Creeks sided with the British against the Americans, spurred on by the great Shawnee war leader, Tecumseh. Andrew Jackson dealt the Creek "Red Sticks" a crushing defeat at Horseshoe Bend, Alabama, which virtually ended the Creek military threat. The Lower Creeks had remained loyal to Georgia, but were not rewarded for it. The United States forced the Creeks to surrender a very large stretch of land in southern Georgia and Alabama, but thanks to the intervention of Benjamin Hawkins the heart of the Creek territory was spared. Unfortunately for the Creeks, Hawkins died two years later in 1816 and Governor David B. Mitchell of Georgia was appointed the new Indian Agent.

The state and federal governments continued to pressure the Muskogees to sign additional treaties selling more land. After the War of 1812, a new leader, Chief William McIntosh, had risen in prominence among the Lower Creeks, but remained generally friendly toward Georgia.

---

[13]Tim Thompson, translator for Muskogee-Creek Nation, personal interview, 20 January 1995.

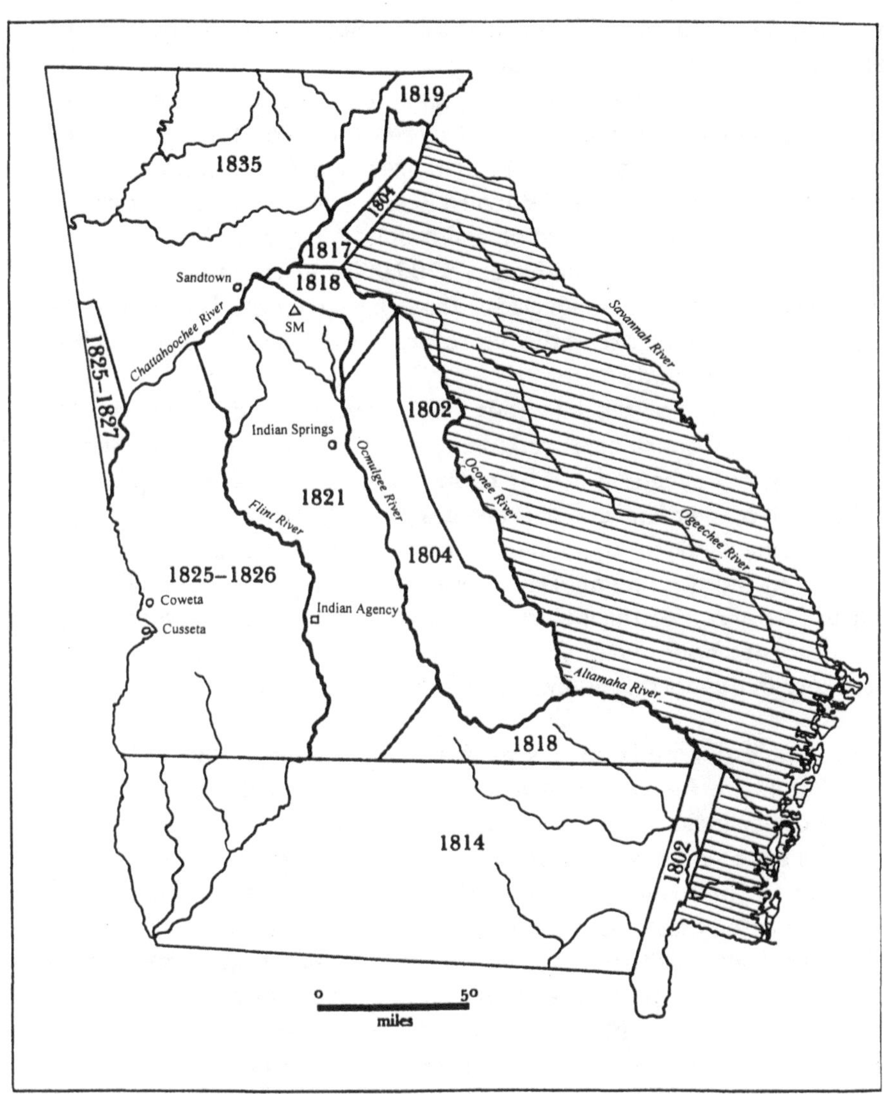

Georgia in 1800 and Indian Land Cessions 1800-1835.
SM indicates the location of Stone Mountain.

McIntosh's initial opposition toward forced removal later waned; he hoped that a new life west of the Mississippi River would bring peace and prosperity for his people. He felt that the Creeks could only hope to sell their lands for as much as they could get.

To this end, in 1821 McIntosh and several other micos signed a treaty at Indian Springs in Butts County. This agreement ceded a five million-acre stretch of territory between the Ocmulgee and Flint Rivers, with the exception of the Indian town of Buzzard Roost, one thousand acres around Indian Springs, and a small tract of land around McIntosh's home. For this land the United States paid the Indians $200,000 and assumed the debts of the Creeks as claimed by Georgia for their depredations. The land sold in this treaty included the site of the future city of Atlanta and the granite boss known as Stone Mountain.

This treaty is not the infamous 1825 Treaty of Indian Springs. The Creek National Council censured McIntosh and the others for signing the 1821 treaty, but accepted it. The council also vowed never to part with another inch of their land and decreed death to anyone who signed another treaty ceding land to the United States. Four years later, however, McIntosh signed the second Treaty of Indian Springs, giving up all Creek lands in Georgia. For this he was executed by his angry tribesmen. With the Muskogees now out of the way, Georgia turned its attention to the Cherokees in the north, and by 1837 had succeeded in driving them out as well.

An interesting aside to this main story occurred in the 1810s near Stone Mountain. Although the federal government had promised to rid Georgia of her Indians, the issue was not as pressing a matter for them as it was the state, and this often caused tension between the two. The state winked at trappers, hunters, and settlers who trespassed on Indian lands, while the United States took a dim view of such violations.

The land around Stone Mountain was still Creek territory, but since no Indians actually lived in the area it was one of the places encroached upon by white settlers. The Muskogees' complaints to the "White Father" in Washington seldom were answered for fear of worsening the already strained relations with the state. The Indians sometimes took matters into their own hands with a raid on the offending settlers. A Mr. R. Fullwood wrote to Governor Mitchell in August, 1813, and offered to "take command of a few persons" and "to keep a sharp lookout from Alcofa Mountain to Stone Mountain and from thence up to the frontier of Jackson

County" in order to quiet the alarm felt by the inhabitants.[14] This letter shows that as early as 1813 whites were encroaching on Creek land around Stone Mountain. President Monroe, however, decided in 1818 to put a stop to the flagrant treaty violations and sent Andrew Jackson, later to become President Jackson, down to Georgia to drive the white settlers off the Indian's land.

John B. Stewart, an attorney in Stone Mountain in the 1860s and 1870s, told of how his father had crossed the Yellow River and established a farm near the Hightower Trail in the vicinity of Rock Chapel, a couple of miles from the mountain. The elder Stewart was doing quite well, having "arrived at that point when abundance and comfort was [sic] his in a marked degree for a new country," until Jackson's troops came through.[15] "Old Hickory" carried out his orders with an iron fist. He followed a scorched earth policy and burned not only every vestige of a farm building, but the crops in the field as well. At least two stubborn pioneers were hanged for firing on federal troops. Those who surrendered peacefully were marched back to Gwinnett County on the east side of the Yellow River.

It is ironic that Jackson was chosen for this assignment given his reputation was as a fighter of Indians, and that in the 1830s as President he would be responsible for the expulsion of the Cherokees from Georgia. Just three years after Jackson's actions enforcing the Creek's claim, McIntosh sold the land off, opening the way for further legal expansion of the settlers.

---

[14]R. Fullwood to Governor David B. Mitchell, 26 August 1813, Creek Indian Letters, 1813-1829, Part 3, 84, Georgia State Archives.

[15]"'Old Hickory' Burned Trail Through Area, Too," *Lithonia Observer*, 12 July 1979 (citing an article from the *DeKalb New Era*, 6 January 1897).

Chapter Two

A Village Grows

The 1821 Treaty of Indian Springs opened for white settlement a vast area running down the center of the state. Out of this land were originally created five giant counties: Dooly, Houston, Monroe, Fayette, and Henry. Stone Mountain was located in Henry County, named for Revolutionary War hero Patrick Henry. The counties were divided into districts and land lots, with the latter being squares of 202.5 acres.

The mountain was located in the Eighteenth District in Henry County until December 1822, when the district became part of the newly created DeKalb County. DeKalb County, named for the Baron von DeKalb, another Revolutionary War hero, was then much larger than it is today. The creation of Fulton County out of DeKalb in 1853 gave DeKalb County its present size. Stone Mountain lies partly in seven different land lots: 75, 76, 77, 86, 87, 88, and 127.

The state disposed of its new territory through a process called the land lottery. To be eligible for the drawing, each applicant had to swear an oath that he or she had resided in the state for at least three years. The number of draws allowed for each individual depended on his or her situation. Bachelors, widows, minor orphans, and dependents of convicts were allowed one draw; married men, widows or orphans of a war veteran, and minor orphans of three or more in a family got two draws. Winners of previous land lotteries were ineligible and war veterans were not given special advantage as they were in prior lotteries.[1]

The drawing for the Fourth Land Lottery was held on May 15, 1821, in the state capital at Milledgeville under the supervision of the governor. The winners of land lots were notified by the state and the fortunate individuals could receive their grants by paying the nineteen dollar fee.

The Stone Mountain lot grants were recorded between 1822 and 1829, according to when the fee was paid. Land Lot (LL) 75 was granted to

---

[1]Rev. Silas E. Lucas, *The Fourth Land Lottery* (Easley, SC: Southern Historical Press , 1986), n.p.

George Marable of Clark County, while LL 76 went to Arnold Seale of Jones County. LL 77 was awarded to Nathaniel M. Clanton of Columbus County, and the orphans of John Murray of Warren County received LL 86. LL 87 was granted to John Murrey of Liberty County, while LL 88 went to Frederick Starnes of Habersham County. Finally, LL 127 was granted to the orphans of Jones County's William D. Williams.[2]

Census records indicate that none of these seven original owners of Stone Mountain ever lived on their granted land, nor are their purchasers or dates of purchase known because an 1842 courthouse fire destroyed all the deed records for the county. Only a few were ever re-recorded. The earliest known resident at the mountain was Augustine Young, who probably bought Lot 86 or 87 from the original owner and from 1822 to 1833 lived on a small hill at the foot of the steep side. Other than this single fact, the earliest exchanges of the Stone Mountain property are traceable only to a few colorful legends passed down through the years.

One of these tales is about a man from Athens, Georgia, who received one of the grants and walked sixty miles to see his newly-acquired property. Discovering it to be merely a big barren rock, he supposedly traded his grant for a mule to ride back home. There may be some truth to this story since George Marable, the holder of Land Lot 75, hailed from Clark County, which includes the city of Athens.

Another early settler named John W. Beauchamp owned a piece of Stone Mountain. Legend says he gave the Indians forty dollars and a pony for the mountain. He probably did not trade with the Indians because he would have known from the publicity surrounding the 1821 treaty and later land lottery that the Indians had surrendered their claim to the land. Beauchamp supposedly sold his claim on the mountain to Andrew Johnson for a muzzle-loading gun and twenty dollars. Johnson acquired a great deal of land in the area during the 1830s, including most of the mountain. Where and precisely how much land he bought, however, is uncertain, again because of the destruction of the records.

The descendants of Jesse Lanford still tell how their great-great-grandfather was offered the mountain, or at least part of it, in exchange for a flintlock musket. Lanford refused the offer, replying that he could hunt to feed himself with the gun, but had no use for a mountain. Besides, he added,

---

[2]Index to land grants, Fourth Land Lottery, 1821. On microfilm at State Archives, Atlanta, Georgia.

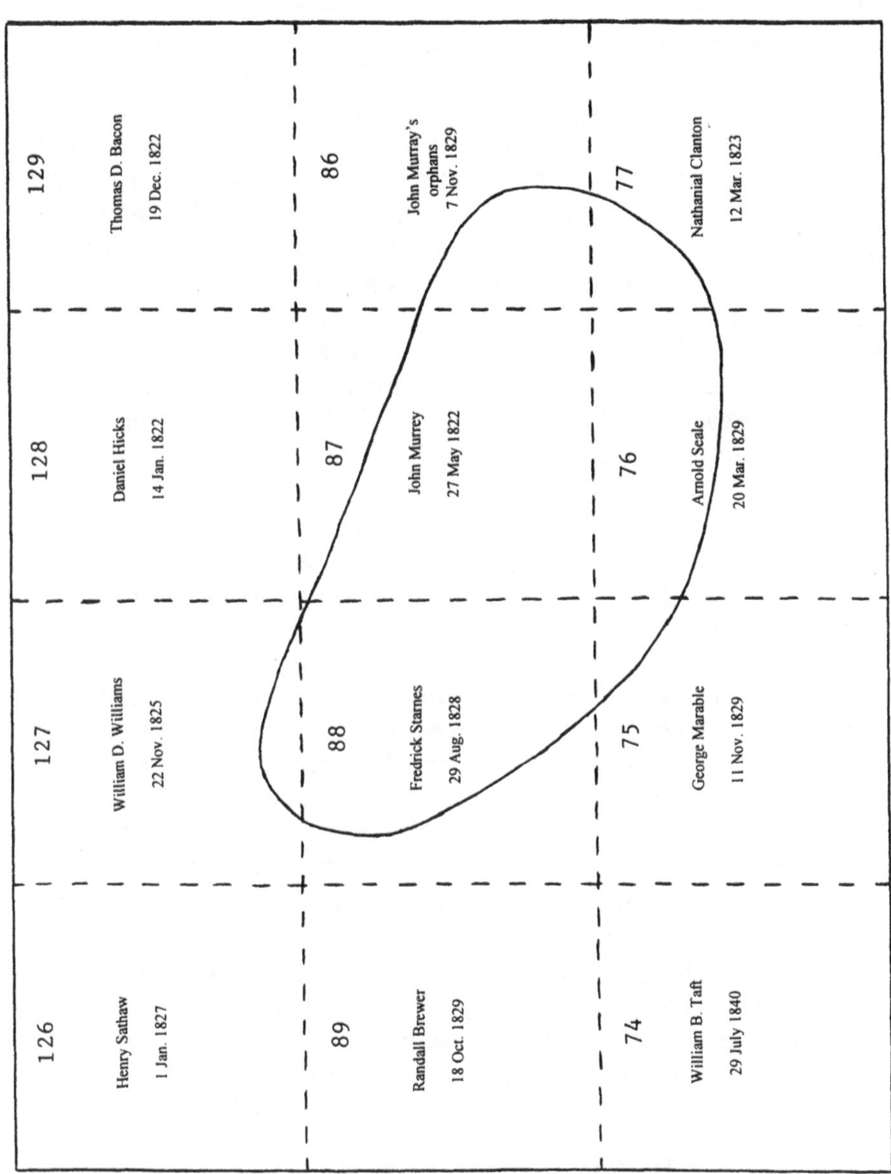

Land Lots in which Stone Mountain lies, original grantees, and dates each grant was recorded with the state.

he already had enough rock on his own land. His descendants came to regret his unfortunate decision, but he did leave them his gun.

As more people came into the Stone Mountain area in the early part of the nineteenth century, the renown of this natural wonder spread. A gold assayer from Dahlonega named M. F. Stephenson wrote in the 1830s that an Englishman had visited the mountain in 1808 and returned to London with his story. But the mountain's distance from the Appalachian peaks made him believe it was man-made. Other visitors, fooled by the white color of freshly broken Stone Mountain granite, thought it was made of marble. The view of the steep cliff inspired such awe that visitors frequently estimated its height at two or three thousand feet, several times its actual height of 780 feet. Such misconceptions became rather widespread back in Europe. The president of the Academy of Arts and Sciences in Paris wrote to Savannah attorney Richard W. Habersham asking for the dimensions and other data concerning this "vast relic of *architectural* grandeur."[3]

In the same year that the state legislature prepared the original land grants, the Reverend Francis Goulding and his party made their visit to Stone Mountain. He provided a vivid description of the mountain on the eve of settlement:

> The country around had, at that time, barely passed into the hands of the white man, and there were few roads and fewer houses of accommodation. Our tent was pitched beside a spring near the mountain's base. . . . From this point the rock rose majestically, with an almost perpendicular face of a thousand feet. We enjoyed its rough grandeur almost as much by the soft light of the moon as we did by the red light of the setting sun. . . .
>
> We found the summit as irregularly flat oval about a furlong [660 feet] in length. The view from it was superb. Not another mountain could be seen in any direction within a distance of twenty-five or thirty miles. The country all around seemed to be an immense level, or rather a basin, the rim of which rose on all sides to meet the blue of the sky. To the east and south appeared

---

[3]Willard Neal, *Georgia's Stone Mountain* (Stone Mountain, GA: Stone Mountain Memorial Association, 1970), 18.

a few clearings, but in every other direction the forest was unbroken.[4]

Goulding's party stopped under a cavern formed by a pile of boulders to escape the heat and eat lunch. A thunderstorm coming up from the other side of the mountain interrupted their repast and bombarded the mountain's surface with lightning bolts. Emerging from their shelter after the storm, the Gouldings discovered, "a great flake of rock scaled off from a ledge not fifty feet from our place of refuge."

At their camp that evening, they had a surprise visit from two members of the "Pony Club," a gang of horse thieves who specialized in stealing riding stock from unwary travelers. The camp was prepared for such an eventuality, however, and the two rode off with a shot from Scipio's gun.

When the territory surrounding Stone Mountain was opened for settlement, the only method of travel into the area was on foot or horseback. Pioneers generally made use of the existing Indian trails and Stone Mountain, situated at the junction of two major trails, naturally became one of the first areas in the new county to be settled. Tradition has it that there was a settlement at the foot of the mountain before the first house was built some ten miles west in the county seat of Decatur (1823). In the early days, the mountain was called Stoney Mountain, or more commonly Rock Mountain, and the tiny community at its base bore the name of New Gibraltar. In the 1830s some began to call the prominent landmark Stone Mountain, and the town changed its name in 1847 to reflect this general usage.

By 1825, traffic coming past Stone Mountain into DeKalb County had increased enough to warrant regular stagecoach service. The stagecoach line ran from Milledgeville to Stone Mountain through Eatonton, Madison, and Covington. Another stage line ran to Winder and Athens. At New Gibraltar a house of accommodation awaited the weary traveler. In 1828 another stage line began making daily trips from Stone Mountain to Dahlonega--where gold had just been discovered--by way of Lawrenceville and Gainesville. A fourth stage line connected the little community to Macon, making it a major travel center in the region. This traffic naturally added to the prosperity of the businesses there.

Practically no one enjoyed the bone-jarring experience of stagecoach travel. Passengers sat on uncushioned wooden seats, and the coaches had

---

[4]Goulding, 121-126.

no suspension system. The best roads were narrow, rutted, bumpy tracks that were dusty in dry weather and turned into sticky mud when wet. Coaches frequently became bogged down in the mud, and accidents such as breaking a wheel or overturning were always a threat. Stage travel was also expensive, with the usual fare being ten cents per mile. The stagecoach continued to be a major means of travel to Stone Mountain for twenty years until the Georgia Railroad was built.

Even in these early days, Stone Mountain served as a place of recreation for the people of the region, a place where families enjoyed picnics and young couples courted. Levi Willard, an early resident of Decatur, described in 1879 how such affairs often went:

> . . . As there were few or no carriages of any kind in use in the first settlement of the country, these little excursions [to the mountain] were taken on horseback. It was an agreeable way of traveling, paired off, two and two abreast.
>
> It was easy to lag behind the company--Sallie's saddle was turning and must be girt tighter, or the blanket was slipping out of place, or some other excuse for stopping a minute. As the company has gone forward, he [the beau] says to himself, 'Now's my time, as no one is near, to pop the question,' as the expression is.[5]

Adiel Sherwood's 1829 *Georgia Gazetteer* indicated that hundreds of people visited Rock Mountain in the summer and that a house of entertainment was near. Sherwood also recorded that in 1828 a number of citizens celebrated the Fourth of July by dining on top of the mountain. Among the performances given was the recital of a poem entitled "Spirits of '76." The Devil's Cross Roads on top of the mountain was a popular spot for picnics and daring young men seeking to demonstrate their bravery often descended the northwest side of the mountain with the Buzzard's Roost as their goal.

The coming of so many visitors led some entrepreneurs to recognize the money-making potential of the great rock, and a few capitalized on it by adding attractions of their own. The first of these was Aaron Cloud, of McDonough, Georgia, who in 1838 purchased from Andrew Johnson a lot

---

[5]Levi Willard, *Early History of Decatur,* 1879, manuscript at the DeKalb Historical Society, 6.

atop the mountain 150 feet square (22,500 sq. ft.). Cloud intended to build an observation tower on the summit, a project that cost him $5,000 and gained him a great deal of notoriety. William C. Richards described Cloud's Tower in his 1842 book, *Georgia Illustrated*, as similar to a lighthouse, octagonal in shape, and built entirely of wood. The 165-foot high structure was not anchored to the rock in any way other than by its own weight, an omission that proved to be its downfall a few years later. Concerning the view from the top of the tower, Richards wrote that with a telescope he could distinguish five county towns, including Atlanta, which at that time amounted to only "a few straggling huts just beyond Decatur."[6]

The Reverend Thomas Porter, of Monticello, Georgia, toured the mountain in 1846 and gave a vivid account of the magnificent spectacle visible from Cloud's Tower:

> A strong fresh breeze drove up volumes of mists, rolling in huge waves like a wide, tumbling ocean, parting occasionally to show spots of sunshine on woods and fields far below. . . . To crown the glory there sprang up . . . a broad, brilliant sunbow, or mistbow, in the shape of an eclipse, and in its center the tower and our moving shadows were clearly defined.[7]

Rebecca Latimer Felton, who later became the first woman to serve in the United States Congress, visited Stone Mountain as a small child. Later, in her autobiography she wrote of "dancing galore" in the lower hall of the tower and a candy vendor selling white candy doves with buckshot for eyes.[8]

Around 1849 a severe storm blew down Cloud's Tower and Thomas Henry built a second tower a couple of years later. Henry's Tower was smaller than Cloud's, being only forty feet square at the base and eighty feet tall. It is said that when the tower was finished, Henry stood on his head on a brass ball on top of the tower. An advertisement from the *Augusta Chronicle & Sentinel* of June 25, 1852, told of plans to convert the summit of

---

[6]As quoted in Lucian Lamar Knight, *Georgia's Landmarks, Memorials and Legends* (Atlanta: Byrd Printing Co., 1916), 247-248.

[7]Letter from Rev. Thomas Porter to cousins in Philadelphia, as quoted by Hugh Park, "Beauty of Georgia in 1846," *Atlanta Journal*, 9 July 1974.

[8]Rebecca Latimer Felton, *Country Life In Georgia In the Days of My Youth* (Atlanta: Index Printing Company, 1919), 69.

the tower into a popular observatory with the finest telescopes available in the South to "exhibit the wonders of Heaven in their utmost glory." The article explains that a Professor L. Harper, LL.D. had been hired to give astronomy lectures on the "glorious Sun" in the daytime, and the "Wonders of the Heavens" at night. The hotels, the notice continued, were being "kept at the same time in the very best style, all luxuries of the table provided for." Not surprisingly, the observatory was sponsored by Stone Mountain hotel keepers Thomas Johnson and John G. Quack.

Another daring entrepreneur of the 1840s was a man named Weldon Wright, whose workmanship can still be seen. Using blasting powder, he cut a trail 250 feet long and about two feet wide high up on the steep face of the mountain, extending from the walk-up trail on the western slope. Visitors adventurous enough to walk out to the end and back paid twenty-five cents for the privilege. Even with an iron safety rail, it must have been a nerve-wracking trip. Wright's ambition, however, proved to be his undoing. While extending his trail even further in 1846, he blew himself off the mountain with a premature explosion of blasting powder.

Another entrepreneur named White took a less hazardous approach to making money from mountain visitors. He built a small "Halfway House" on the walk-up trail where climbers could rest before pushing on to the top and sold cups of cool water for five cents.

With an ever-increasing number of visitors, some accidents naturally occurred. The slope of the mountain is deceptive, having no well-defined edge at the top, even on the sheer north side. The downward curve of the dome is so gradual that an intrepid explorer might not detect trouble until beginning to slide--by then, too late. The lichens on the surface of the rock become very slippery when wet, thereby increasing the danger. There is no record of the number of people who have fallen to their deaths at the mountain in the past two centuries, but it may well be more than a hundred.

One of the earliest accounts of a fall from the mountain appeared in the 3 April 1830 *Macon Telegraph*:

> A pathetic story is told of a couple of hounds that a year or two ago followed their owners to the top of the mountain, and in performing their gambols around the edge of the precipice, had gone too far down to be able to get back. One slid immediately over, and was dashed to pieces on the rocks below, not a whole bone being left in his skin; the other held to the rock for two days,

howling piteously, but at last became exhausted, fell, and shared the fate of his companion.[9]

Another recorded fall had a happier ending. In 1879 an Augusta family named Holmes was enjoying a picnic on top of the mountain when their nine-year old daughter, Emily, slipped and fell into a shallow depression down on the north side. She might never have been found had not a man coming into town spotted a small white form high up on the north side. Upon learning that a little girl was missing, the man reported his observation, and a physician named George Goldsmith volunteered to be lowered down the side of the mountain on a rope to help young Emily. Goldsmith accomplished the rescue, carried the little girl to her distraught parents, and received a gold-headed walking cane in appreciation. Fifty-eight years later, in 1937, Emily Holmes Wetsell returned to the mountain to revisit the scene of her narrow escape.

Due to the destruction of county records, little is known about the development of the village of New Gibraltar prior to 1840. The town was designated as the Rock Mountain Post Office on 18 July 1834, indicating a community of note by that time. William Cochran served as the first Postmaster until January, 1835, when he was succeeded by Andrew Browning. The office was eliminated in January, 1836, and was re-established as the Stone Mountain Post Office in June of the same year with William Meador as Postmaster.

The town of New Gibraltar was incorporated by an act of the Georgia General Assembly on December 21, 1839. Andrew Johnson, Isaiah Parker, Silas Pool, William Beauchamp, and Drury Lee served as the first Commissioners. An 1843 amendment to the act of incorporation extended the town limits to 600 yards in every direction from the house of Andrew Johnson. Four years later, in December, 1847, the corporate limits were extended again to embrace all of Land Lot 89, and the town's name was changed from New Gibraltar to Stone Mountain.

The name change of the post office clearly indicates that the term "stone" was gradually replacing "rock" as the preferred appellation for the mountain. The change of the town name eleven years later reflected this common usage. The town was already so closely identified with its giant neighbor that it was probably being called Stone Mountain well before the official change. The author of the *Gazetteer of Georgia*, Adiel Sherwood,

---

[9]As quoted in Garrett, 81-82.

however, strongly rejected the new town name as inappropriate. As late as 1860, the mountain and the town were listed in the *Gazetteer* under "Rock Mountain." The entry insisted that "rock, instead of stone, mountain is the true name; it is a vast mass of rock--not a high pile or heap of stones."

Of the founding fathers of Stone Mountain, the name Andrew Johnson deserves special mention. A South Carolina native who moved to Stone Mountain with his wife, Eliza, sometime around 1830, Johnson amassed a great deal of property and soon headed the most prosperous family in the area. His holdings included a 2,300-acre plantation on the north side of the mountain, as well as most of the lots in the town. (Many of the early residents purchased their lots from him.) He also owned and operated a hotel in town and held about a dozen slaves. His estate was valued in 1850 at $30,000, and Johnson was so important in the affairs of the town that the city limits were drawn in a circle around his house. Perhaps more than anyone else, he earned the title of "founder" of the town of Stone Mountain. Johnson and his wife were buried in a small cemetery on the side of Memorial Drive, about two miles west of Stone Mountain. Some years after their deaths, their sons Thomas and William sold off the family's landholdings on the mountain.

Undoubtedly the most important development in the history of Stone Mountain was the building of the Georgia Railroad, which came about as the result of a mudhole between Augusta and Athens. On one particular instance a wagonload of machinery bound for a cotton mill in Athens became stuck for several weeks until the mud dried. The incident demonstrated to several Athens businessmen the necessity of a railroad. As a result, in December, 1833, the legislature consented granted a charter to the Georgia Railroad, the first railroad company in the state, and only the third in the nation.

Actual construction began at Augusta in 1835 with trains running by 1839 at the unprecedented speed of twelve miles per hour. The stretch of railroad between Covington and Marthasville (later renamed Atlanta) was surveyed in December 1843 and completed two years later in order to connect with the Western & Atlantic Railroad. The route of the railroad curved twenty miles out of the straightest course to bring it right past New Gibraltar, assuring the future prosperity of the young town.

Many of the leading citizens of Marthasville came out to New Gibraltar to ride the first train into their town. Rebecca Latimer Felton, ten years old when the railroad was built, later recalled the impact of the railroad and one of its first conductors, Colonel George Adair:

> Imagine, if you can, the advent of a real railroad in a poor section where no railroads had been expected and what the travel to Stone Mountain stood for with a popular conductor who provided sugar plums for the children and rare and racy jokes for the grown-ups![10]

The railroad very quickly became more important to the town than the stagecoach lines, and the focus of development shifted from the mountain to the train depot. In fact, land records show that the town essentially moved over about half a mile to take full advantage of the railroad. This shift may have begun prior to 1845 in anticipation of the railroad's completion. Local tradition holds that in order that no favoritism be shown the depot was built equidistant from the hotels of Andrew Johnson and Aaron Cloud.[11]

Deeds from this period of time refer to lots in the "old Town of Gibraltar," indicating that each section had a distinct identity. This is not surprising given that the railroad lay outside of the 1200 yard diameter of the town's corporate limits. The extension of the limits in 1847 to all of Land Lot 89 brought both locales together under the name City of Stone Mountain.

While a town plan is referred to in several deeds, no comprehensive plan from this time period has ever come to light. A local myth attributes the layout of the town to Alexander H. Stephens, the future Vice-President of the Confederate States. This, however, is highly unlikely. Stephens, a resident of Crawfordville, Georgia, was an attorney and in 1843 was the Whig candidate for a seat in the state legislature. None of his biographers mention any connection with Stone Mountain or experience as a surveyor or town planner.

It is much more likely that the railroad itself was responsible for the layout of the town. According to the historical and archaeological firm of New South Associates, the arrangement parallel streets along the railroad

---

[10]Felton, 69.

[11]This legend cannot be substantiated by the historical record. There is an 1847 deed granting to Aaron Cloud a right-of-way twenty-seven feet wide through Johnson's town lots from the Georgia Railroad Depot to a specific spot between their two hotels "to stop just halfway through said hotels and no further." We do not know what this right-of-way was for; it may have been a street. This arrangement could also be the source of the legend.

right-of-way in Stone Mountain is typical of a railroad strip town. Railroad officials may have circulated generic plans to aid land owners in carving their property into marketable real estate.[12]

The coming of the railroad was a great boon to the economy of the town. It made day trips to the mountain quicker and easier for more people and its popularity grew, especially with the city people in Atlanta and Decatur. Parties would pay the fifty cent round-trip fare and spend the day rambling around the mountain and picnicking before heading home in the afternoon. The combination of natural scenery, man-made attractions, good hotels, and railroad access turned Stone Mountain into a budding resort.

The hotel owners in town were not content to rely on the mountain to draw visitors who usually went home in the afternoon. Instead they wanted to create some other attraction that would bring patrons into their hotels for the night. Thomas Johnson has already been mentioned as sponsoring lectures on astronomy on the mountain, but undoubtedly the most successful scheme was hatched by John W. Graves, a Newton County planter and owner of the Stone Mountain Inn. In searching for an idea to popularize his newly-built establishment, decided to promote an agricultural fair. Graves contacted his numerous acquaintances and soon the Southern Central Agricultural Society was formed with sixty-one members, each of whom paid the one dollar dues. The purported goal of the Society was to inquire "into the resources and facilities of agricultural pursuits, and the advancement of the arts and sciences connected therewith, and into the best method of developing the one and illustrating the other."[13]

The first Agricultural Fair and Internal Improvement Jubilee was held in August, 1846, in a grove that the Society leased from Andrew Johnson. This small fair boasted only one exhibit--three horses and two cows, belonging to Graves, and their groom, "a sprightly negro, 82 years old, once the servant of George Washington."[14]

The next year's fair was better organized and attended. Visitors and exhibits filled the Ten Pin Alley in front of the Stone Mountain Hotel. Admission to the fair was ten cents, and some small premiums were awarded as prizes. Articles on display included caskets, marble, embroidery,

---

[12]Historic Sites Survey: City of Stone Mountain, New South Associates, January 1994, 9.

[13]Elizabeth Austin Ford, *Stone Mountain* (n.p., 1959), 17.

[14]David W. Lewis, *Transactions of the Southern Central Agricultural Society* (Macon: n.p., 1852, xi.

brooms, bed-spreads, vegetables, blooded stock, wheat, farm tools, and the magnetic telegraph.

A reporter for the Savannah *Georgian* complained that the hotels "were filled to suffocation," and he was required to spend the night in a room with twenty-eight other men, "many of whom broke the stillness of the night by snoring." Another chronicler of the fair noted that "the portly form of Graves was seen in a large arm chair in the piazza; the old man surveying, with evident gratification, the bright prospect of the success of his scheme."[15] No doubt the other hotel and shop keepers were also pleased with the fair.

The fairs of 1848 and 1849 included various side shows to entertain the crowds. One of these was the world-renowned show of Phineas T. Barnum featuring "General Tom Thumb." Two other gentlemen, Banigan and Kelley, exhibited a caravan of trained animals. Tipo Sultan, a large elephant, became enraged by the taunting of some drunken men and chased the frightened spectators out of the tent before being calmed.

Fighting within the Society over the location of the fair necessitated moving the fair to Atlanta in 1850 before moving permanently to Macon in 1851. The fair's success ultimately worked against Stone Mountain, as the event grew too large for the small town to accommodate.

Besides tourism, another industry to benefit from the coming of the railroad was quarrying. Previously, the vast amount of granite in the mountain had little commercial value due to the difficulty of getting it to market. The Georgia Railroad connected Stone Mountain to the river port of Augusta and the seaport of Savannah. By connecting with other rail lines in Atlanta, the way was open to other cities north and west, thus creating the outlet necessary to make quarrying economically viable.

First efforts at quarrying were probably made shortly after the railroad opened in 1845, largely from exposed and partially disintegrated ledges that were easy to cut up, but that yielded poorer quality stone. The 1850 census lists five stonecutters or stonemasons, indicating small-scale quarrying at this time. The granite industry remained a minor part of the local economy until after the Civil War.

The great majority of the people in the nineteenth century were farmers. The farms of Stone Mountain and environs were typical of the Piedmont region across the South. The large plantations of the antebellum period popularized in films and novels did not exist here. Scarcely one in a

---

[15]Ibid., xii.

hundred agricultural families could count themselves as members of the planter class. The plantation belt was further south in middle Georgia. In the Piedmont, subsistence farms were the rule.

A typical farm extended for two to three hundred acres, with perhaps only a hundred or so acres under cultivation. The rest of the acreage was forest or rocky wasteland given over to grazing. The main crop of these farmers was corn, and a number grew wheat during the winter. Only about one half the farmers grew cotton, normally less than three bales, to make a little extra cash. At ten cents a pound during the 1850s, a four-hundred-pound bale of cotton could bring in forty dollars.

In addition to their crops, most farmers kept chickens, a couple of cows, a half dozen cattle, about a dozen sheep and a score of pigs. From these animals they produced eggs, milk and butter, wool, and meat. What they did not consume themselves they sold in town. Stone Mountain farms produced lumber, honey, molasses, peaches, scuppernongs, and a variety of vegetables. On market days the streets of the town would be crowded with farmers bringing in their goods for sale or barter.

While only about twenty-five percent of whites owned slaves, among farmers the figure was about sixty percent. Few, however, owned more than three or four. Costing from two hundred dollars for a female cook to more than five hundred dollars for a male field hand, a slave represented a farmer's most expensive investment--even greater than his land.

The farmer's house was modest, generally one to one-and-a-half stories, and one room deep, with a covered porch across the front. A detached kitchen typically lay behind the house. Due to the warm, humid climate of the South, most work was done outdoors when possible, the back yard being the main work space. Farms of the Deep South tended to be rather ramshackle and unkempt. Buildings were unpainted, the animals roamed free, and only small efforts were made to beautify the dirt yards with shrubs and flowers. Despite this lack of attention to appearances, the subsistence farmers could set a bountiful table.

The decade of the 1850s was a good one for the town of Stone Mountain. Known as the "Golden Era" of Georgia agriculture, production levels were high and the price of cotton rose in response to strong European demand. According to the 1860 *Gazetteer*, the town boasted some forty houses, and the 1860 census lists 164 white households in the Stone Mountain district, plus 290 slaves. The *Gazetteer* makes note of large quantities of granite sent out from the mountain, while the census lists twenty-five individuals involved in the stone quarries. This indicated strong development in that industry. Merchandizing and the building trades were also major growth areas, and tourism, of course, was booming. The town sat poised to enter a new decade with confidence, but the outbreak of the Civil War cast a pall of concern over the future.

DeKalb County supported the Union, favoring further efforts to resolve the nation's differences. The county's representative to the state convention to consider secession was George K. Smith, an attorney from Stone Mountain. In speaking for the people of DeKalb, he twice voted against leaving the Union. But when the vote went in favor of secession by 166 to 130, the entire state pulled together for the war effort. The great granite rock served its part in the war preparations by being used as a firing range for Confederate artillery trials.

Cornelius R. Hanleiter, a pioneer Atlanta printer, publisher and telegraph operator, wrote a letter to the *Atlanta Intelligencer* on October 10, 1861, concerning the testing of some big guns at the mountain by the Wright Legion. The guns, made by William Rushton of Atlanta, were positioned 1,500 yards from the mountain and a target was hung from the north face. Nine shots were fired at the target from the improved breech-loading cannon to test for accuracy. Three shots were then fired over Henry's Tower on the summit to demonstrate the gun's superior range. The apparent success of the trials prompted Hanleiter to assert that "no regiment will have more effective arms."[16]

The Wright Legion was only one regiment in which DeKalb County residents served. They also filled the ranks of the Murphey Guards (Company A, 39th Infantry), the Bartow Avengers (Company K, 38th Infantry), and the McCullough Rifles (Company D, 38th Infantry), just to name a few.

During the first three years of the conflict, Stone Mountain was not directly affected, apart from the absence of some local men who were off serving in the military. Business went on as usual and pleasure seekers still came to the mountain, though perhaps in reduced numbers. At the height of the war, Atlantan Samuel P. Richards recorded in his diary an excursion to the mountain on July 21, 1863. In his entry he noted, "the refreshment saloon half way up is now deserted and in ruins, also the Tower on the tip is nothing but a pile of unsightly stones and lumber, 'wrecks of the past'."[17]

---

[16]William S. Smedlund, *Campfires of Georgia Troops* (Lithonia, GA: William Smedland, Publisher, 1994), 377.

[17]"S.P. Richards Diary," as quoted in Garrett, 558.

From this we see that the tower mentioned in Hanleiter's 1861 letter was gone less that two years later, as was White's halfway house. Richards does mention that the hotels were still operating, but some of the tourist attractions seem to have fallen on hard times during the war.

Stone Mountain's contact with the war became much more intimate during the summer of 1864 when the Union Army, under General W.T. Sherman, laid siege to nearby Atlanta and the bloody campaign spilled over to many surrounding communities. Sherman planned to cut the four railroads coming into Atlanta in order to isolate the city. The most important line was the Georgia Railroad since it was the most likely route for Confederate reinforcements.

A number of skirmishes occurred around Stone Mountain in mid-July as the Union forces sought to destroy the railroad between there and Decatur. On July 15, there was a small battle on Stone Mountain Road, just a couple of miles to the north of town, in which twenty-five Confederate and ninety Union soldiers were killed.

Union forces under MajorGeneral James B. McPherson attacked the railroad just two miles west of Stone Mountain on July 18, and began working west toward Decatur while Brigadier General Kenner Gerrard's Cavalry was sent east to raid the town. The raiders encountered little resistance as the main body of Confederates was engaging McPherson's divisions. Gerrard's Cavalry destroyed some two miles of track and burned the depot, a water tower, the commissary stores, and 200 bales of cotton before moving toward Decatur to cover McPherson's rear.

Thomas Maguire, owner of the "Promised Land" Plantation near Rockbridge, a few miles southeast of Stone Mountain, mentioned Gerrard's raid in his journal:

> July 18--Yankees at Stone Mountain--water station burned, part of track torn up--great excitement.
> July 19--Fighting at Atlanta--Yankees at the mountain--folks badly scared in this settlement.[18]

Three days later Gerrard reported light fighting continuing around the town, writing that his pickets, left to guard the roads in the vicinity of Stone Mountain, "are constantly exchanging shots with rebel cavalry pickets."[19]

---

[18]"Farm Journal" of Thomas Maguire, manuscript at Atlanta History Center.
[19]*Official Records of the Union and Confederate Armies*, Series I, Vol. 38, 221.

During the course of the seven-week battle, hundreds of homes, churches, and inns in the Atlanta area were converted into hospitals to care for the wounded. Many Confederate, and some Union, casualties were removed from the areas of heavy combat and brought to Stone Mountain because of its proximity. Stone Mountain had two doctors in 1860, but one of them, R. M. Johnson, enlisted and served with the Army of Northern Virginia. The other, Benjamin Hollinsworth, remained in town during the battle of Atlanta and would have been called upon to render what aid he could for the wounded soldiers. The women of the town were pressed to become temporary nurses and provided most of the help for these make-shift hospitals. Approximately 150 soldiers died from wounds and disease and are buried in mass graves in the Stone Mountain Cemetery. Two of the homes reportedly used as hospitals still exist today.

Local family stories passed down for generations poignantly expressed the sorrow and despair of the townspeople:

> I was sixteen years old when the war began, and the first call took my father. He went north to Virginia and was soon dead of smallpox. He died among strangers. The next call for recruits took my eldest brother, and he was shot dead by Sherman's marauders close to Macon. It was more than my mother could bear, and when it was over, she was broken down by her sorrows.[20]

In the summer of 1864 residents, under the imminent threat of Union assault, struggled against deprivation and palpable fear to make a meager crop. A local girl wrote in her diary: "When Sherman burned Atlanta, we could see the smoke, and my mother cried all day, praying he wouldn't come and burn us out. Where would we go? What would we do?"[21]

With the surrender of Atlanta on 2 September 1864, the Union forces moved in to occupy the city. For ten weeks foraging parties and individual looters plundered the surrounding countryside for food, animals, and other valuables. Sherman issued orders that soldiers were not to "enter the dwellings of the inhabitants, or commit any trespass," and that "they will endeavor to leave with each family a reasonable portion of their maintenance," but his instructions in this regard went largely ignored.

---

[20]As given in Kathryn Patton, *A Sketchbook of Stone Mountain* (Stone Mountain, GA: Sue Kellog Library, 1995), 16.

[21]Ibid., 17.

Thomas Maguire received several visits from the Federals and kept a vivid account of these trying times:

> July 21--At 12 or 1 o'clock at night the Yankees came here in force. Knocked us up. The house was soon full of thieving Yankees--robbed us of everything they could carry off. . . . They must have practiced roguery from their childhood up, so well they appeared to know the art.
>
> July 22--Yankees left about 8 o'clock on their way to Covington. . . . The Yankees set Rockbridge on fire.
>
> Oct. 19--This day devoted to hiding out wheat . . . making preparation for the evil time coming.
>
> Oct. 27--At 10 ½ o'clock some 30 Yankees rode up. Took Philip's wagon and two horses, all our meal and flour, one keg of syrup and several articles . . . that I do not know of.[22]

Colonel Francis West, of the 31st Wisconsin Infantry, reported that during the occupation of Atlanta, his regiment twice engaged in foraging expeditions to the vicinity of Stone Mountain, and that on each of these occasions "some 800 wagon loads of forage were obtained."[23] Foraging trips near the mountain are also mentioned by other units.

Miss Mary Gay, who fled Decatur during the Battle of Atlanta, recorded in her memoirs that she saw the depressing results of these foraging trips during her return home after the fighting had ceased. Nearing Stone Mountain, she entered a devastated section of the country where prosperity had once ruled, but where now stood only blackened chimneys. "Ah, those chimneys standing in the midst of smoldering ruins," she wrote, "No wonder they were called 'Sherman's Sentinels' as they seemed to be keeping guard over those scenes of desolation."[24]

Federal troops evacuated Atlanta on 15 November 1864, beginning their famous "march to the sea." The right wing of the army went south toward Jonesboro, while the left wing went east toward Madison. On the first day the left wing marched as far as Stone Mountain. Several officers reported the location of their units in reference to the mountain. The

---

[22]Maguire "Farm Journal."

[23]*Official Records*, Vol. 44, 267.

[24]Mary A. H. Gay, *Life In Dixie During the War* (Atlanta: *Atlanta Constitution* Job Office, 1892; reprinted by the DeKalb Historical Society, 1979). 208.

twentieth Corps, First Division, camped the night "one and a half miles southeast of Stone Mountain;" the 134th New York Volunteers "marched to near Stone Mountain and encamped the night;" the 119th New York Volunteers "marched to the vicinity of Stone Mountain;" and the 29th Ohio Infantry "reached the base of the mountain at 11 pm and encamped the night."[25] The next day the 2nd Massachusetts Volunteers remained behind to destroy the public property in the city before rejoining their command.

General Sherman traveled with the 14th Corps in the rear guard. They traveled east on the Covington Road, stopping the first night out near Lithonia. In his memoirs of the war, Sherman wrote that, "Stone Mountain, a mass of granite, was in plain view, cut out in clear outline against the blue sky; the whole horizon was lurid with the bonfires of rail-ties, and groups of men all night were carrying the heated rails to the nearest trees, and bending them around the trunks."[26] Soldiers who took particular pride in this work periodically left the rails twisted into the letters U and S, as a reminder of the futility of the rebellion.

Tearing up the railroad was not the only activity of the soldiers on their march; many still found time to loot and pillage the homes they passed. Most of the inhabitants of the area made an effort to bury their valuables in hopes of preserving them, but it was often in vain. Major George Ward Nichols, aide-de-camp to General Sherman, noted the treasure hunts of the Union soldiers:

> Whenever the army halted, almost every inch of ground in the vicinity of the dwellings was poked by ramrods, pierced with sabres, or upturned with spades. The universal digging was good for the garden land, but its results were distressing for the Rebel owners of exhumed property, who saw it rapidly and irretrievably "confiscated." . . . It was all fair spoil of war, and the search made one of the excitements of the march.[27]

Thomas Maguire wrote in his journal that on the night of November 15, Slocum's Corps camped at his house, slaughtering his remaining hogs and

---

[25]*Official Records*, Vol. 44, 216-301.

[26]William T. Sherman, *Memoirs of General William T. Sherman* (New York: Charles L. Webster & Co., 1891), 180.

[27]George Ward Nichols, *Story of the Great March* (New York: Harper & Brothers, 1865), 112.

sheep to feed themselves. Maguire and a neighbor spent the night hiding in the woods. When he returned to his "Promised Land" the following morning he found "great destruction of property." The gin house, stables, barn, and fencing were in ashes, and the corn cribs, straw, and bales of cotton were still smoldering. Cotton bales had been slashed open and laid out as beds by the soldiers. It was, he concluded, "the destruction of Jerusalem on a small scale." Meanwhile, according to the recollections of Major Henry Hitchcock, in the vicinity a detachment from a Federal signal corps climbed Pine Mountain near Lithonia to keep a lookout for the enemy. Presumably, the invaders kept a vigil on top of Stone Mountain, as well.

The surrender of the Confederacy in April 1865 began a twelve year period known as Reconstruction, when the Southern states were under military rule, and daily life, though closer to normal than the previous year, was still not what it had been before the war. Agriculture particularly suffered as a result of the conflict. Even after five years of recovery production remained in decline, as is evident from the 1870 agricultural census.

Stone Mountain farmers showed a decline in farm animals of thirty to seventy percent from prewar levels, which led directly to a drop in animal products. The amount of butter, for instance, declined seventy-five percent. Crop production dropped twenty-five to near one hundred percent, depending on the type of crop. Corn declined forty-five percent, cotton dropped forty percent, and sweet potatoes fell ninety-two percent.

The decline in crops was related to the number of acres under cultivation, which for most farmers was about half of what it was before. This was due to several factors, including the loss of tools and draft animals, short supply of good seed, and fewer farm laborers as the result of war casualties and the emancipation of the slaves. The food shortage was so critical that 35,000 people around Atlanta were dependent on the federal government's food distribution office for three years after the war to ward off starvation.

Many families, including some around Stone Mountain, lost their farms because they could not pay the land taxes imposed by the Reconstruction government. Among those fortunate enough to have retained some of their gold (Confederate notes being worthless), a few bought up the confiscated land for a fraction of its value. The 1870 agricultural census shows three Stone Mountain farmers who each doubled their landholding to 800 acres.

Freed slaves continued to work in the fields, but as hired laborers for those who could afford to hire them, or more often as sharecroppers. Their newfound freedom allowed them to leave the homes of their former owners and many of them congregated together to begin a new neighborhood on the southern edge of town. They called this new community Sherman town in honor of their liberator.

The hard times, the deprivation of the legal rights of white Southerners, and resentment against northern domination led to the rise of the Ku Klux Klan in 1866 to fight against what many Southerners viewed as Yankee oppression. The usual targets for the Klan's nocturnal raids were the most defenseless segment of society--the freed slaves. The Klan was ordered disbanded by its leader, General Nathan Bedford Forrest, in 1869, but isolated remnants continued to operate through 1871. One can only speculate about the level of Klan activity in DeKalb County after the war, but the twentieth century Klan would eventually become much more important in the history of Stone Mountain.

Even if the farmers were having a difficult time, the businesses in the village proper recovered quickly by comparison. The railroads were soon rebuilt and the various establishments were again vying for tourist dollars. An advertisement in the 4 October 1866 edition of the *Atlanta Intelligencer* boasted about the dining experience awaiting at the New Georgia Railroad Eating House, M.D. Lee & Co., Proprietors. "Pleasure Parties" could be accommodated on short notice with lunch, dinner or dancing, should they desire, at the "House With the Blue Front!"

In fairly short order, Stone Mountain regained its reputation as "Atlanta's favorite picnic ground," and as a summer resort. In August 1871 the editor of the *Albany News* wrote to the editor of the *Daily Constitution* in Atlanta to praise Stone Mountain as "a delightful summer retreat," and went on at length about the virtues of the King House hotel run by White. Attractions in town for visitors at this time included a velocipede rink near the depot, wrestling exhibitions, croquet, foot races, and watermelon cuttings.

A unique event in the annals of Stone Mountain tourism took place a few years later for the Centennial Celebration on 4 July 1876. To commemorate the hundredth anniversary of the nation's birth, the townsfolk were not content with the customary hoe-down and shooting of the anvil; they wanted a really big show. They got one when Miles A. Killiam, a local blacksmith, sent two huge boulders tumbling down the steep side of the mountain with a hefty charge of dynamite. Newspaper advertisements encouraged people to come out and enjoy this once-in-a-life-time spectacle, and no doubt thousands did.

Tom Willingham was another area resident known for his exploits on the mountain. Newspaper accounts from the 1870s document his adventures as an amateur explorer and rescuer of stranded people who had fallen part way down the steep side of the mountain. Willingham made an attempt in 1876 to explore a cavity high on the mountain's north face, but this quest turned into a fiasco. He was lowered down the side of the mountain in a basket to the level of the shallow hole, and just as he looked inside he was attacked by a swarm of bees. He screamed to his cohorts to pull him back up, but halfway to safety he fainted. George Jones, one of his companions, then climbed down the rope and held the unconscious Willingham in the basket as both were pulled up. Later, a story developed concerning someone who did finally climb down a rope to look inside that hole. They reportedly found a folded piece of paper with the message, "You are not the first darn fool who has been here."

Apart from the tourism, which was mostly seasonal, the mercantile and building trades profited handsomely from all the rebuilding around Atlanta after the war. At this time quarrying began to take off as an organized industry. A study of the deed records concerning the Stone Mountain property shows that the heirs of Andrew Johnson sold his holdings on the mountain (which amounted to most of it) in 1853 to William B. W. Dent, congressman for the fourth district. Dent paid $25,000 for the mountain, which his heirs sold in 1863 for only $22,638 to William B. Wood and John T. Meador. Wood and Meador resold the mountain six years later to the Stone Mountain Granite Company. This company was formed in 1869, marking the first systematic effort for large-scale commercial production of Stone Mountain granite. The Stone Mountain Granite Company bought up some remaining partial interests in the mountain owned by other people, bringing the total purchase price for the mountain to $45,400. The act of incorporation granted the right to build a spur line from the mountain to connect with the Georgia Railroad in the village. Much of the quarrying at this time was done on the northwest side of the mountain.

In 1878 the Stone Mountain Railway and Granite Company was incorporated. It bought up what interests in the mountain the other company did not own (for $5,012), and then in 1880 bought the controlling interest in the Stone Mountain Granite Company, renaming the merged companies the Stone Mountain Granite and Railroad Company.

The demand for skilled stonecutters to work in the granite quarries at Stone Mountain, Lithonia, and Rock Chapel attracted immigrants from England, Wales, Scotland, Sweden, Norway, and Italy, thus giving an international flavor to these small towns. Quarry workers, whether immigrants or natives, tended to be a rough and tumble lot. Their work was hard and dangerous, with the specter of injury or death facing them each day. Most newcomers had to live in crowded boarding houses because new house construction lagged behind the rapid increase in population. To compensate for the demanding labor and crowded living conditions, these men played as hard as they worked.

Quarry workers were noted for their rowdiness, and frequent complaints against them included card playing, drunkenness, dancing, brawling, profanity, chicken shooting, disorderly walking, and violating the Sabbath. One curb cutter noted of late nineteenth-century life, that "compared to Lithonia on a Saturday afternoon, Dodge City would be like a Sunday School picnic."[28]

The local churches fought back against such conduct with only limited success. When behavior got wildly out of hand, the law stepped in, usually resulting in a little jail time and a fine. Serious offenses, however, could lead to a hanging. A retired quarry worker once wrote, "Local people like to think all the real bad characters were hanged publicly and thus excluded from their ancestry."[29] Many of these immigrant workers married local girls and settled down in Stone Mountain and Lithonia, where their descendants have become leading citizens.

The *Georgia Gazetteer* attested to the rapid growth of the village of Stone Mountain. The 1879-80 *Gazetteer* lists the population at around 750, while the 1886-87 edition estimates 1,200 inhabitants--an increase of sixty percent in just seven years. The *Gazetteer* also notes that granite, cotton (4,000 bales annually), and produce were the principal shipments. The 1881-82 edition listed whiskey as one of the principal shipments due to the presence of the Coxon Hill Distillery built on the south base of the mountain in the 1850s. According to Atlanta historian Franklin Garrett, Stone Mountain's four saloons were the last in the county to close with the onset of prohibition in November 1885.

---

[28]New South Associates, *Stone Mountain Historic Sites Survey* (Stone Mountain, GA: New South Associates, 1994), 29.

[29]Patton, 10.

As for schools and churches, the *Gazetteer* shows a strong presence, with one common school, two academies, and three churches--Baptist, Methodist, and Presbyterian. Interestingly, the bars in town outnumbered the churches. The first school in town was the Stone Mountain Academy, chartered in 1838. This was followed by the Stone Mountain Female College in 1866, and a common school sometime in the 1870s. The Stone Mountain University School for Boys was founded in 1900 by W. H. Conter and W. B. Griffin.

In 1886 the Stone Mountain Granite and Railway Company sold its holdings for $70,000 to the newly-formed Southern Granite Company, composed of the following partners: George Morelin, of Cincinnati, president; Charles Horne, of Atlanta, secretary and treasurer; William Hoyt Venable, of Atlanta, vice-president; and Samuel Hoyt Venable, of Atlanta, general manager. This marked the beginning of the long and close association of the Venable name with Stone Mountain.

William Hoyt Venable (1852-1905) and Samuel Hoyt Venable (1856-1939) were the two eldest of the eight children of William R. and Sarah Hoyt Venable. The boys both grew up during the Civil War and Reconstruction and well remembered the suffering their once-prosperous family endured. Their father died in 1874, putting the financial responsibility for the family on them. William had just been admitted to the bar after completing his studies at Oglethorpe University and tried practicing law.

Samuel tried his luck in the business world, but his early ventures were not very successful. He took a job as a bookkeeper for the Atlanta National Bank, but lost all of his savings when he made a bad investment in cotton futures. Other employees at the bank, noting his ability, honesty, and recent bad luck, persuaded him to ask for a raise. This request cost him his job. On borrowed money he established a small grocery store, but a fire completely destroyed the business a year later, one day after his insurance expired. He next entered the grain elevator business with his brother William, but this concern also failed.

Disappointed but not discouraged, Samuel learned of the thriving granite industry in DeKalb County and foresaw great possibilities for expansion. He persuaded his brother to form another partnership with him, and in 1879 the firm of Venable Brothers Contractors was born. They purchased a small ledge of granite near Lithonia and the venture was successful until the ledge was exhausted. The technique for getting at granite for cutting, called raising a ledge, had not yet been perfected. The Venables faced a crisis as the Scotch quarrymen working for them grew impatient for the new ledge to be raised. They would not stay without being paid, but to pay the sixty men during the idle period would bankrupt the company.

According to what may be an apocryphal tale, Samuel invited the "blockers," as the quarry workers were known, over for beer and to discuss the matter. He then made them an unusual proposition; he would wrestle with them, one at a time, and for every man who threw him down he would pay full wages of six dollars a day to keep them on, but every man whom he threw down had to remain at his house for a week without wages. He reserved the right to select the men he would wrestle first and to rest for five minutes after each bout.

This sporting arrangement appealed to the blockers and they accepted his terms. Sam Venable's tall, thin build belied his iron strength. He threw down nine of the men, rested for ten minutes, then threw down ten more. The others refused to wrestle and they all agreed to remain with him for another week. Fortunately, the new ledge was raised just three days later, allowing the blockers to go back to work and the Venables to pay them.[30]

In just one year, the Venables were able to expand, acquiring the "Big Ledge" quarry at Lithonia, and the Pine Mountain and Arabia Mountain properties. Six years later the made their greatest expansion of all when they went into partnership with Morelin and Horne to buy Stone Mountain. A year after the purchase, Morelin and Horne sold their interests in the company to William and Samuel Venable and George W. Foster for the sum of $45,000. In less than ten years, Samuel and William controlled most of the granite industry in DeKalb County through their two companies. The Venables bought out Foster's stake in 1893 for $1,800, and purchased 325 additional acres from John Meador for another $3,600. Since they were now the sole owners of Stone Mountain, the Venables folded up the Southern Granite Company and added its holdings to the granite empire of Venable Brothers Contractors.

A brochure published by the Venables in 1901 billed Stone Mountain as "the largest deposit of merchantable granite in the world," and claimed that the property, including its developments, represented an investment to the company of $350,000. Developments included the stone cutting shed and other buildings, all machinery, wagons and mules, three miles of track connecting with the Georgia Railroad, and the "Dinky" train that hauled the men into the quarries each morning and brought them back in the evening

---

[30]Mildred Lewis Rutherford, *Miss Rutherford's Scrapbook* (October, 1924), 9.

loaded with "white gold" destined for points across the nation. The Venables boasted a production capacity at the Stone Mountain quarry of 2,000 feet of curbing and 200,000 paving blocks daily, a testament to the scope of the granite business around the turn of the century.[31]

Much of the Stone Mountain granite was used to pave streets in cities across the country. The push for paved streets toward the end of the nineteenth century created an enormous demand for vast quantities of paving and curb stones, and because of its hardness and durability granite was the favored material. These paving stones became known as "Belgian Blocks" in recognition of the immigrant workers who fashioned them and which were first used to pave many of Atlanta's downtown streets.

Its low iron content, poor water absorption, and uniform color made Stone Mountain granite desirable for use as building stone. Stone Mountain granite has been used in hundreds of post offices and courthouses across the country, as well as the steps of the east wing of the U.S. Capitol, the vaults of the Treasury Building, the Arlington Memorial Bridge, the federal gold depository at Fort Knox, four Federal Reserve banks (including the one in Atlanta), the locks of the Panama Canal, the Detroit tunnel to Canada, the Norfolk naval base, the capitol of Cuba, the Cuban National University, and the Imperial Hotel in Tokyo.

In Georgia, the granite has been used in the state capitol (for the foundation), classroom buildings of the University of Georgia, the barracks at Fort Benning, the Savannah Public Library, the Carnegie Library in Atlanta, the Fulton County Courthouse, and the Atlanta Federal Penitentiary. It also found its way into thousands of homes and commercial buildings. In addition, it has been used for countless headstones, mausoleums, and monuments across the country, including the Chickamauga National Battlefield. The greatest monument of all, of course, is the Confederate Memorial carved into the mountain itself.

During a century of active quarrying at the mountain, the techniques employed to remove the stone changed considerably. As first, stone workers still used ancient manual methods. They drilled holes along the top of the exposed ledge, hammered in wooden wedges, and then poured water over them, causing the wood to expand and the stone to split. Later, they placed two half-round pieces in the holes and drove iron wedges in between them with sledge hammers to accomplish the same thing.

---

[31]The output of the Venable's Lithonia quarries was even greater.

To ease handling the large blocks of stone were cut into the approximate shapes and sizes needed. This was accomplished by snapping a chalk line on the block to mark it off appropriately and then drilling more holes and hammering more wedges. The lines were scored with a tracing tool to facilitate a straight tearing of the granite. This was done as often as necessary to break the block down to the correct size for its intended use, whether it be for paving, curbing, or building. From the quarry site the roughed out blocks were carried over to the cutting shed to be finished properly by skilled stonecutters. Small dimension stone, such as paving blocks, were loaded by hand into a mule-drawn wagon for the trip to the shed. Larger pieces, such as curbing and building stones, had to be handled differently because of their great weight. A wagon frame with no bottom was backed over the stones and with the use of chains and winches they were slung up and fastened underneath the carriage. The average curb stone was seventy-two by six by sixteen inches and weighed over 600 pounds. One or two of these was all that could be carried at one time.

Once in the cutting shed, the stonecutters, the craftsmen of the trade, began their work. By using special concave-faced hammer, paving stonecutters would quickly render the blocks the correct size, shape, and smoothness for paving stones.

Curbing was finished in different ways depending on the desired appearance. Most of it only required the use of a special pointing chisel to knock off the most offending protrusions. For a smoother finish the curb cutters would use a bush hammer, which had from four to ten chisel-like blades, or "cuts," clamped together. The more cuts the hammer had the smoother it would pulverize the surface of the stone. The ends of the curbing had to be made flat and smooth so that the pieces would join properly.

Highest in status among stonecutters were those who cut building stone. Building blocks had to be cut in order, according to a blueprint, and numbered so that the builder could assemble them correctly for an exact fit. Each stone was unique and stonecutters had to cut them precisely, using little more than a straight edge and an experienced eye to guide them. On the face of the stone to be exposed, the cutter also had to be able to render a variety of surfaces, whether textured in some fashion, fluted (for columns), flat, or polished. Depending on the design of the building, the work could demand no small amount of artistry from the stonecutter.

The act of quarrying produced large quantities of irregularly shaped stone called rubble. Rough rubble was used as is out of the quarry. Coursed rubble, to be usable, first had to be bankered up, or squared into a more regular rectangular form. No finish work was done on rubble, which was used for less expensive work.

Toward the end of the nineteenth century, new technologies became available to aid the quarrying process. The air compressor was one of the most important innovations of the day. To raise a new ledge from a flat expanse of rock, holes ten or twelve feet deep were drilled and packed with black powder, which was detonated with a burning fuse. This was repeated every day with ever-increasing loads of powder for as long as a month. The resulting explosions cracked the rock laterally. The more time given to this step the smoother the separation along the crystalline layers of the stone.

The air compressor was then used to force air underneath the loosened sheet of rock. This was done on hot summer days, so that he heat would expand the air and increase the underground pressure. Eventually, the pressure was great enough to cause the ledge to pop up, accompanied by a very loud cracking and booming, like a combined earthquake and explosion, as the pent-up pressure was released. The air compressor also made possible the pneumatic drill, which was much faster and easier that the old method.

The pointed tools used by stonecutters required constant sharpening. A blacksmith was always on site to reheat the iron tools and hammer a fresh point on them. In the early twentieth century, however, carbide tips were introduced that did not dull as quickly and could be resharpened on an emery wheel. The twentieth century also saw the introduction of pneumatic shears and saws, comprised of a steel cable embedded with tiny pieces of carbide running along a series of pulleys to cut the stone faster and easier, although finishing was still done by hand.

For all the benefits it brought the town, the granite industry committed one unpardonable act on the mountain--the destruction of the Devil's Cross Roads. In 1896 quarry workers discovered that this amazing geological feature was composed of superior quality granite for building stone. Since better stone brought a higher price, they broke it up and lowered it down the mountain by winches, much to the dismay of visitors and to the regret of future generations. Unfortunately, not even a photograph of the Cross Roads seems to have survived.

Some of the public objected to the quarrying activities there. James Randall lamented in *Walker's Magazine* that the Venable Brothers had "no sentiment in the premises." He continued:

> For years they have, as they had the right to do technically or absolutely, been hacking, mutilating, gashing and defacing this grand mountain. . . . I wish, in common with many others, that this lawful vandalism should cease; that the mountain be saved, and that, if not too late, some effort made to bring it into state ownership and protection for all time to come.[32]

William H. Venable died in 1905 and his brother Samuel took over as head of the company. A few years later he began to lease the company's holdings to other quarrying companies, profiting from lease fees while leaving the hard work for others. He leased the Stone Mountain property in 1911 to the Weiblen Brothers of New Orleans, Louisiana, who operated there for twenty-four years as the Stone Mountain Granite Corporation.

Largely as a result of the quarry industry, Stone Mountain became the second largest city in DeKalb County by the 1890s, surpassed only by the county seat of Decatur. When created in 1822, the site chosen to be the seat was close to the center of the county. However, when the western half was cut off in 1853 to form Fulton County, Decatur was left on the western edge of DeKalb. This was used as an excuse by some to agitate for the removal of the county government from Decatur.

The issue came to a head in 1896 when the county decided to build a new courthouse to replace the inadequate structure that had been built fifty years earlier. The solicitation for bids by the County Ordinary was met with an injunction from proponents of Stone Mountain as the county seat. The matter was put to popular election in December, 1896, to determine the question of removal. Much to the chagrin of the Decaturites, Stone Mountain won by a vote of 814 to 160, and despite objections, the Georgia Supreme Court held that the election was valid.

Supporters of Decatur as the county seat had one more card to play. They appealed to the state legislature, and accordingly, a bill was introduced in November, 1897. The vote went 85 for removal and 60 against, but since removal required a two-thirds majority, the measure failed. Despite the public vote, a motion to reconsider was squashed, thus ending Stone Mountain's bid to become the county seat,. The new courthouse was built of granite, but from Lithonia, not Stone Mountain.

Of the many activities that occurred at Stone Mountain, the most nationally significant was the revival of the Ku Klux Klan on November 25,

---

[32]James R. Randall, "Stone Mountain," *Walker's Magazine* (October, 1905), 10.

1915. The original Klan was officially disbanded in 1869, but was romanticized in folk legend for decades after. The revived Klan was founded by "Colonel" William J. Simmons, a former minister and organizer for fraternal associations. Born in Alabama in 1880, Simmons grew up on stories of his father's war service and the Ku Klux Klan. He long thought of founding his own fraternal order based on the Klan, and in the fall of 1915 the moment seemed right. The first American feature film, *The Birth of A Nation*, was making its way across the country at this time. It glorified the old South and the original Klan, and created quite a stir of interest among the public.

Simmons timed the creation of his Knights of the Ku Klux Klan to coincide with the premiere of the film in Atlanta. He gathered together nearly forty men from various fraternal orders, including two members of the original Klan, the Speaker of the Georgia legislature, and Samuel H. Venable, owner of Stone Mountain. Formal induction ceremonies were set for Thanksgiving Eve. The members gathered at Atlanta's Piedmont Hotel, but Simmons had a surprise prepared for them. He ushered them onto a hired bus and took them out to Stone Mountain where they picked their way up the dark slope by flashlight.

Under Simmons' direction, the fifteen shivering men gathered stones to build a base for the cross of pine boards he had brought up earlier that day, and a crude altar upon which he laid an American flag, an open Bible, an unsheathed sword, and a canteen of water. They put on the bed-sheet robes and pointed masked caps and then gathered around in a semi-circle as Simmons touched a match to the kerosene-soaked cross, the dancing light of the wind-blown flames creating an eerie backdrop for the ceremony. With practiced oratory he then called forth the Invisible Empire from its slumber of nearly half a century. When *The Birth of A Nation* opened in Atlanta a week later, the local newspapers carried Simmons's announcement of "The World's Greatest Secret, Social, Patriotic, Fraternal, Beneficiary Order" next to the advertisement for the movie.

Initially, Simmons' Klan proved very successful, but within a few years internal power struggles and a reputation for fraud and violence tore the organization apart. It exists now only as independent splinter groups, a feeble shadow of its early strength.

For over forty years, Stone Mountain had the dubious honor of being sacred soil for members of the Klan. In 1923 Sam Venable granted to the Atlanta Klavern an easement to the top of the mountain to hold their annual rallies. The Klan used the mountain until the state took possession in 1958 and canceled the easement, thereby booting them out. Shermantown residents report that they never had any trouble with the Klan, and some of the children would follow the marches of hooded men out of curiosity.

Modern Stone Mountain slowly began to emerge in the first two decades of the twentieth century. Many of the existing houses and commercial buildings in the heart of the village date from this period. A fire in January 1918 destroyed a large part of the old business district. The nineteenth century wooden structures were replaced with masonry buildings and a volunteer fire department organized to prevent future catastrophes of this nature. Many of the town's craftsman bungalows and present church buildings date from this period, as does the old train depot turned city hall. The introduction of mass transit in 1915 brought an electric street car line to link Stone Mountain with Decatur and Atlanta, allowing more convenient access between the country town and the big city.

At this point the village and the mountain were about to be thrust onto the national and eventually the world stage by an ambitious dream, a colorful cast of characters, and a drama of unforeseen proportions.

Chapter Three

Guardians of Imperishable Glory

Each year millions of visitors stream into Stone Mountain Park to take in the natural wonders of the great monadnock, as others before them have done for nearly two centuries. Today, however, they also come to view a man-made wonder, a unique achievement in the annals of sculptured art. The great Confederate Memorial carved into the northern face of the mountain, the world's largest piece of sculpture, measures ninety feet tall, 190 feet wide, and eleven feet deep. The three mounted figures ride 400 feet above the ground in a frame that covers an area of three acres.

Who first conceived of a Confederate memorial on the side of Stone Mountain has long been a matter of debate. After all, there is no way to know when an idea first comes to mind unless a person takes pains to record it. The written evidence in this case points to Francis Tichnor, a nineteenth-century physician and poet from Jones County, Georgia. During the Civil War, he was in charge of the Confederate hospitals in Columbus and wrote many stirring lyrics about the conflict.

Tichnor proposed a monument on Stone Mountain dedicated to Alexander Stephens and other heroes of the Confederacy in an 1869 poem. In his verse he asks the question:

May we not mate the mountain and the man--
The granite dome and the great Georgian? . . .
One in their grandeur! Who shall bid apart
Those stalwart coils that clasp our Georgia's heart?

At the time, it was just a poet's dream. But William H. Terrell, an Atlanta attorney and son of a Confederate veteran, entertained the notion again in the twentieth century. He first suggested it publicly on May 26, 1914 in an editorial for the *Atlanta Constitution*. Initially he proposed to carve niches into the vertical face of the mountain where might be placed great statues of leading Confederates. A museum in the form of a Greek temple could be erected on top of the mountain, which would be dedicated as a public park. Terrell recommended that the Sons of Confederate Veterans and the United Daughters of the Confederacy take the lead in the movement for such a memorial.

For many years he had been disturbed by the perception that the Southern perspective had been neglected in modern histories and that Northern states and the Grand Army of the Republic had spent millions of dollars on memorials to their heroes while the South had not. Sitting in his Atlanta office one afternoon in late 1913, with Stone Mountain in view through the window, the idea struck him that it would make an ideal place for a giant memorial.[1] He may have been influenced subconsciously by Tichnor's poem, but he never credited it as a source of his inspiration.

The call for a memorial on Stone Mountain was echoed three weeks later by John Temple Graves, editor of the *New York American*. A former Atlantan, Graves was in the city for his son's graduation when he heard talk of Terrell's suggestion. He thought it was a tremendous idea and wrote a lengthy and favorable editorial in June 14 issue of the *Georgian*. Graves argued eloquently for "Nature's matchless plan for a memorial" and elaborated on Terrell's idea by suggesting a single statue seventy feet high of General Robert E. Lee in the uniform of the Confederate Army "of which the grey stone is the natural base." He even specifically called for the great sculptor Lorado Taft to create the "object of artistic, romantic and sentimental interest unique among the wonders of the age."[2]

Now the memorial idea had taken on a more concrete form than in the more generalized statements of William Terrell. These two editorials, particularly the rousing piece by Graves, fired the imagination of C. Helen Plane, a diminutive widow and member of the United Daughters of the Confederacy (UDC).

Helen Plane, nee Jemison, was born in 1829 on a plantation near Tuscaloosa, Alabama. A true Southern belle, she eventually captured the heart of the dashing William F. Plane. They were married in 1854 and moved to Columbus, Georgia. When the Civil War erupted, her husband, a doctor, became a captain in the Confederate army. He was killed in 1862 at the Battle of Sharpsburg, and for the rest of her life, Helen devoted herself to preserving the memory of her husband and the cause he served.

---

[1]George Raffalovich, "Stone Mountain's Memorial Controversy," 1938, manuscript at the Atlanta History Center, Atlanta, Georgia.

[2]Lucian Lamar Knight, *Georgia's Landmarks, Memorials and Legends* (Atlanta: Byrd Printing Company, 1916), 250-251.

One of the organizers of the Atlanta Chapter of the United Daughters of the Confederacy in the 1890s, Plane later organized the Georgia State Division of the UDC and served as its first president. She considered her greatest contribution to be the establishment of college scholarships to descendants of Confederate Veterans.

In 1914 the eighty-five-year-old Confederate widow was no longer an active officer in the UDC, but she held the title of Honorary Life President of the Georgia Division and maintained a strong interest in the work. When she read the editorials by Terrell and Graves she became possessed of a "wonderful vision" of a carved figure of General Lee standing proudly on the face of the mountain. In a letter to the Philadelphia *Public Ledger*, Plane noted:

> Now the time has arrived for us to cease the erection of small and perishable local monuments such as were erected before the UDC organization began the more costly ones to Davis, Lee and others, and more recently the one to our dead at Arlington, and concentrate our efforts on one which shall be a shrine for the South and of which all Americans may be justly proud.[3]

Plane's first step was to contact John T. Graves and William Terrell to refine the concept and discuss ways of turning it into reality. She also wrote to Sam Venable to confirm his willingness to allow a carving on the side of Stone Mountain. Secure in their enthusiastic support, Plane prepared a resolution to present at the next meeting of the Atlanta Chapter of the UDC suggesting the carving of a seventy-foot bust of Lee on the side of the mountain. The chapter unanimously adopted her resolution and, at the suggestion of Mrs. A. McD. Wilson, voted one hundred dollars out of the treasury to forward the work.

She next went before the annual convention of the Georgia Division of the UDC in October, 1914, at Eastman. There she received further endorsement of the project. With the approval of the Atlanta Chapter and the Georgia Division, Plane organized a special committee called the UDC Stone Mountain Memorial Association, which she served as president, to take charge of the project.

---

[3]Helen Plane to the Philadelphia *Pubic Ledger*, 14 January 1916, Helen Plane Papers, Special Collections Department, Robert W. Woodruff Library, Emory University, Atlanta, Georgia.

The first task before the Association was to select a sculptor to design and execute the monument. Initial thoughts on the matter turned to some of the best known names of the day--Lorado Taft, Auguste Rodin, and the South's favorite son, Moses Ezekiel--but all were considered too old for such rigorous work and rejected. Eventually, Plane and the Association hit upon the name of Gutzon Borglum.

John Gutzon de la Mothe Borglum was born of Danish parents in March 25, 1867, in Idaho. He first studied painting in San Francisco and then at the Ecole des Beaux Arts in Paris. He developed a reputation as a painter before turning to sculpture in the late 1890s. He distinguished himself in the art world for such works as *Mares of Diomedes* in New York's Metropolitan Museum of Art, the figures of the Apostles in the Cathedral of St. John the Divine in New York, the statues of General Sheridan and James Smithson (for whom the Smithsonian is named) in Washington DC, and for his statue of a seated Lincoln in Newark, New Jersey. At the time Helen Plane was trying to get the Stone Mountain memorial project started, Borglum was receiving kudos for his sculptured head of Abraham Lincoln on display at the Capitol rotunda. Lincoln was a hero of Borglum and the artist's feeling for the subject is evident in the work. Robert Todd Lincoln claimed that it was by far the finest portrayal of his father ever done.

Plane was aware of Borglum's creation, and of the General John Gordon equestrian statue on the grounds of the Georgia capitol executed by his younger brother, Solon. On her own initiative and without consulting anyone else, Plane wrote to Gutzon in June, 1915, outlining her proposal and inviting him to come see the mountain for himself. She included a copy of Graves' stirring editorial as an additional persuasive voice.

Borglum wrote back the following month that he would be glad to come to Atlanta to inspect the mountain and submit a cost estimate. He warned, however, that competitive bidding did not serve well the interests of great art and that the Association would do better to "find a sculptor who has the ability, the imagination, the courage, as well as the sympathy to place Lee in the unique position he holds among great men and great generals . . . ." adding that he had an idea grand enough to be "fitting for Lee and his cause."[4]

Obviously excited by the concept of carving Stone Mountain and with his imagination already beginning to play with the possibilities, Borglum agreed to visit Atlanta in August. Greeting Borglum at the train station

[4]Gutzon Borglum to Helen Plane, 9 July 1915, Plane Papers.

along with other members of the UDC, Plane was polite, but would not shake his hand--he was, after all, a Yankee. The women took him to Stone Mountain and introduced him to Sam Venable at the family's summer home, Mont Rest, at the foot of the mountain. During his visit he explored the great rock, climbing over it, walking around it, studying the contours and the lighting from all angles, making measurements and photographing each surface. He expressed amazement at the magnitude of the rock and was fascinated by the quarries around it. In the evenings, after supper, he sat on the porch with Sam Venable and watched the mountain turn shades of lavender, mauve, and purple in the setting sun. In the twilight he listened to Venable's stories of the War, Reconstruction, and the South's struggles to retain its pride and heritage.

After examining the mountain for three days, Borglum reported to the Association that the single figure they had in mind was not commensurate with the great size of the mountain and that the face of Robert E. Lee would be dwarfed into significance. He asked for time to draw up a proposal that would do credit to the mountain and to the Southern cause. In a brief note to Plane before leaving Atlanta, the sculptor wrote that he would begin at once upon models and drawings and would keep her informed of the progress, adding, "I can see Lee's, Jackson's, Johnson's Army finding their way over that Mountain."[5] The vague idea mentioned in his first letter was beginning to take on concrete form.

Borglum returned to Atlanta a few weeks later to present his plan to the UDC Association. His concept was as spectacular as he had promised--a veritable army of colossal figures riding across the face of the mountain. The design called for five groups of figures, each representing an aspect of the Confederate fighting forces. The central group consisted of Generals Lee and Jackson and President Jefferson Davis as Commander in Chief, plus four others to be decided later, on horseback symbolizing the top leadership of the military. The second group called for cluster of sixty-five mounted officers to represent each of the thirteen Confederate states. Exactly which officers was to be determined by the states themselves. The third group, to the right of the central figures, consisted of General Forrest and his cavalry. The infantry and artillery groups would be descending from above as if marching to join the cavalry.

All the figures, an estimated 700 to 1,000 of them, would be facing east to greet the dawn of a new day. The figures would range in height from

---

[5]As quoted by *The Emory University Quarterly* 8 (June 1952), 111.

thirty-five to fifty feet, and the total length of the carving would be 1,200 feet. Borglum wanted to create the impression that the figures were alive and moving silently over the surface of the mountain and not simply across its side.

The sculpted army on the mountain's scarp was only half of the memorial, however. Borglum also proposed to carve into the mountain, at its base and underneath the central group, a colonnade of thirteen columns. Behind these columns would be cut a room extending sixty feet into the mountain and stretching the 320 feet of the colonnade, with a height of forty feet. This Memorial Hall would be decorated with the seals of each state and would be dedicated to the women of the Confederacy. In the center of the Hall would be sculpted from the rock the seated figure of a Southern woman entitled *Memory*, which would be as large as the figure being carved for the Lincoln Memorial in the nation's capital. The UDC was encouraged to make this hall their archive to store and preserve the relics and records of Confederate history.

Borglum reported to the ladies that the work would take eight years to complete and would cost two million dollars, an amount, he pointed out, comparable to the Lincoln Memorial then under construction. The central group of figures, he noted however, could be finished for $250,000. This was a frightening prospect for the Association with its limited fundraising experience. Nevertheless, they were swept up in the sculptor's vision and approved the plan, appointing him the official sculptor of Stone Mountain.

Plane prevailed upon Borglum personally to lay his scheme before the UDC national convention in San Francisco that October. She believed that his eloquence would persuade the national body to adopt the Stone Mountain project.

At the UDC convention, Borglum captivated the audience with a stirring speech filled with heroic imagery, his voice ringing out words of duty, sacrifice, and honor. He compared his plan to other great monuments of history--the Egyptian pyramids, the Acropolis of Greece, and the Colossus of Rhodes. Only Stone Mountain, he proclaimed, would be greater than these because of the imperishable nature of the mountain. The Confederate host would ride across Stone Mountain long after all other works of men had crumbled to dust. He assured the UDC of the practicality of such a project and that financing would not be an obstacle.

In closing he said, "The Confederacy furnished the story, God furnished the mountain. If I can furnish the craftsmanship and if you will furnish the financial support, then we will put there something before which the world will stand amazed. The whole world is waiting for us to begin."[6]

Plane was correct in believing that Borglum could win the support of the national UDC, but she was mistaken in believing that the organization would adopt the project. The convention delegates voted to endorse it, but did not want to take on any new works, particularly one so costly, because they were already heavily obligated to existing projects. There was also a faction that thought the whole idea was crazy and could never be accomplished.

Not deterred by the setback, Helen Plane went before the annual convention of the Georgia Division of the UDC the following month to solicit its support once again. She reported on the progress made thus far and read the text of Borglum's San Francisco speech. There was a motion to accept the memorial as a work of the Georgia Division and a second, but the measure failed to pass when put to a vote. Instead, individual chapters were permitted to make voluntary contributions to the memorial. Plane left the convention with pledges from thirty-two chapters totaling $5,905. On three occasions the UDC organization had endorsed but refused to underwrite the Stone Mountain Memorial. Now Plane's small Association would be solely responsible for seeing the project through.

At the same time that Plane went before the Georgia Division convention, "Colonel" William Simmons was orchestrating the revival of the Ku Klux Klan. He possibly selected Stone Mountain as the place for the nocturnal ceremony precisely because of the planned Confederate memorial. Sam Venable, the owner of the mountain, was also a Klansman. From the very beginning a circumstantial link existed between the Klan and the Confederate memorial, a fact that would taint public perception of the project in the future.

In December, 1915, just three weeks after Simmons burned that first cross, Helen Plane wrote to Borglum:

> The 'Birth of A Nation' will give us a percentage of the next Monday's matinee. Since seeing this wonderful and beautiful picture of Reconstruction in the South, I feel that it is due to the Ku Klux Klan which saved us from Negro domination and carpet-bag rule, that it be immortalized on Stone Mountain. "Why not represent a

---

[6]Minutes of the Georgia Division, United Daughters of the Confederacy, 16-20 November 1915.

small group of them in their nightly uniform approaching in the distance?[7]

As the Klan had not existed when Borglum first visited, he did not know anything about the organization or exactly how to respond to Plane's request. He decided against amending his carving design, but not wanting to offend his patron, he included a KKK altar in the overall plan for the memorial. A little later, probably at the urging of Sam Venable, Borglum actually joined the Klan and within a few years participated actively at the highest levels.

Early in 1916 Borglum moved his family from Stamford, Connecticut, to Stone Mountain to begin the project in earnest. The Borglums were provided with a house in Avondale Estates by G. F. Willis, founder of the upscale, Alpine-inspired community about seven miles west of the mountain.

To mark the official start of the work, the Association planned a dedication on 20 May 1916. For the ceremony, Borglum wanted to drape a huge Confederate battle flag over the spot on the mountain where he planned to carve the figure of General Lee. All of the stonecutters he approached, however, refused to cross the red warning line painted on the summit, which marked the limits of how far one could safely go. This meant no one would be willing to work on the mountainside.

Fortunately, a handyman and jack-of-all-trades by the name of Jesse Tucker happened to be working on the speaker's platform for the ceremony and volunteered to help Borglum with his problem. With rope around waist, Tucker carefully worked his way past the red line and down the slope. He hammered two metal anchors into the rock from which the flag could be suspended by 300-foot long ropes. In accomplishing this task, Tucker exhibited resourcefulness and ingenuity, two qualities indispensable for mountain carving. Borglum hired him on the spot to be the superintendent of the carving project.

With the Confederate flag hanging high above, the dedication ceremony went forward as planned. Master Mason N. H. Ballard performed the rites for the unveiling of a cornerstone erected in a grove at the base of the mountain to mark the boundary of the deeded property.

---

[7]Helen Plane to Gutzon Borglum, 17 December 1915, Plane Papers.

Sick and unable to attend, Sam Venable sent his brother-in-law, James Ellis, to deliver a short address in his place. Coribel Venable Kellogg, daughter of the late William H. Venable, presented the warranty deed to Helen Plane. The deed granted to the Stone Mountain Confederate Monumental Association the scarp of the mountain, ten acres at the base, and a protective easement over the skyline of the mountain. The deed stipulated that the memorial include a tomb to the memory of William and Samuel Venable, and that the land revert back to the donors if the memorial was not completed within twelve years.

One member of the Venable family nearly prevented the granting of the land. Mrs. Robert ("Aunt Bob") Venable Roper, sister of Coribel Kellogg, filed an injunction against any transfer of property on the basis that she, as the other beneficiary of William Venable's estate, had not been consulted in business matters of the company and that her uncle had exceeded his authority in making the grant without her consent. Plane conferred with Mrs. Roper about the project and persuaded her to deed her one-fourth interest in the mountain separately. Her deed carried the same stipulations as the other one, with the added provisos that the property never be used for commercial purposes and that the memorial executed be the plan contemplated by Gutzon Borglum.

In order to take possession of the property, Plane, with the assistance of William Terrell as attorney, had incorporated her group a month prior as the Stone Mountain Confederate Monumental Association and opened the membership to business leaders who wished to support the project. Among the original incorporators were such notable Atlantans as J. K. Orr, Lucian Lamar Knight, Hooper Alexander, William Plane, Clark Howell, Alex C. King, Mell R. Wilkinson, William Terrell, and John T. Graves of New York.

In December of 1916, business and community leaders were invited to a meeting at Decatur to hear the sculptor give an address on the Stone Mountain carving. According to his wife, before the meeting started Borglum happened to overhear the conversation of two men sitting in front of him.

"What's this meeting being held for?" asked one of them.

"Oh," the other sniffed, "some damn fool artist from New York has a notion he can carve up Stone Mountain, and they want him to tell us about it."[8]

This second man turned out to be Forrest Adair, one of the most prominent realtors in Atlanta. After Borglum's speech, however, Adair became a steadfast supporter of the memorial project.

Although Borglum managed to make others believe in mountain carving, privately he harbored doubts. The episode of hanging the Confederate flag underscored the numerous difficulties to be overcome. Foremost among these was the matter of how to get workers to their work site on the cliff. Borglum and Tucker designed a strong leather harness, to be buckled around the waist, which was attached to a cable running to a winch anchored on the mountain. With this device a man could sit and push himself around with his feet and have his hands free to work. Another man operated the winch to raise and lower the worker. Borglum used the harness to go all over the face of the mountain exploring surface imperfections and locating the high points of his design.

Borglum then decided to have a ten-foot wide work platform halfway down the cliff, just above where the carving would be done, with a set of steps down the slope from the top. Jesse Tucker was in charge of this work. He depended largely on black laborers, some of whom came from Venable's stone quarries. Tucker inspired confidence by doing difficult tasks first to show his workers exactly how they could be done. He soon had them crossing the red line to drill holes designed to receive the iron anchors for the 480-foot long stairway. All the materials in the work had to be carted up the west side by oxen because at that time there were no trucks capable of climbing such a steep slope. The oxen pulled lumber, cement, iron rods, and tools three-fifths of the way up the mountain. When the slope became too steep for them, the materials were transferred to the arms and shoulders of Tucker's workers. Mary Borglum, the sculptor's wife, fondly recalled one of the men known as Homer, who "could take a piece of timber four by eight inches and eighteen feet long, put it on his shoulders, carry it to the top of the cliff and down the stairs without dropping it or pausing for breath."[9]

---

[8]Robert Casey and Mary Borglum, *Give The Man Room: The Story of Gutzon Borglum* (New York: Bobbs-Merrill Company, 1952), 177.

[9]Ibid., 179.

The heavy air compressor was perhaps the most difficult piece of equipment. It took two days to drag it up the slope on rollers, with two men crawling beside it on hands and knees every foot of the way to keep the rollers adjusted.

Work on the mountain paused in the winter, and the following spring, on 6 April 6 1917, Congress declared war on Germany, launching the United States into World War I. The country needed all the engineers it could get, so Jesse Tucker joined the army and was shipped overseas. Borglum shut down the operation and returned with his family to their Stamford estate. The sculptor was very active politically and became a government investigator during the war to look into reports of corruption in the aircraft industry.

In light of these events and other urgent demands for time and money created by war-related activities, the Stone Mountain Confederate Monumental Association executive committee reported to its members that under the circumstances the only proper thing to do was to suspend the activities of the Association until the return of peace. This hiatus was to last for three years.

Biographers of the Borglum brothers have noted that the Venables and some of the ladies of the UDC may have been expecting Solon in 1915 instead of Gutzon. Some years earlier Solon had executed the General Gordon statue for the state capitol and it was he with whom they would have been acquainted. Even if Helen Plane had not been specific as to which Borglum she had invited, the issue would have been cleared up the moment the sculptor stepped off the train. Gutzon, however, did expect Solon to work with him on the massive Stone Mountain project. Solon made a few visits to the mountain with Gutzon and made suggestions as to the design of the memorial and even helped to raise some funds in the early stages. He expected to do more when he finished some other commissions, but then the war intervened. By the time the carving project was solidly under way once more, Solon was dead from a ruptured appendix.

Jesse Tucker returned to the mountain after being mustered out of the army in the summer of 1919 to find the scaffolding and stairs in need of repair. He reported to Borglum that he should return to the site if he did not want to lose everything he had accomplished before the war. At the time, Borglum was working on some other large commissions, the sponsors of which wanted to have his undivided attention. He told Tucker that things had waited this long; they could wait a while longer. The main problem, as always, was a matter of money. The Association treasury was nearly depleted and the general public, having dug deeply into its pockets to support the recent war, had little interest in shelling out more for a Confederate memorial. Helen Plane was now past ninety years of age, and though still deeply committed to the project, she no longer had the energy to continue the difficult fundraising that lay ahead.

If the effort was going to move forward, the Association needed younger, more vigorous leadership. Borglum made a quick trip to Atlanta to meet with Sam Venable, Helen Plane, and several other Association members in early 1920 to discuss the situation. Plane agreed to retire with the title President Emeritus and Halle Rounsaville was elected the new president. Many of the other officers changed as well, with members of the UDC still holding most positions.

Executive committee members Sam Venable and Forrest Adair took on the assignment of raising more money. Borglum asked them to consider a fundraising offer made by E. Y. Clarke, a professional solicitor and chief recruiter for the national KKK. At the time the Klan heavily recruited Masonic lodges for new members. Several members of the Monumental Association, particularly the Freemasons, objected to accepting any help from Clarke and the Klan for fear that the carving would be seen as a Klan project. They were unable to reach any compromise for more than a year. Clarke was forced solicit funds through his own Southern Advertising Association rather than the Klan--a purely cosmetic solution that deceived no one.

For his part, Borglum took it upon himself to raise money from the state of Georgia by appealing to Governor Hugh Dorsey:

> You were one of the first to recognize the value to Atlanta and the country of this great memorial. I want to ask you to help me go on with the work now. . . . There are many rich men in Virginia and North Carolina who would contribute heavily to this work if they get some expression of definite activity from your city and state . . . . I receive inquiries about it from all over the country. It would not require much money to carve. . . .[10]

---

[10]As quoted in Howard and Audrey Shaff, *Six Wars At A Time: The Life and Times of Gutzon Borglum* (Sioux Falls, SD: Center for Western Studies, Augustana College, 1985), 188.

This would not be the first or the last time that Borglum claimed he could raise vast sums of money for a project. Unconvinced, Dorsey wrote back that he was "very dubious" as to the sculptor meeting with success. While project leaders revived fundraising efforts, Jesse Tucker began the preparatory work at the mountain. Borglum had decided to scaffold the entire area for the central group. Tucker repaired the staircase from the top of the mountain and a new one, seven hundred feet long, was built to the carving site from the base of the escarpment five hundred feet below. Several large platforms housed the blacksmith shop, machine shop, supply shed, and cable hoist. A new air compressor was installed at the base, out of the danger zone, with 1,700 feet of air hoses reaching up the mountain. The Georgia Power Company estimated the cost of bringing electricity to the carving site at $15,000, but Preston Arkright, president of the company, reduced the bill by eighty percent, and then canceled it altogether.

Borglum was unable to free himself from other work to return to the Stone Mountain memorial until the summer of 1921, but his thoughts were never very far from it. During his absence he had hit upon some new ideas about which he was quite enthusiastic.

One of these was for an amphitheater at the base of the cliff. This idea was actually suggested by Nan Stephens, of Atlanta, who discovered the sounding board qualities of the granite wall. At the first opportunity, Borglum arranged for Marie Tiffany, of the Metropolitan Opera Company, to come sing for the members of the Association and demonstrate the acoustics of the place. The test was so successful that the Association approved plans for the amphitheater.

Another idea addressed the repeated inquiries about the place of the Confederate Navy in the memorial. To commemorate these oft-neglected heroes, Borglum planned a large bronze group to be placed in front of the Memorial Hall. His third idea evolved out of his need for a studio at the mountain. He envisioned a great building made from the mountain's granite which could house an art school. The students, he explained, could learn sculpture by being part of the great work, as they did in Renaissance Italy. In this case his scheme did not win out. He got his studio, but it was a more modest wooden structure.

As to the main project, Borglum still wrestled with the technical aspects of the work. He had determined how to get his carving crew on the side of the mountain, but putting his design there was still problematic. The scale of the figures was so great and the curving surface such that it was impossible to get any correct sense of proportion from up close. Borglum attempted to solve the problem by hanging large drawings over the cliff, but this proved unsuccessful. Then he announced that he would pour photographic emulsion on the carving area, flash an image of his model through a giant enlarger, and then pour more chemicals down to develop the picture on the surface of the rock. It was an imaginative solution, but one that professional photographers assured him was impossible. By that time, however, newspapers and magazines around the world had described his plan in detail and given the project an incalculable amount of free publicity.

Borglum did find a way to use the projection concept when he and Tucker began experimenting with a giant photographic slide projector. At the time, the largest projectors had a range of only 300 feet. Borglum needed a projector that would cast an image more than 1000 feet, but the manufacturers of such machines declared that a lamp that powerful would create so much heat that the lens would crack and the slide melt. He secured the assistance of photographic engineer Charles d'Emery who helped design a special projector to meet the sculptor's requirements. Borglum then went to E. S. Porter, of the Precision Machine Company of New York, who agreed to build the projector. After several months, the experimental machine was delivered to Borglum's Stamford estate where he had returned to work on other commissions.

According to his wife, the sculptor could not seem to get the projector to focus his design on the sheets hung several hundred feet away. As he struggled to adjust the lenses, his six-year-old daughter, Mary Ellis, pointed and exclaimed: "Oh, Daddy, look! Horses riding through the woods." The light from the projector was passing through the sheets, which were much too close to the lens, and throwing the image in sharp focus against the distant trees. He now had a way of putting his design on the mountain.

He brought the one-ton projector down to Stone Mountain and had it set up a quarter of a mile from the mountain and bolted to a concrete foundation to avoid even the slightest vibration. The projector itself could swivel to any angle, up or down, left or right. At this stage he encountered another difficulty. The location for the carving was five hundred feet up, which meant that the beam of light would have to travel upward at an angle of a little more than fifty degrees and would cause a greatly distorted image.

To overcome this, he photographed the model from above at a reciprocal angle to cancel out the distorting effect. When he put the new slide in, the image appeared on the mountain as if it were on a level with the lens. The picture was so clear and the illusion so convincing that a passing motorist stopped and commented that he thought the carving had been finished.[11]

The sculptor's only guideline for developing the scale of the carving was the rule that governed the size of courthouse clocks--an inch in height for every twelve feet of distance from the viewer. By this scale, the carved figures should have been nine feet high to be clearly seen from the studio 1,300 feet away. At this size, however, the men and horses would have appeared as mere dolls. Borglum enlarged the image until it assumed a more impressive size and then called for two of his men to measure it. They swung over to the projection in their harnesses and stretched a tape measure from the top of the image to the bottom. The man at the bottom called out, "One hundred and sixty-eight feet." This information was relayed to the sculptor via the telephone he had installed between the studio and the carving platform.

The next step was for men equipped with brushes and buckets of paint to descend and outline the picture. When they tried, however, they encountered another problem. The magnification was so great that the thinnest line on the glass slide widened to more than six feet on the mountain and sharp edges became diffused. The workmen could not tell one figure from another or even where on a figure they were. Borglum tried to sharpen the focus more, but to no avail.

Not to be discouraged by this latest setback, he made a drawing of his model in the thinnest lines possible and then made a new slide from the drawing. Choosing a night with no moon to be assured of the greatest possible enhancement of the projection, Borglum sent Tucker over the cliff to try painting the outline. Even though Tucker felt as if he were in a spotlight, he discovered that filling the area with paint was not as difficult as he had anticipated. He did, however, get a scare when he began to descend through an unlit area. As he moved away from the cliff, his harness began to rotate wildly. Fortunately he swung back toward the cliff so that he was able to arrest the spinning before reaching the next illuminated area. Borglum was never aware of the danger.

The next day the two worked out a system of guide ropes to keep the men from spinning out of control, and the painting of the outline began in earnest. Each night crowds of people came out to view the projection on the mountain and to watch the men perform their nocturnal task like spiders suspended from silken threads high above the ground.

---

[11]Casey and Borglum, 185-186.

With the design on the mountain, actual carving could begin at long last. Always ready to take advantage of an opportunity for publicity, Borglum planned an elaborate ceremony. As Robert E. Lee, a Virginia native, was the first figure to be carved, he declared June 18, 1923, to be Virginia Day at Stone Mountain and invited Virginia Governor E. Lee Trinkle to attend and give the dedicatory address. A motorcade of dignitaries and officials made its way through Atlanta, out to Stone Mountain where the throngs gathered. Trinkle, Governor Thomas Hardwick of Georgia, Hollins Randolph, an Atlanta attorney and member of the Monumental Association, and others accompanied the sculptor down the steps to the main platform at the carving site.

From this lofty perch, Trinkle spoke through a megaphone to the audience on the ground. He made a few appropriate remarks, then dedicated the chisels and handed them to Borglum. Randolph gave official authorization to begin the carving, as the sculptor donned a harness and positioned himself on the rock. The audience below cheered while he drilled a few holes to mark the start of the carving--almost eight years after he had first begun the work. An airplane flew high above, and dropped three hundred roses onto the side of the mountain. Everyone then retired to the picnic tables for a barbecue dinner and more speeches. Here the sculptor presented the first chips of granite from the memorial to the dignitaries. Trinkle then gave the keynote address, speaking to the hopes of everyone there when he said:

> We shall have erected a monument which will outlive the centuries and which will carry the history of our Southern War to a future so distant that the mind of man is not gifted to grasp it. . . . Centuries will be born to die--age will follow age down the unending pathway of the years; cities, government, people will change and perish--while yet, our heroes carved in stone, will stand on guard--the custodians of imperishable glory, the sentinels of time.[12]

The day after the show, the real drilling began. To block out the figures, workers buckled into bosun's chairs, or flat boards attached to a bridle of rope, and used jackhammers to drill a row of holes almost touching along

---

[12]Address by Governor E. Lee Trinkle, 18 June 1923, Mary Carter Winter Collection, Georgia State Department of Archives.

the sides and across the bottom of a marked area. They drilled another row of holes across the top slanting downward and hammered wedges into the top holes until the block broke free and plummeted to the ground. This was slow work because the iron bits were good for only a few holes before the point was dulled and a fresh one had to be inserted. The dull bits were sent up to the blacksmith shop to be resharpened.

The slow pace of the work was frustrating to Borglum, who wrote that he spent weeks experimenting with ways of removing stone, but his efforts proved "childish and inadequate." He despaired that the work would be next to interminable with the labor he could afford and by the known means at his disposal.[13]

Borglum at first rejected explosives as too unpredictable in their results. Then he began to reason that if firearms could use a controlled explosion, there should be some way he could, as well. As he was pondering this problem, a vacationing Belgian engineer named Jean Vanophem stopped by to see the carving about which he had heard so much. When Borglum explained his difficulty, Vanophem told him of his success with small charges of dynamite for precision blasting. He explained that by drilling holes the required depth a few inches apart and then scattering light charges in a zig-zag fashion, the stone would be cracked loose by the detonation and could be easily freed with a pry bar.

After some experimentation, Jesse Tucker found that a half-ounce of dynamite sufficed for a successful charge and began to train some of his crew in its proper use. One of these men, Cliff Davis, became such an expert in this artistic form of blasting that he became known as "Dynamite Davis." The use of explosives hastened the work considerably and removed the last obstacle to completing the carving. All Borglum needed now was a steady supply of money.

The ongoing need for funds continued to be of great concern to the sculptor. Sam Venable and Forrest Adair had managed to raise several thousand dollars, but it was only a pittance compared to what was needed. E. Y. Clarke's efforts had likewise been disappointing. Most people were interested in the idea, but many were not convinced it could be done and took a wait-and-see attitude toward the project. Borglum had mortgaged his estate to obtain equipment and meet the payroll. The sculptor's agreement with the Association entitled him to a percentage of the total cost as his fee, but he could collect nothing until the actual carving began.

---

[13]As quoted in Casey and Borglum, 186.

Several Atlanta business leaders were invited to join the Association executive board in order to aid in financing the memorial. In March, 1923, Hollins Randolph was elected as the new president, and realtor E. "Pete" Rivers was named chairman of the executive committee, while journalist Rogers Winter served as publicity director. The UDC was still well represented, holding several other positions on the board.

When these men took office, they intended to make the operations of the Association more business-like. First, they opened an office in the Hurt Building in the heart of downtown Atlanta and hired an office staff to keep business hours. David Webb, Secretary of the executive committee, became the paid business manager of the Association. The committee discovered that E. Y. Clarke received a twenty-five percent commission on the money he raised and decided to drop him as a fundraiser. Instead, they formed their own salaried fundraising organization under the direct control of the executive committee. The committee also tried to get Borglum to enter into a formal contract, but for some reason the sculptor delayed, a decision which later caused him trouble.

As Borglum had earlier predicted, the real financing did not come until there was noticeable progress on the carving. The first campaign of the reorganized Association was targeted at the citizens of Atlanta. Albert S. Adams, a well-known and respected business leader, chaired the citizen's committee for the Association and netted pledges totaling $40,000 from the general public. The City of Atlanta offered $100,000, payable in five years, and Fulton County agreed to contribute a like amount. Memorial supporters and Association members across the country were asked to spearhead campaigns in their own cities.

Efforts to get a grant from the federal government failed, but President Warren G. Harding sent his personal endorsement of the project:

> [T]his gigantic work, certain to rank among the immortal memorials created by men, has always made a special appeal to my imagination. . . . I know of no equally magnificent and ambitious memorial conception. . . . The imagination runs riot as the thought of such a panorama in granite.[14]

---

[14]President Warren G. Harding to Hollins Randolph, 16 April 1923. Records of the Stone Mountain Confederate Monumental Association, Special Collections Department, Robert W. Woodruff Library, Emory University, Atlanta, Georgia.

Another strategy of the Association involved a case pending against the Atlanta Gas Light Company in the United States Supreme Court regarding excessive gas rates. The Association sent out letters to Atlanta Gas Light customers asking them to consider donating their rebates should the company lose its case. This simple effort netted the Association over $19,000.

Association Secretary David Webb suggested that tablets be placed in the planned Memorial Hall upon which would be engraved the names of Confederate veterans whose families contributed $1,000 or more. This was known as the Founder's Roll, and proved to be very popular with the public and very lucrative to the Association. A spin-off of this idea was the Children's Founder's Roll, which was established in March 1924. Through this fund, school children could subscribe one dollar to have their names recorded in a special book in Memorial Hall and receive an octagonal bronze medal depicting Borglum's design for the memorial.

Despite the increased cash flow, Borglum and Tucker were nonetheless advised to proceed cautiously. Borglum responded that the carving was the most important thing and cautioned against spending more money in the Association office than on the mountain. Since its beginning, Borglum had poured $20,000 of his own money into the project and his creditors were pressing him for many unpaid debts. Concerned that he might not get paid under his present gentleman's agreement with the Association, in August, 1923 he demanded a formal contract specifying a monthly amount he was to receive. The Association reminded him that they had asked for a contract three months earlier and requested that he submit a proposed contract for them to review. They rejected his initial submission, prompting him to halt the work. The Association responded angrily and the two sides exchanged some harsh words before a contract was signed and the work resumed. Borglum's relationship with the Association, however, was irreparably damaged.

The contract called for Borglum to complete the central group of figures by June, 1926, for a cost of $250,000. The other groups were to be completed at specified times in the following eight years, at a total cost of $1.5 million. The Memorial Hall work was to be covered under a separate agreement and cost an additional million dollars. All workers' salaries and equipment purchases were to be paid by Borglum out of the fee paid to him. Paragraph seven of the contract stipulated that the sculptor was to be paid monthly installments of $3,000 plus actual carving expenditures, the total paid not to exceed $250,000 for the central group.

As the months progressed, the head of Lee slowly emerged from the cold stone. During the early stages, Borglum was gone much of the time, either to his Stamford studio to work on other commissions, or on the lecture circuit promoting the Confederate memorial. He was in great demand to speak to UDC gatherings, women's clubs and veteran's groups all over the country. In addition, the Association expected him to show his designs whenever there was a convention in Atlanta, and there were many of them. Whenever he had to be away from the mountain, he left the work in charge of Jesse Tucker and Hugo Villa. An Italian sculptor from Milan, Villa had gone to Mexico to work on a monument many years before. A revolution put an end to the project and he fled to the United States, where he eventually came into the employee of Gutzon Borglum.

During the fall and winter of 1923, as the head of Lee came closer to completion, the sculptor spent more and more time on the side of the mountain, as it was his practice to do the finishing work himself. He aimed at finishing the head by January 19, the hundredth anniversary of the general's birth. In the six weeks prior to this date, the men worked around the clock, in three eight-hour shifts. Borglum was there with them nearly all of the time. Working conditions on the mountainside were miserable in the cold winter weather. The men stretched canvas tarpaulins around the scaffolding as wind breaks, bundled up in heavy clothes, and hung pots of burning coals along the rock as heaters. Many of the men undoubtedly would have quit were it not for the jubilant presence of the sculptor. As Tucker remarked years later, "Men didn't work *for* Mr. Borglum. They worked *with* him."[15] By the time Lee's head was finished, Borglum was very tired, but also very pleased. Nobody would ever again tell him that he could not carve a mountain. The proof was staring out from the stone.

On the day before the unveiling Borglum invited a select party of dignitaries to a luncheon on Lee's shoulder. Included in this group were Governors William Brandon of Alabama, Pat Neff of Texas, and Lee Trinkle of Virginia, all of whom had arrived for the unveiling a day early. Mary Borglum made arrangements with Hettye McCurdy, who ran a restaurant in Stone Mountain called The Golden Glow Tearoom, to prepare the meal. Miss Hettye later revealed a little-known secret about the catered chicken. While carrying the meal out to the mountain, she dropped a basket and dumped the chicken all over the ground. Mrs. Borglum, whom Miss Hettye described as "the essence of a lady," told her not to worry about it because

---

[15]Casey and Borglum, 179.

they had probably eaten worse than that. So they wiped off the chicken and sent it up to the waiting diners.[16]

The workmen set up a table on the scaffolding, so that one end was actually resting on the general's shoulder. By means of a pulley, the hot chicken, biscuits, and coffee were served with little trouble. Some of the guests probably wished they had not been quite so honored, but they all smiled gamely for the camera.

Unveiling day, January 19, 1924, was cold and rainy, but that did not stop an estimated 5,000 people from showing up to witness the event. Visitors came from all over the United States, including artists, engineers, Civil War veterans, politicians, and everyday citizens. Three more governors--Clifford Walker of Georgia, Thomas McLeod of South Carolina, and Cameron Morrison of North Carolina--joined the three who had arrived early, and President Coolidge sent his official representative.

Ninety-four-year-old Helen Plane arrived shortly after noon. When she first met Borglum in 1915 she would not shake his hand, but on this day she allowed him to carry her to her place of honor on the speaker's platform. David Marx, rabbi of the Jewish Temple of Atlanta, delivered the invocation and prayed for God's blessings on the Southern people represented by General Lee and for the indissoluble union. The ceremony that followed was accompanied by all the pageantry and oratory that the organizers could muster, and at which the South excelled. At the appointed time, Mrs. Plane raised a small Confederate flag in her trembling hand. A giant American flag slowly rose, accompanied by a cascade of falling boulders. The head of Lee appeared to the thunderous acclaim of crashing rocks below.

There was a long silence as the throng of spectators stared in awe. Out of the stillness came the quavering voice of an elderly veteran dressed in grey: "It's General Lee! Its the General!"[17] Following this acknowledgment applause, screams, cheers, and even Rebel yells of the assembled multitude echoed off the mountain in a thunderous din.

When called upon for a speech, Borglum confessed that he was too wrapped up in his own thoughts and too stunned by this partial realization of his dream to talk. "But," he said, "the head of Lee is on Stone Mountain! And if a tidal wave should sweep over this fair land of ours and cover it all, tearing away the last vestige of our commercial, all too commercial

---

[16]William Schemmel, "Will Success Spoil Stone Mountain?," *Atlanta Magazine* (April 1970), 74.

[17]"Robert E. Lee's Head Unveiled," *Stone Mountain Magazine* 1(3 January 1923), 4.

existence, and if in time the tide should break and roll away--the head of Lee would remain on Stone Mountain for all time, immutable and imperishable."[18]

The entire ceremony was carefully chronicled in the press and in the *Stone Mountain Magazine*, a publicity tool published by the Association. One of the articles read:

> The dream of the world's greatest memorial began to come true Saturday afternoon at 3 o'clock. With a stately dignity that held something of a caress, a bright, broad national emblem was lifted and gathered as a flowing coronet on the majestic brow of Robert E. Lee, looking now and forever from the sheer wall of Stone Mountain.[19]

No one could guess at that time how wrong these statements were. The unveiling of Lee's head was the highlight of Borglum's Stone Mountain career. A few months later the sculptor's relationship with the Association began to sour.

The head of "Stonewall" Jackson was the next to be carved. As before, Borglum left the day-to-day supervision of the rough work to Tucker and Villa, though he made all the important decisions himself. This time, however, an unexpected crack in the granite was discovered which slowed down this part of the work. The crack was where the bridge of Jackson's nose would be, and although it was small, water getting into it and freezing could turn it into a serious flaw over time. Borglum tried shifting the location of Jackson's head, but the crack still plagued him. In the original design, Jackson's face was turned toward Lee, as if speaking to his commander. He decided to turn Jackson's head to look in the direction of his pointing arm. The crack was thus buried in the six-foot hole of the eye socket where it posed no threat.

While Borglum wrestled with the fissure, another struggle bedeviled the Monumental Association. Elections of new officers were scheduled for the annual meeting in April, 1924. Prior to the meeting, Hollins Randolph approached Sam Venable and asked him not to oppose his bid for re-election as president. Randolph, a member of the state Democratic party felt that being president of the Monumental Association would enhance his

---

[18]"Lee's Monument to Last Forever," *Atlanta Constitution*, 20 January, 1924.
[19]"Robert E. Lee's Head Unveiled."

standing at the upcoming Democratic convention. Once the convention was over, Randolph promised, he would resign from the board. He knew that Venable, one of the most influential members of the executive committee, was critical of his handling of the Association's finances. Venable took him at his word, however, and agreed, hoping that this would the matter peacefully.

At the meeting, Randolph showed up with eighty-six political and business associates who were not members of the Association. He put them forth for membership, and the question of dues came up. The Secretary reminded him that two years earlier dues had been raised from one dollar to five dollars. The secretary at that time had since died and the minutes of that meeting had been lost. Since no minutes could be produced, Randolph decided the Association should return to the original dues of one dollar and declared his eighty-six supporters to be members on those terms. Delighted with this apparent strong interest in the project, the Association members welcomed these newcomers. They did not, however, suspect what was coming.

With a promise of noninterference from Sam Venable and a stacked membership, Randolph easily won re-election. By the votes of his new members he reorganized the executive committee of the Monumental Association, leaving out all the members of the UDC except for Mrs. T. T. Stephens, who was given the office of Second Vice-President, and Mildred Lewis Rutherford, the Association historian. Many of the sitting members of the executive committee were replaced by Randolph's cronies. Other members of the Association were scandalized by Randolph's brazen takeover, but there was little they could do. He accomplished it legally according to the by-laws of the organization. Two committee members who were not replaced, Sam Venable and David Webb, resigned in protest shortly thereafter.

One of the first changes the Randolph regime made was a resolution barring any new members in the Association who did not have the approval of a special committee appointed by the president. He next enlarged the executive committee from nine to fifteen members (enlarging it again to nineteen later on) and declared a quorum to be five members. He also made himself chairman of the executive committee as well as president of the Association. As a result of these arrangements, Randolph and Pete Rivers, who became the business manager, exercised almost absolute control of the organization. They were supported in this by Reuben Arnold, the Association's legal counsel, and Rogers Winter, who controlled all of the publicity for the Association.

There was, of course, a great deal of complaining against the Randolph administration, but his opponents avoided a public squabble for the sake of the memorial and the image of the Association. Borglum kept working though he was angered at the betrayal of the UDC and was losing faith in Randolph's leadership. Regarding the action, he complained, "I feel like a father who comes suddenly upon his child in the woods and finds it asleep--yet in the coil of a snake, himself fearful to act lest he might endanger or wound what he must and will save."[20]

He was suspicious of the timing of the coup, which came just as the Association was beginning to receive substantial financial contributions with good prospects for more. This suspicion was supported by Rivers' parsimonious attitude toward carving expenditures. There seemed to be plenty of money coming into the Association's coffers, but most of it disappeared in the Atlanta office. The sculptor complained that there was always enough money to hire stenographers, pay the committee's travel expenses, and print public relations material, but not for the one thing of real importance--the carving.

Shortly after the Randolph coup, the newly inaugurated Children's Founder's Roll roiled the Association's waters. The dispute centered on the medal, designed by Borglum, to be given for a one dollar contribution. He was authorized to make arrangements for its manufacture with any company he saw fit so long as he obtained a reasonable price. At the same time that he had entered into a contract with the Medallic Art Company of New York to make 25,000 medals at eight cents apiece, a subcommittee for the Children's Founder's Roll began negotiations with the Whitehead & Hoag Company. The misunderstanding that arose from this was eventually cleared up and the contract was given to Whitehead & Hoag to make 100,000 medals at five cents each. The whole thing was attributed to poor communications within the executive committee, but for some reason a few of the committee held it against Borglum and the issue would later become distorted and used against him.

Two other factors in 1924 helped drive a wedge between Borglum and Randolph--national politics and the Ku Klux Klan. Borglum was very active on the national level of the Republican party, while Randolph was trying to

---

[20]Minutes of Association annual meeting, April, 1924. Robert W. Woodruff Library, Emory University, Atlanta, Georgia.

build his prestige in the Democratic leadership circles, and 1924 was a presidential election year.

Even more central to the friction between them was the fact that both Borglum and Randolph were active in the Klan, as was Sam Venable. At the time there was a serious power struggle within the Klan between its founder, William Simmons, and a rival, Hiram Evans, of Texas. The fight was taking them in and out of court and all over the front pages of the newspapers. The adverse publicity helped splinter the Klan into factions. As a result, the Klan lost credibility as a national fraternal organization and saw its membership fall sharply. Simmons and Evans fought primarily over control of Klan income and the power to influence national politics. Evans seemed to be gaining support, but the more he and Simmons fought, the less there was to fight over. Among the Stone Mountain leaders, Venable and Borglum supported Simmons, while Randolph backed Evans.

To confuse the issue even more was the 1924 presidential election. The Klan had dreams of becoming a powerful force on Capitol Hill and in the White House. Hollins Randolph and the Klan backed William G. McAdoo as the Democratic candidate for President, but being labeled as a Klan candidate doomed his bid from the start. Had McAdoo won, Randolph might have been more magnanimous toward Borglum and events at Stone Mountain may have turned out differently. Instead, McAdoo lost and Randolph channeled his bitterness over the defeat to his Klan and political opponents, which included Borglum.

There was a certain amount of confusion at the time over the depth of Klan involvement in the Stone Mountain project. It was widely believed, particularly in the north, that the Association was governed by the Klan, that the mountain was a Klan stronghold, and that by association with E. Y. Clarke the carving was a Klan project. It is true that some members of the executive committee and board of directors, as well as the sculptor, were members of the Klan and that the Klan contributed money, but the influence of the Klan over the memorial has been overemphasized and exaggerated.

Rogers Winter, publicity director for the Association, pointed out, and quite correctly, that there were also Freemasons and Rotarians on the committee and that Jewish and Catholic groups gave money to the cause, yet nobody accused them of taking control of the Association. Winter also addressed the subject of the annual Klan gathering at the mountain on Thanksgiving. He reiterated that the Association had no control over the mountain other than the small part deeded to them for the carving, and that a hike to the top of mountain by the Ku Klux Klan had no more significance to the memorial than did a party of Boy Scouts hiking up the mountain.[21]

Despite public impressions, the only real impact of the Klan on the Association was the fratricidal power struggle within the Klan that may have been carried over to the Stone Mountain memorial by men who belonged to both groups. As Borglum's working relationship with the Randolph-led committee deteriorated, their clashes over money became angrier than they might otherwise have been. When Borglum was upset he made no attempt to hide the fact. One carver, recalling the scathing criticisms he overheard on the mountain, commented that Borglum was "a pretty good stone carver--but he ain't no sweet talker."[22]

In the winter of 1923-1924, a suggestion was made that promised to end the Association's money troubles--the minting of a memorial half-dollar by the U. S. government. Harry Stillwell Edwards, a journalist and Randolph supporter, received the official credit for the idea, as well as several thousand dollars as a reward from the Association.

Edwards claimed that he got the idea in August 1923 when touring the mountain. He noted the interest of many visitors for securing souvenirs, and thought that a medal of some kind might be struck and sold for the benefit of the memorial fund. This idea later developed into a coin when he came across an Alabama Centennial Half-Dollar. He brought the matter before Joseph McCord, head of the Federal Reserve Bank in Atlanta, suggesting the issue of ten million coins of the half-dollar denomination which the Association could sell for a dollar apiece. McCord assured him that such a thing could be done.

Edwards brought the Alabama coin and his idea to Mrs. Samuel Inman, who was at the time, before the Randolph coup, a member of the Association executive committee. After several discussions among the committee, Hollins Randolph drew up a bill to be introduced in the next session of Congress requesting an issue of five million coins.

At this point the versions of what happened are different. The story officially sanctioned by the Monumental Association was that Edwards wrote to Bascom Slemp, Secretary to President Calvin Coolidge, to arrange a meeting between the President and a delegation from the Association.

---

[21]Rogers Winter to Arthur Krock, 2 January 1925, Records of the SMCMA, Special Collections Department, Robert W. Woodruff Library, Emory University.

[22]Casey and Borglum, 201.

According to Edwards, his own efforts resulted in a Presidential blessing on the coin and played a key role and pushing the bill through Congress.

Others, including the sculptor's wife, claim that the Association asked Borglum to make the arrangements to see the President and to get the bill through because of his numerous connections with the Republican administration. Borglum appealed to Henry Cabot Lodge, then the most powerful Republican in the Senate. A few days later, on December 10, 1923, the Stone Mountain coinage bill was introduced into the Senate. On January 11, 1924, Representative L. T. McFadden of Pennsylvania introduced the bill into the House. McFadden stated that he had sponsored the bill out of friendship with the sculptor.[23]

The truth is that both men worked for the passage of the memorial coin and apparently followed different channels to achieve the same end. In any case, the bill sailed through Congress with little opposition. Act S.684 of the sixty-eighth Congress stated:

> An Act to authorize the coinage of 50-cent pieces in commemoration of the commencement on June 18, 1923, of the carving on Stone Mountain, in the state of Georgia, a monument to the valor of the soldiers of the South, which was the inspiration of their sons and daughters and grandsons and granddaughters in the Spanish-American and World Wars, and in memory of Warren G. Harding, President of the United States, in whose administration the work was begun.[24]

The Association's bill included veterans of more recent American wars to give it a broader appeal and to lessen the chances of attack by hard-liners. Congress did insist, however, that there be a tribute to the late President Harding, who died in office shortly after the carving began. The inscription to Harding was later removed from the coin when the Teapot Dome Affair and other scandals of his administration came to light.

President Coolidge signed the Act authorizing the coin on 24 March 1924. This was the largest issue of commemorative coins ever authorized by the U. S. government. Less than a month later Randolph seized control of the Association and its income. Borglum was granted the task of

---

[23]William D. Hyder and R.W. Colbert, *The Selling of the Stone Mountain Half Dollar*, undated reprint from *The Numismatist*, published by the American Numismatic Association.

[24]Records of the SMCMA, Emory University.

designing the coin, perhaps as a way of pacifying his anger over Randolph's actions. The sculptor had made many bas-reliefs and assumed that making one for a coin would be an easy task, but he had never before worked to the exacting requirements of the Treasury Department.

His first hurdle was to get approval for the general design of the coin. Secretary of the Treasury Andrew Mellon demanded to know why he had placed the motto "In God We Trust" over the head of Lee. Borglum responded, "Because they did trust Him, and were sincere in their belief that they were right." Then Mellon wanted to know what the thirteen stars were for. Borglum calmly replied, "It all depends on which side of Mason and Dixon's line you happen to live. They could, of course, stand for the thirteen rebellious colonies." Then Mellon laughed and gave his approval for the design.[25]

With approval from the Secretary, the Treasury Department submitted the model to the Commission of Fine Arts for comment. James E. Frasier, sculptor for the Commission, did not care very much for Borglum, and rejected the design as lacking appreciation for the art of metalwork, being devoid of artistic merit, and for generally being "below the standard of United States coins."[26] He also criticized the style of the lettering, the proportion and arrangement of the figures, and the appearance of the eagle's legs. Borglum cabled Randolph of the Commission, "Damn fool suggestions, but easy to correct. I will meet gracefully. . . ."[27]

The greatest change he had to make was dropping Jefferson Davis from the design so that the figures of Jackson and Lee could be enlarged and to make the design fit better into the circular area of a coin. Other changes were minor. All told, Borglum made nine reliefs before getting the approval of every detail in October, 1924.

Just as the design was finalized, the matter of the tribute to President Harding became an issue. The Fine Arts Commission instructed Borglum to remove the inscription "in memory of Warren G. Harding" because it felt this was in bad taste considering recent revelations concerning his administration. The Philadelphia Mint, however, refused to proceed with production unless the Congressionally-mandated phrase was restored. Borglum had to telegram Coolidge for presidential approval of the omission

---

[25]Casey and Borglum, 203.

[26]As quoted in Harkness Kenimer, *The History of Stone Mountain* (Atlanta: Kenimer Publishing Company, 1994), 34.

[27]Gutzon Borglum to Hollins Randolph, 25 July 1924, Records of the SMCMA.

before the Mint would act. Minting finally began three months later with delivery scheduled for March, 1925.

During the seven months Borglum was trying to please the Commission, the Grand Army of the Republic, a society founded by and for Union Civil War veterans, mounted a campaign against the coin honoring "treason." The GAR lobbied the President, Congress, the Treasury Department, and the Arts Commission to stop the coin. The pressure put on the Commission was undoubtedly one of the reasons it gave Borglum such a hard time. Even though the GAR's effort failed, it made Randolph and the Association nervous. They, in turn, became irritated with Borglum for taking so long. They threatened to turn the affair over to another sculptor if he did not get the design approved quickly. Borglum was insulted at the committee's attitude and again became angry with the members.

Borglum's relationship with the Association continued to worsen during the last half of 1924. Progress on the Jackson head slowed because of the difficulties with the crack in the rock, the sculptor's distraction with designing the coin, and the lack of adequate funding from the Association. Much of the problem stemmed from the fact that the Monumental Association had ceased all other fundraising efforts in anticipation of the coin. When the coin design took far longer to be approved than they expected, the Association began to run short of money and was forced to borrow funds from several Atlanta banks to pay the bills and meet the office payroll. Founder's Roll contributions continued to trickle in, but it was far less than needed.

Money was the root of most of the conflict between Borglum and the Association. In August of 1924, he requested payment of $3,000 for the previous month in accordance with his contract. The Association refused to pay on the basis that he had done no work on the carving that month. He became indignant at their refusal to pay a legitimate bill and directed some bitter language at the committee, which responded in kind and called him mercenary. He resented the charge and in hotly denying it was dubbed irascible

This state of affairs continued through the fall when the committee, desperate for cash, began to promote the Founder's Roll subscriptions more heavily. Through arbitration with a special subcommittee, Borglum stated that he was willing to let his claim rest until the Association was "in funds" if it would help smooth out the differences that had arisen during the year. In November the Association finally paid the sculptor his $3,000 to "avoid a rupture" with him. Upset that he had been paid at all, Rivers claimed that the finances were not sound enough and that the progress on the carving did not justify the payment.

With matters in such a state, it probably was not wise of Borglum to take a trip to South Dakota in September, 1924, to discuss the carving of a national monument in the Black Hills. He did so at the request of Doane Robinson, State Historian of South Dakota, who wrote to the sculptor seeking his expertise at carving mountain. Borglum reasoned that since he had already solved the technical problems of mountain sculpting, it should not be difficult to supervise two carvings at once, particularly if the South Dakotans raised the money they promised.

Of course, the Stone Mountain Monumental Association was not very pleased to hear of this. The committee blamed Borglum for the lack of progress at Stone Mountain, though it was itself responsible for most of the problems holding up the work. Most of what had been done was the roughing out executed by Tucker and his crew when Borglum could pay them. The members pressured Borglum to spend more time at Stone Mountain and produce more finished results. Publicly, of course, Randolph announced that the work was coming along splendidly.

Despite all the points of conflict between Borglum and the committee, it was actually the commemorative coin that ended his career at Stone Mountain. As much a Borglum claimed to deplore being involved with fund-raising, he never could seem to stay out of it. To help the Association underwrite the sale of the coins, the sculptor contacted several wealthy acquaintances who promised to loan the needed money. The Association took no action on his offer, and Randolph, Borglum later claimed, offered him $200,000 to not interfere with the Association's handling of the coins.[28]

The next day Borglum was in Washington to aid a friend of his, Lester Barlow, in his bid to collect $300,000 from the War Indemnities Board for his invention of depth charge during the recent world war. Should the claim be accepted, he was going to donate one third of it to the Stone Mountain memorial. Barlow had in the past headed up fundraising campaigns in the north for the Association. To return the favor, Randolph had promised Borglum in their meeting of the day before that he would also go to Washington to give Barlow's claim the official backing of the Monumental Association. With more than a million dollars expected from the sale of the coins, however, Randolph was not very concerned with a potential $100,000 and he never showed up for the meeting.

---

[28]Shaff and Shaff, 213.

Feeling betrayed, Borglum became incensed. Since Randolph's strange offer of $200,000, he had become convinced that the Association officers were planning to divert the coin money from its intended purposes. He hastily arranged for a meeting with President Coolidge to inform him of his suspicions. Barlow was a witness to the meeting and recalled the two men sitting knee to knee in serious discussion. The President slapped Borglum on the back and told him not to worry about it, that he would halt the issuance of the coins. The President, however, never acted on his promise.

The sculptor then gave a statement to the Associated Press vaguely criticizing the Association's handling of memorial coin. He made no specific charges, but hoped that by drawing public attention to the coin distribution he might prevent Randolph from doing anything dishonest. He knew that the Association would be furious with him, but he counted on that fact that, if push came to shove, they needed him to finish the carving.

Borglum, however, overestimated the strength of his position. Randolph called Jesse Tucker in from the mountain to offer him Borglum's job and a share of the coin money for his cooperation. Tucker flatly refused and immediately cabled Borglum in Washington notifying him of the offer. Back in Atlanta the next day, Borglum was not as concerned as his friend. He believed that he was protected by his contract.

In an emergency meeting on 25 February 1925, the executive committee debated the sculptor's fate. Eleven of the nineteen members present wanted to give Borglum a fair hearing before canceling his contract. Hollins Randolph, Pete E. Rivers, Reuben Arnold, and a few others claimed that any delay would give him a chance to begin litigation harmful to the Association. To protect their best interests, they argued, a vote had to be taken right away. As usual, Randolph managed to persuade the others to adopt his position and the sculptor's contract was canceled that afternoon. The full details of the meeting and the reasons for the decision appeared in the newspaper that same day. Charges against the sculptor included "neglect and virtual abandonment [of the carving], inordinate demands for money not due him, offensive egotism, and delusions of grandeur."[29]

Borglum was at the carving with Tucker, Sam Venable and his sister, and two ladies of the UDC when he received a telephone message that the executive committee had just voted to dismiss him as sculptor. The stone cutters were to be given charge of the work. After some moments of

---

[29]"Memorial Leaders Cancel Contract Held By Borglum," *Atlanta Constitution*, 26 February 1925.

contemplation, he decided that it would be necessary to destroy his models to protect his design. The conditions of the mountain had forced him to make so many changes that the models were useless for anyone else to follow. He believed only a caricature could result from such an attempt. He ordered the plaster models of the Lee and Jackson heads thrown from their place on the scaffolding to the rocks below. He then instructed one of his men to break up the large master model and the model of Jefferson Davis' head that was in the studio. Sam Venable noted that Borglum had tears in his eyes as he turned his back on the mountain and his great work.

Borglum's destruction of the models sparked a great deal of controversy. He believed that they were his to do with as he wished. In a letter to the Association a year earlier he had reminded them that the models and designs and were copyrighted as the property of Gutzon Borglum, "their creator and sole owner. . . ."[30] The Association took the position that anything related to the carving became the property of the Association. They swore out a warrant for the sculptor's arrest on charges of "malicious mischief" and "willful destruction of Association property."[31]

Borglum was at the home of Mrs. Coribel Venable Orme speaking to the ladies of the Atlanta Chapter UDC when Jesse Tucker burst in and hustled "the Chief" out the door with barely a word of explanation. Moments after Tucker's car pulled out of the driveway, a sheriff's deputy arrived to serve the warrant, but not finding his man there, he sat down and accepted a cup of coffee offered by the ladies. Under questioning from Mary Borglum, the deputy revealed that the complaint specified damages amounting to twenty-five dollars, and to make matters more absurd, the only model he was charged with destroying was the plaster head of Lee, which had already served its purpose for the carving.[32]

The ladies' delaying tactics allowed Tucker and Borglum enough lead time to cross the border into North Carolina ahead of the sheriff's posse. The next morning the Atlanta newspapers announced his flight in bold letters and gave the Association's version of the whole affair in sensationalized terms.

There have been various explanations as to why a split developed between Borglum and the Association officers. One insightful newspaper

---

[30]As quoted in Shaff and Shaff, 215.

[31]"Memorial Leaders Cancel Contract Held by Borglum," *Atlanta Constitution*, 26 February 1925.

[32]Casey and Borglum, 212.

There have been various explanations as to why a split developed between Borglum and the Association officers. One insightful newspaper editor surmised that

> the longer Randolph was in charge the more firmly convinced he became that he was not only a great business manager but a great sculptor, and the more Borglum saw of the memorial business methods the surer he became that he not only was a great sculptor but a great business manager.[33]

There was a great deal of truth to this statement, but the reason for the friction was more fundamental. The two men, and their respective supporters, had different perceptions of the very nature of their relationship. Borglum viewed the Association as an entity formed for the purpose of financing of his concept and he had a perfect right to question the job they were doing if it was not forwarding his work. Randolph saw Borglum as an artistic contractor, paid to complete a task and not interfere with the business affairs of the Association. Both men were also dictatorial in their manner and the resulting conflict was inevitable.

When asked for a statement on her husband's behalf, Mary Borglum referred to the case of another sculptor of the ancient world: "It was the Hollins N. Randolphs of Greece who passed a law making it a crime for a sculptor to sign his work, yet the name of Phidias has outlived the ages, while the names of those who drove him into exile had been forgotten."[34]

---

[33]"As Others See Us," *Columbus (GA) Enquirer-Sun*, 15 March 1925.

[34]"Wrecked Models Were Sculptor's His Wife Asserts," *Atlanta Journal*, 26 February 1925.

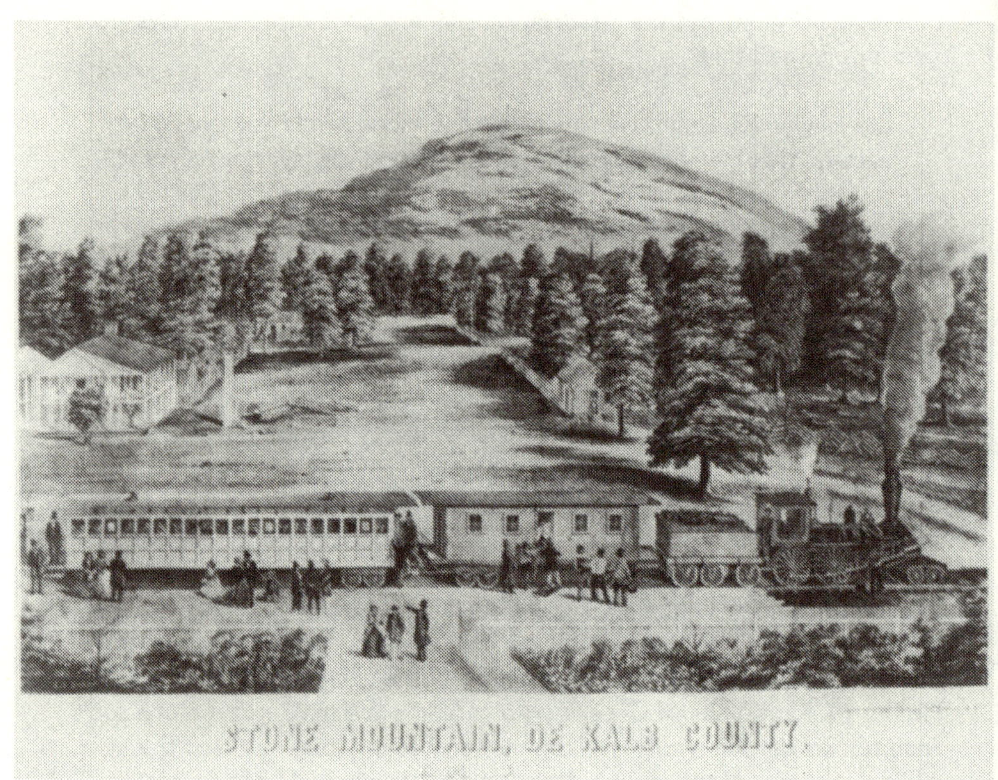

1. The town of Stone Mountain, Georgia as it appeared in the late 1840s in a lithograph by F. Hoppenheimer.

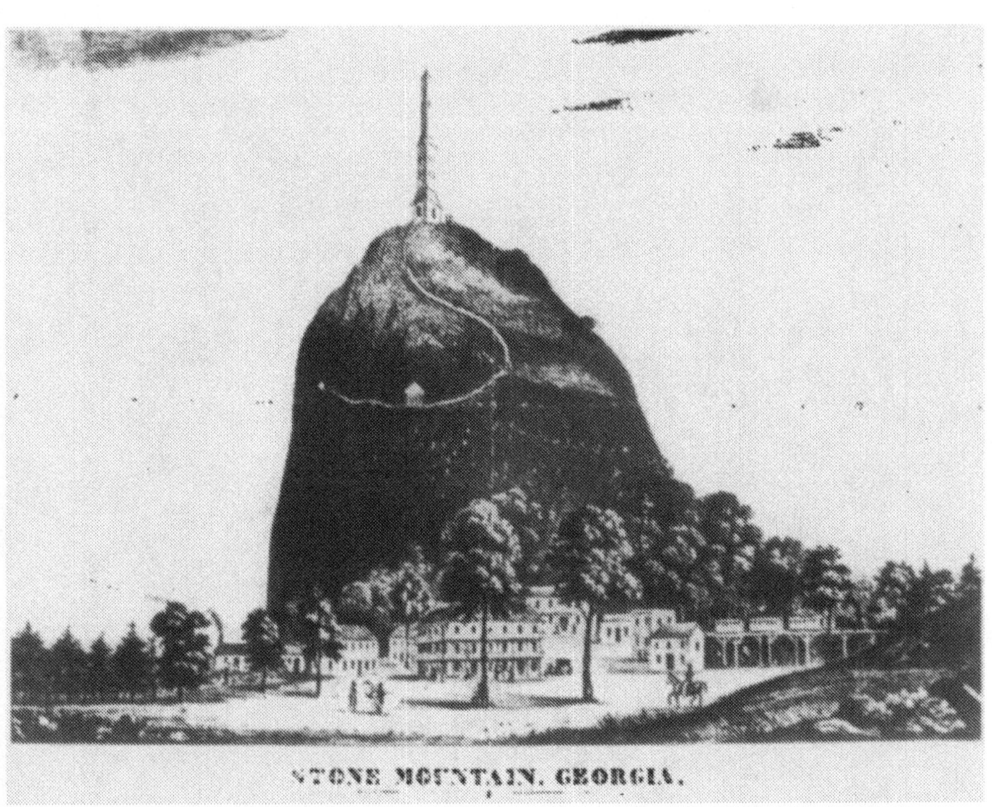

2. An artist's conception of Stone Mountain in the 1890s showing Cloud's Tower on the summit.

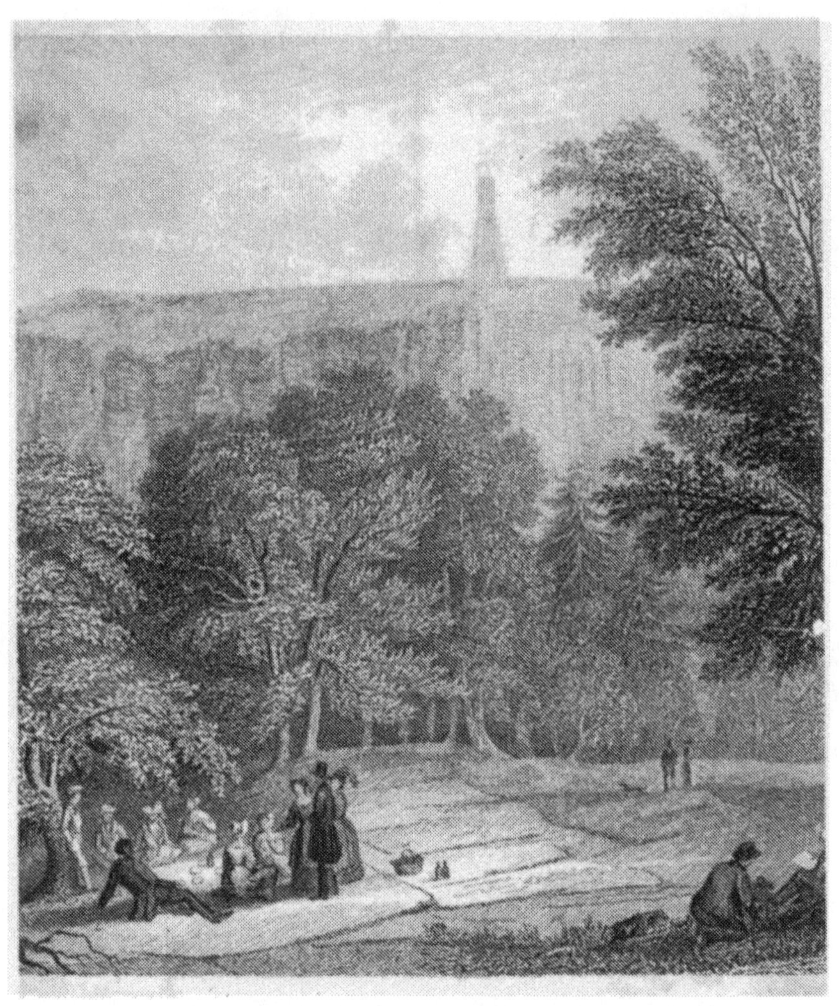

3. The north side of the mountain from an engraving in *Graham's Magazine*, 1845. Stone Mountain was also known as Rock Mountain at this time.

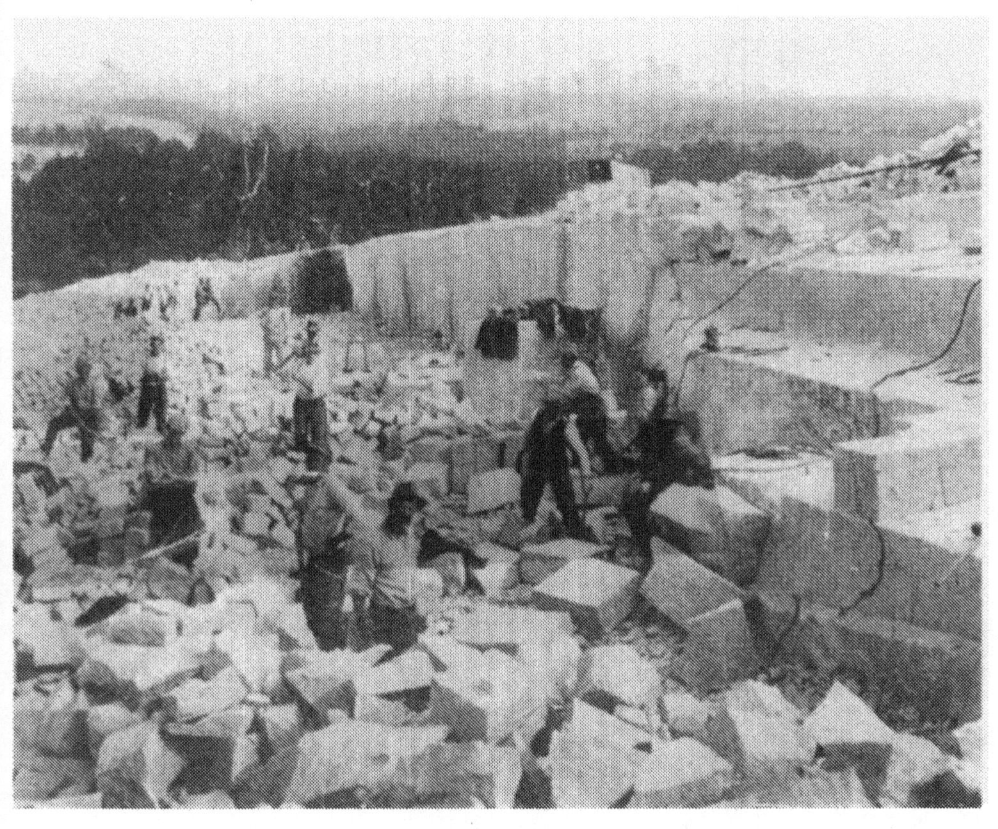

4. One of the quarries operated by the Stone Mountain Granite Company on the southeast side of the mountain.

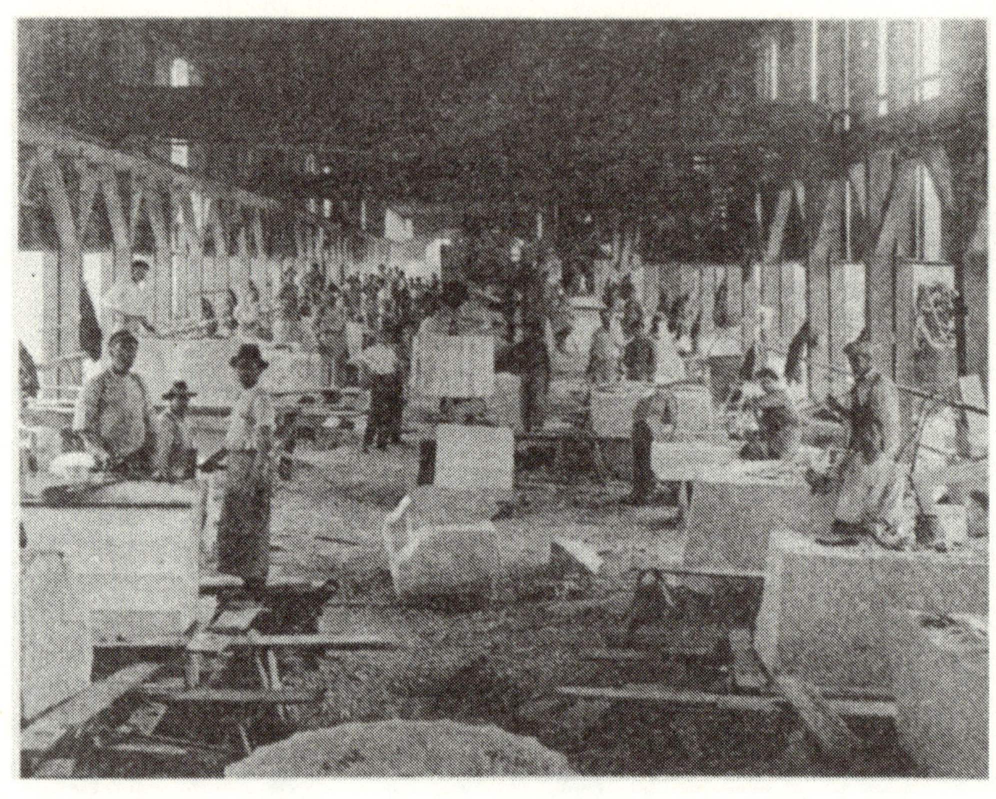

5. Under the cutting shed of the Stone Mountain Granite Company. Skilled craftsmen shape building stones to order.

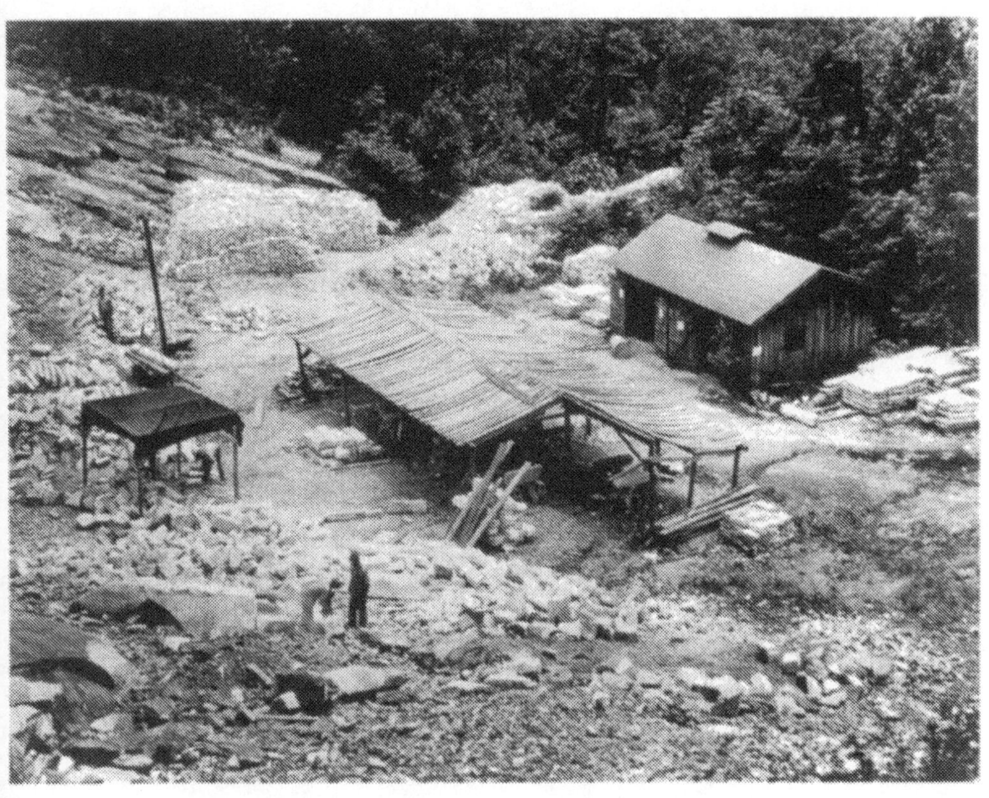

6. One of the smaller quarry operations around the mountain, circa 1930. This operation produced mostly paving and curb stones.

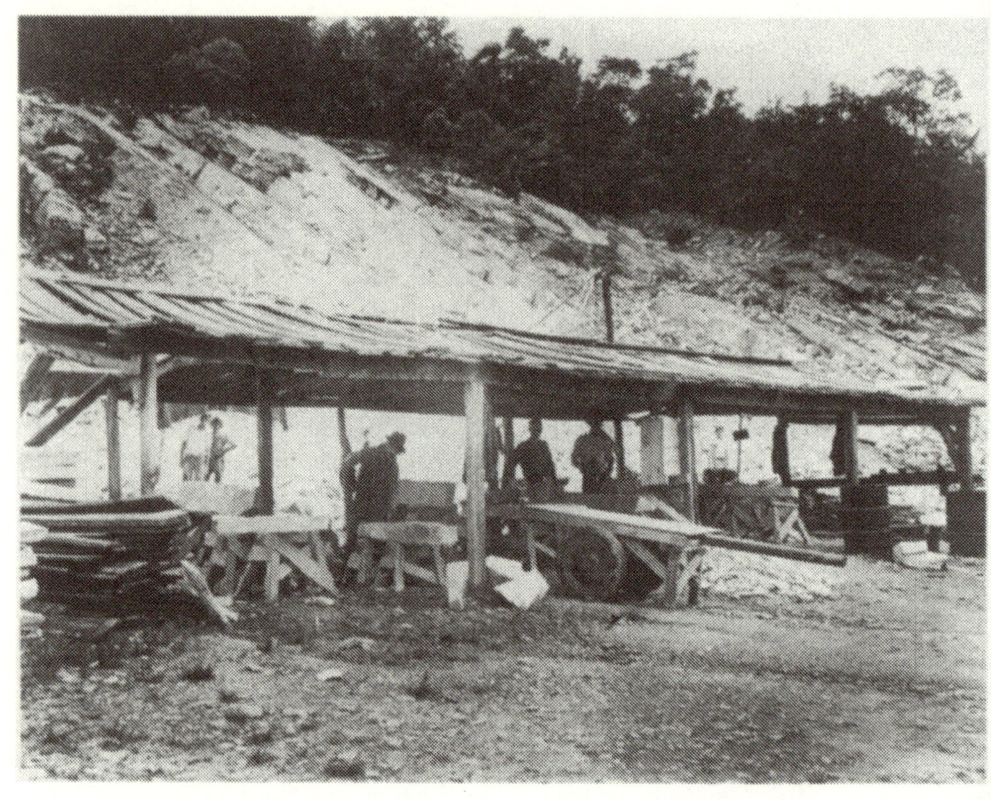

7. Curb cutters used bush hammers to shape up curb stones. Hundreds of miles of granite curbing around Atlanta came from the Stone Mountain quarries.

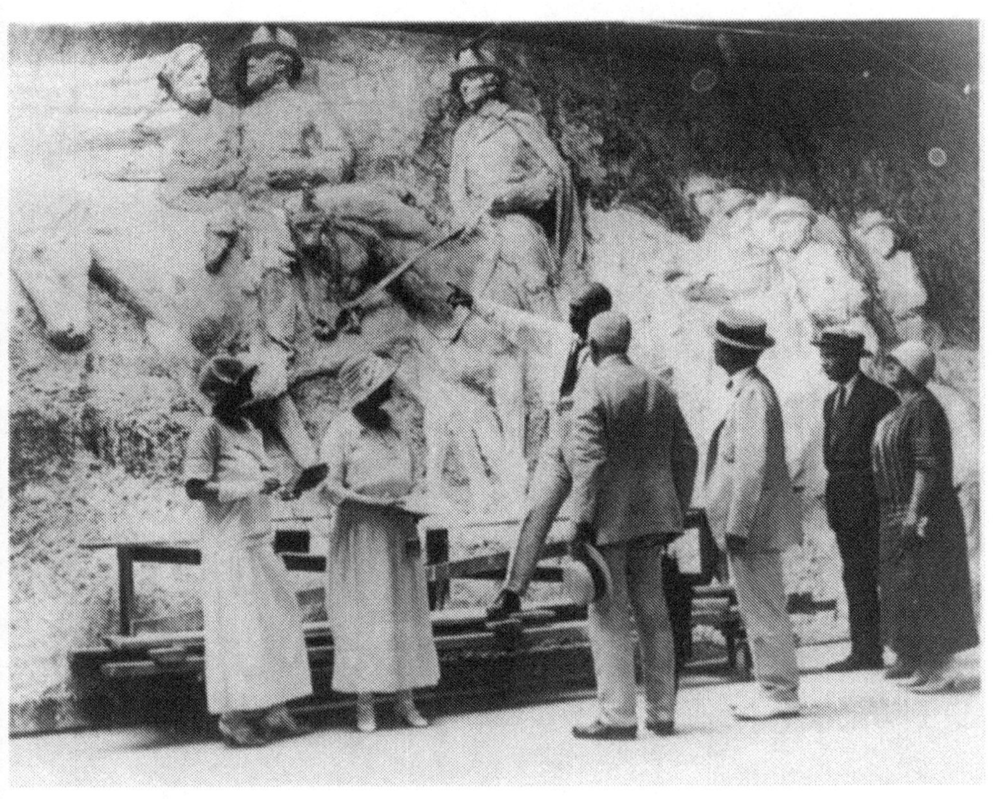

8. Gutzon Borglum showing his model for the Confederate memorial to members of the Monumental Association.

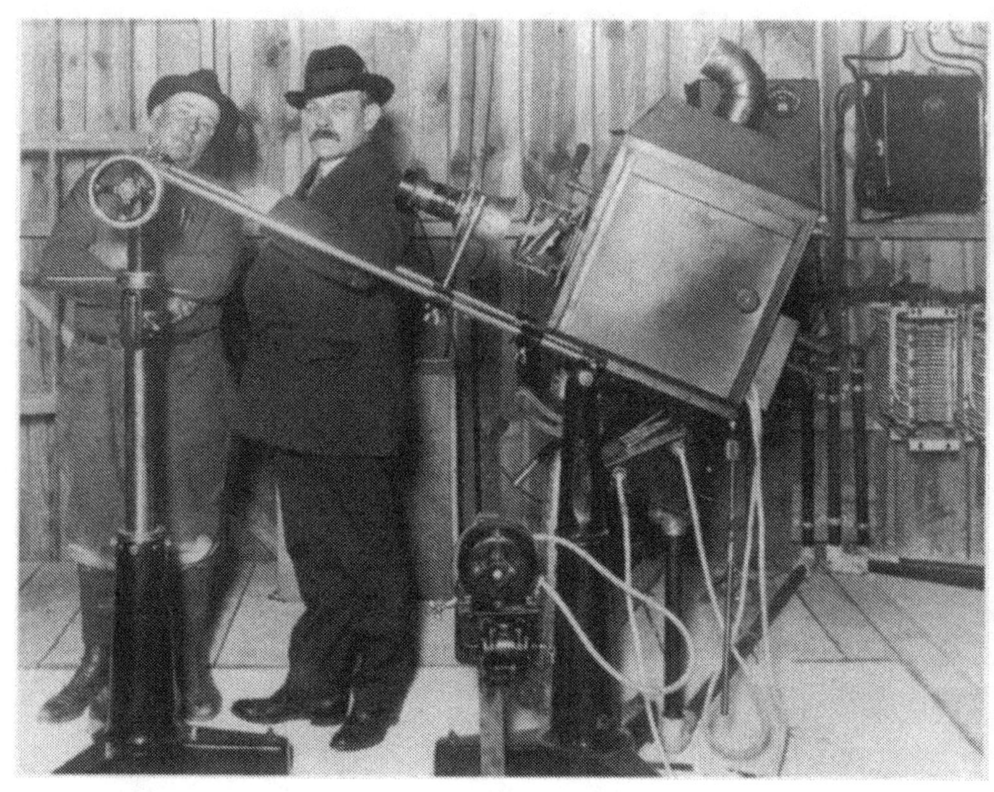

9. Jesse Tucker (left) and Gutzon Borglum (right) with the slide projector specially built to shine Borglum's design on the side of Stone Mountain.

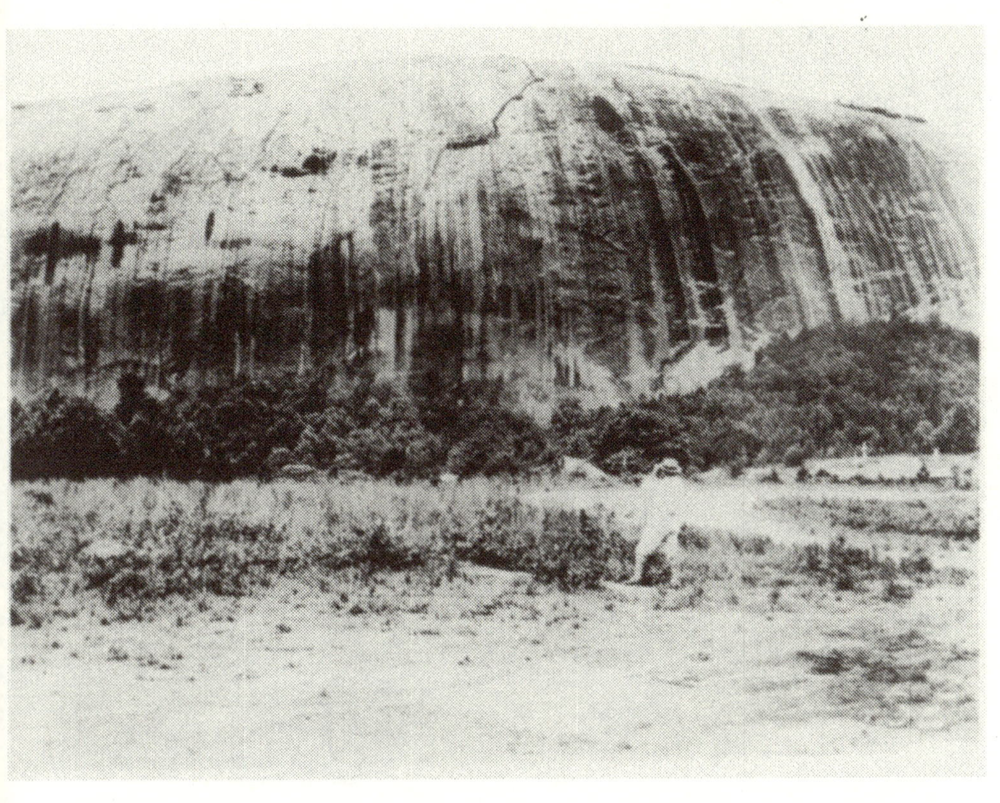

10. Borglum studying the scarp of the mountain throuqh binoculars. The painted outlines of his figures are visible.

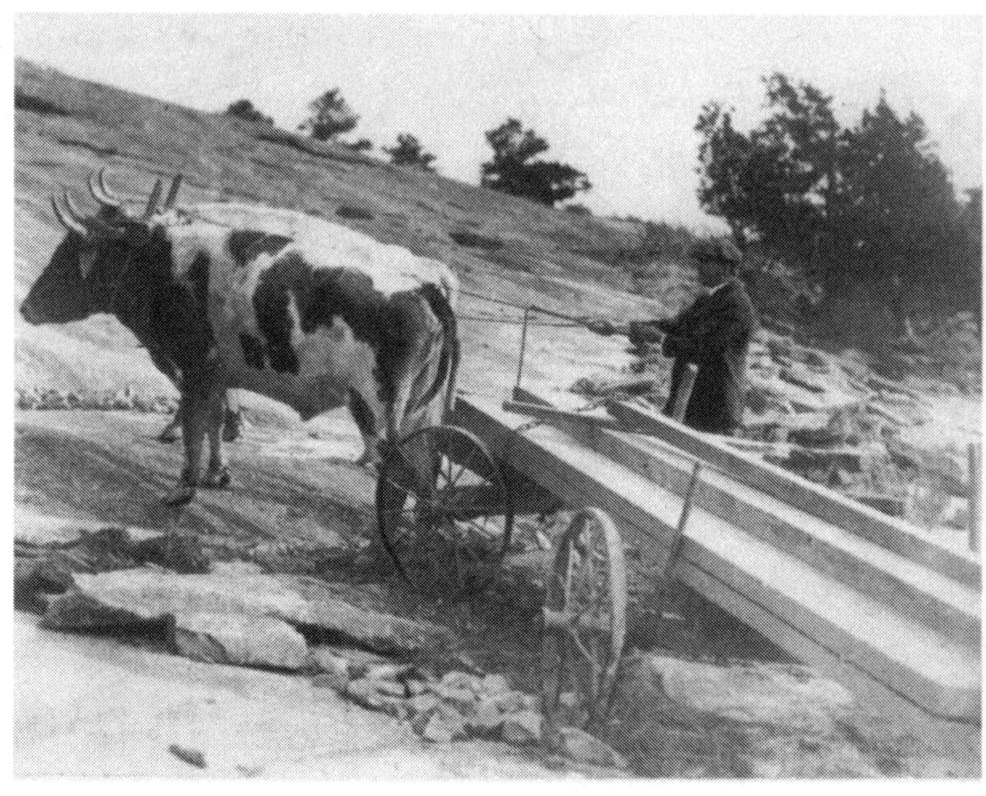

11. Timber to build the carving platform and staircase down from the top of the mountain was hauled up by oxen.

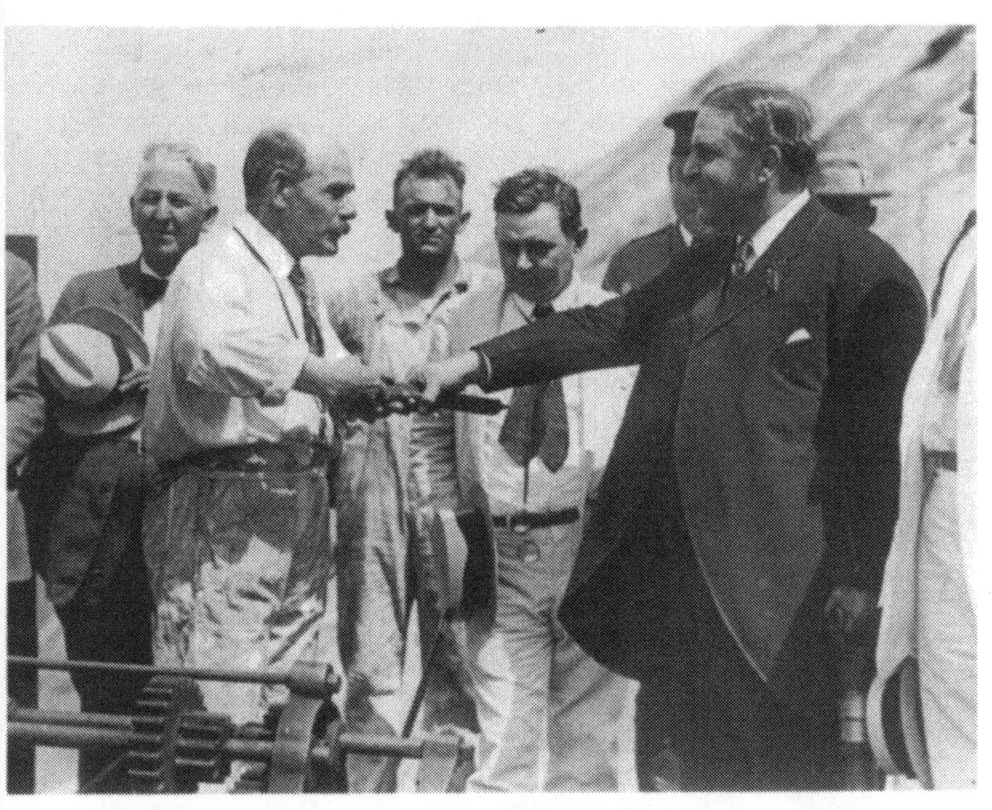

12. Borglum receives the consecrated drill bit from Governor E. Lee Trinkle of Virginia to begin carving the Confederate memorial. Association President Hollins Randolph is at far right.

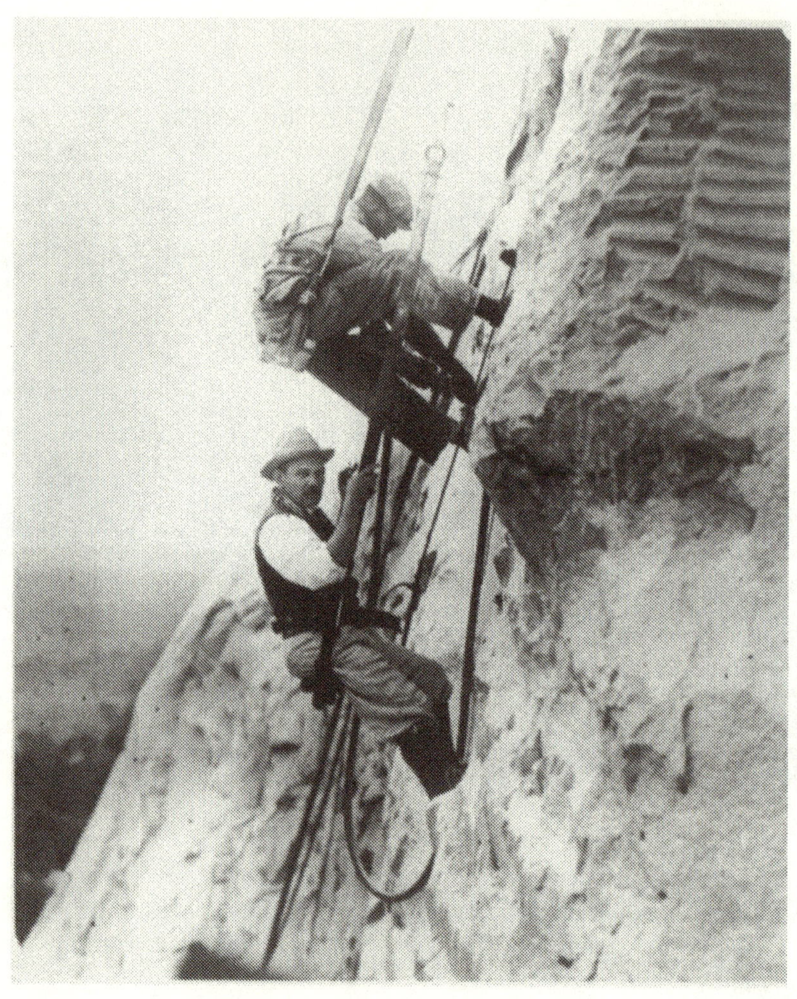

13. Borglum and one of his carving crew at work on the side of the mountain.

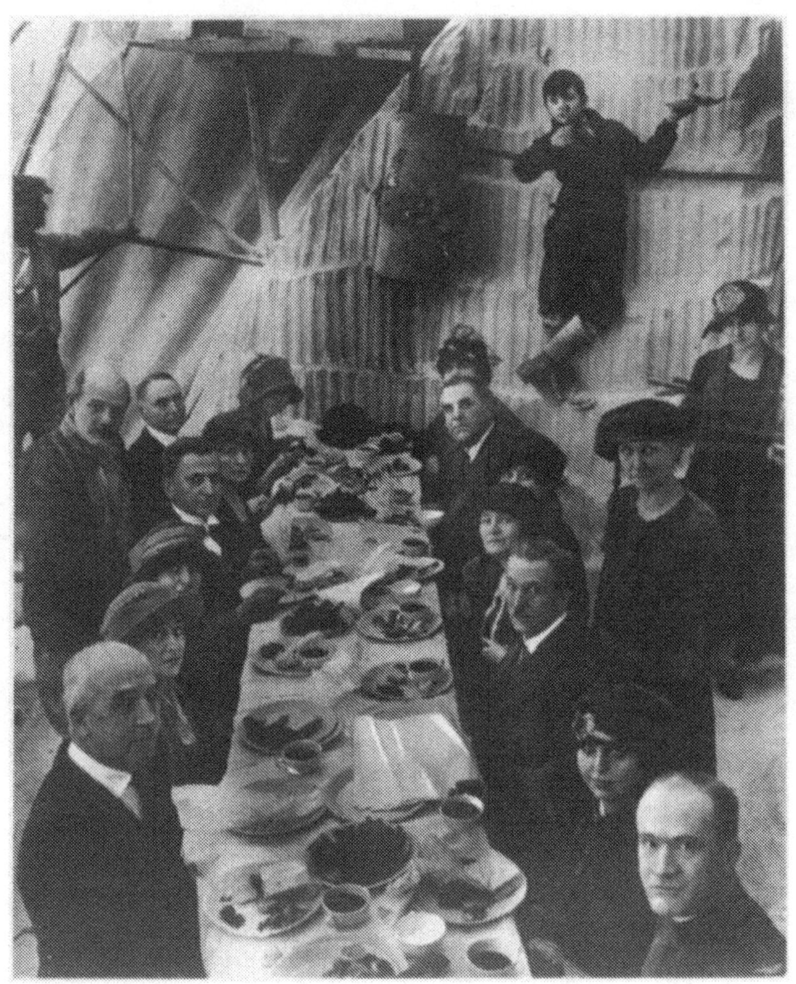

14. The luncheon on the side of the mountain hosted by the Stone Mountain Monumental Association. Left side front to back are Preston Arkwright, Mrs. Robert Roper, Mrs. Hollins Randolph, Governor Neff of Texas, Mrs. Arkwright and Elizabeth Mason. Standing are Gutzon Borglum and Lee Ashcraft. Right side front to back are Col. H.M. Smith, Mrs. Rogers Winter, Governor Brandon of Alabama, Ella Sykes, Mrs. Scotia Dunwody, Governor Trinkle of Virginia and Mrs. Lee Ashcraft. Standing are Mary Borglum, Mrs. J.G. Tucker and Lincoln Borglum.

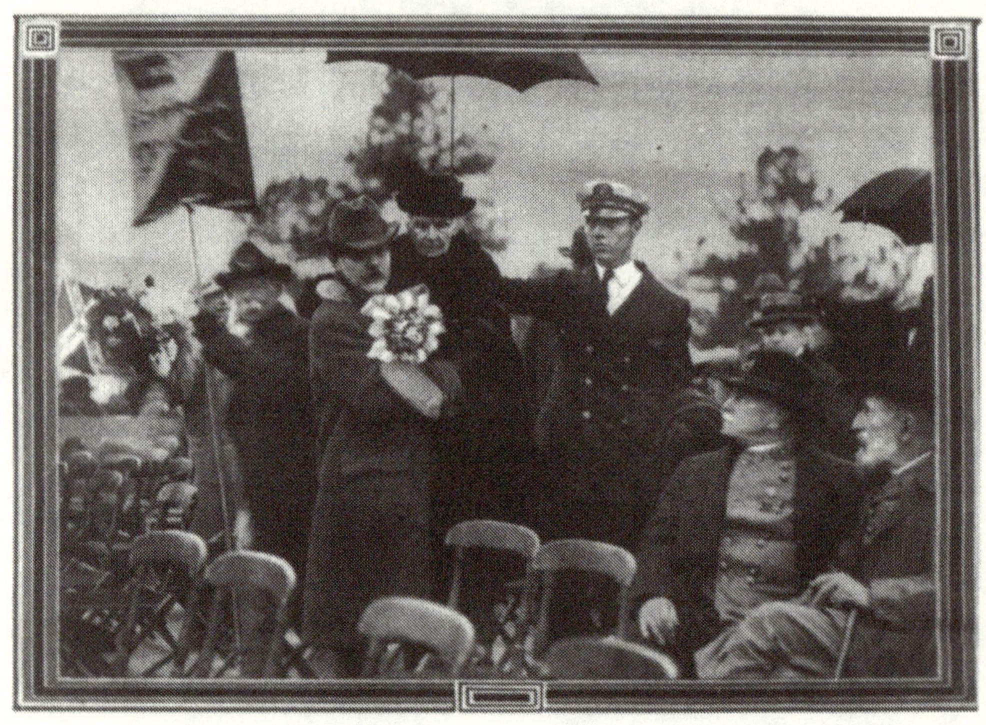

15. Gutzon Borglum carries Helen Plane to the speaker's platform for the 1924 unveiling of General Lee.

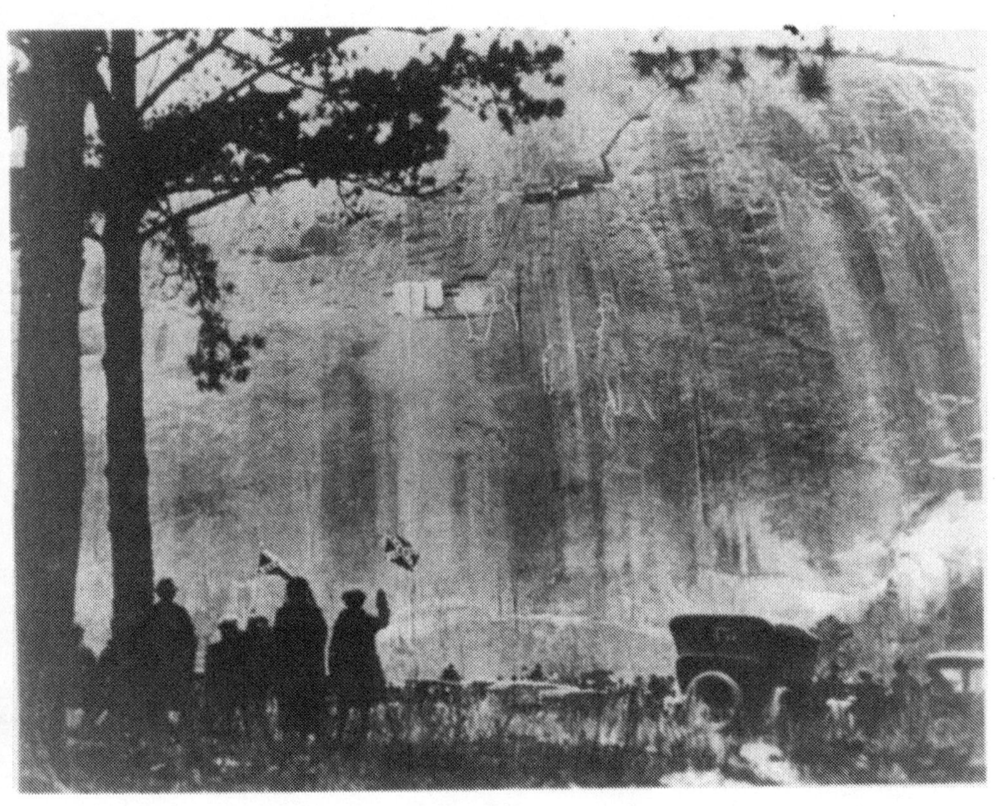

16. Crowds gather at the base of the mountain to watch the unveiling of Borglum's handiwork.

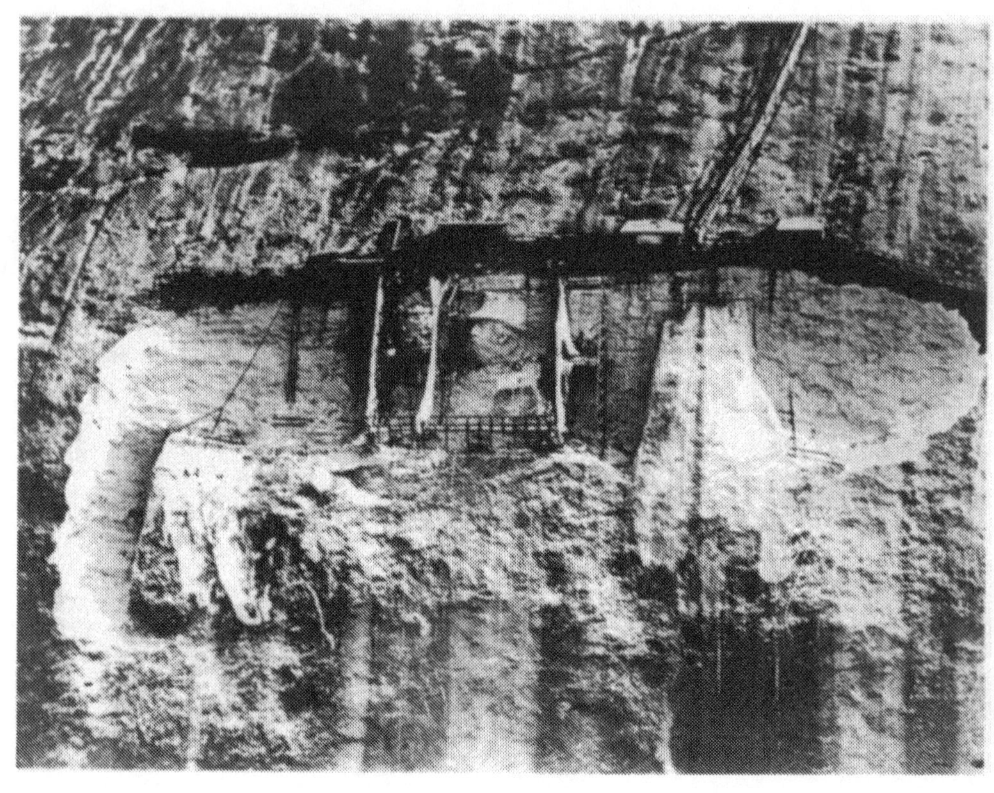

17. The progress of Borglum's carving at the beginning of 1925. The roughed out face of Stonewall Jackson is visible to the left of Lee.

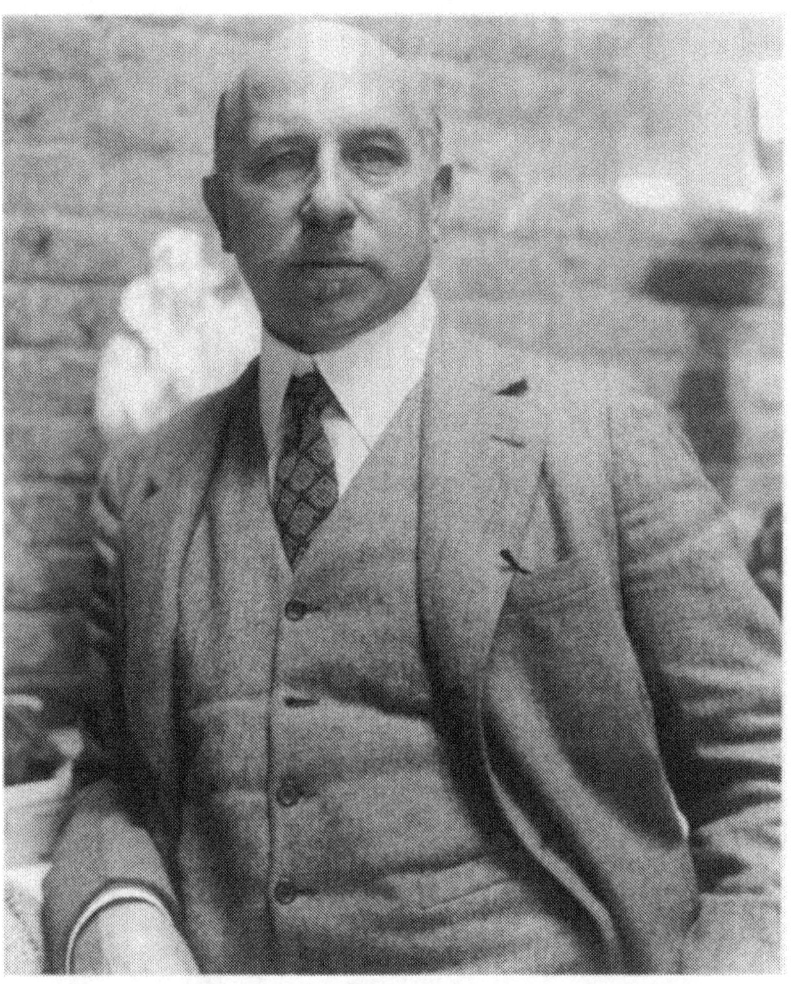

18. Augustus Lukeman, the sculptor who suceeded Gutzon Borglum.

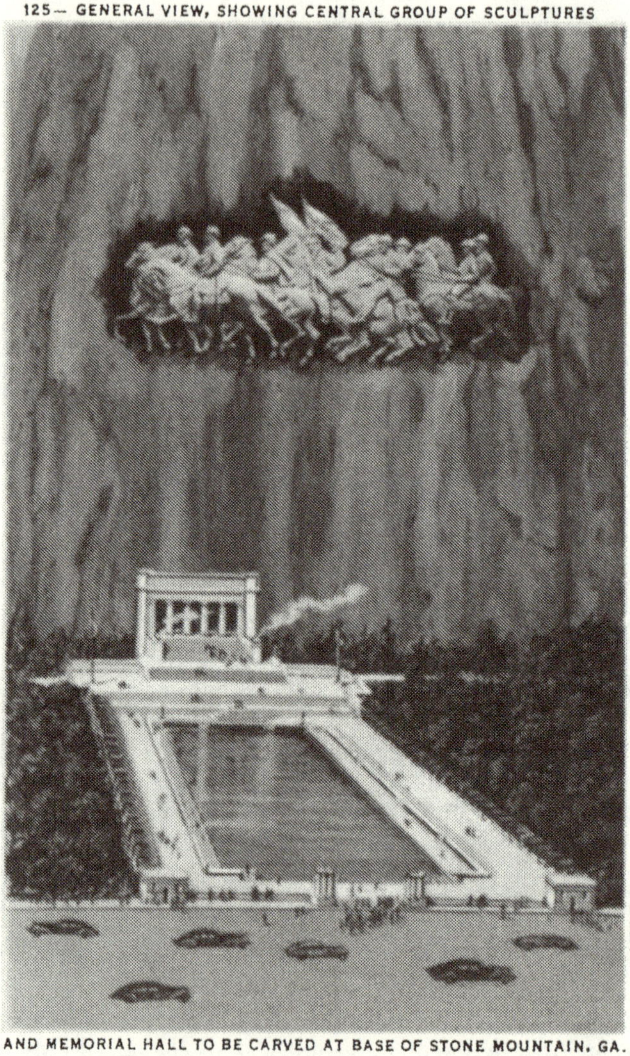

125— GENERAL VIEW, SHOWING CENTRAL GROUP OF SCULPTURES

AND MEMORIAL HALL TO BE CARVED AT BASE OF STONE MOUNTAIN, GA.

19. A postcard showing how Lukeman's original design would look once completed, with Memorial Hall carved into the base of the mountain.

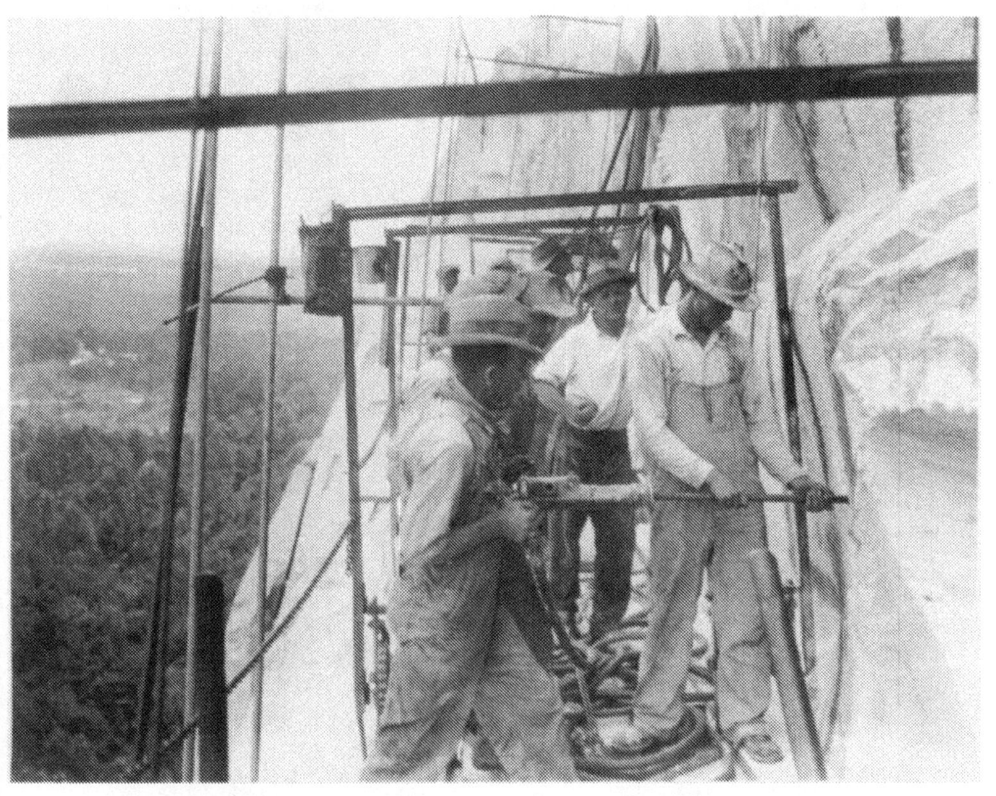

20. Stone cutters recruited from the quarries of the Stone Mountain Granite Company to execute Lukeman's design on the mountain.

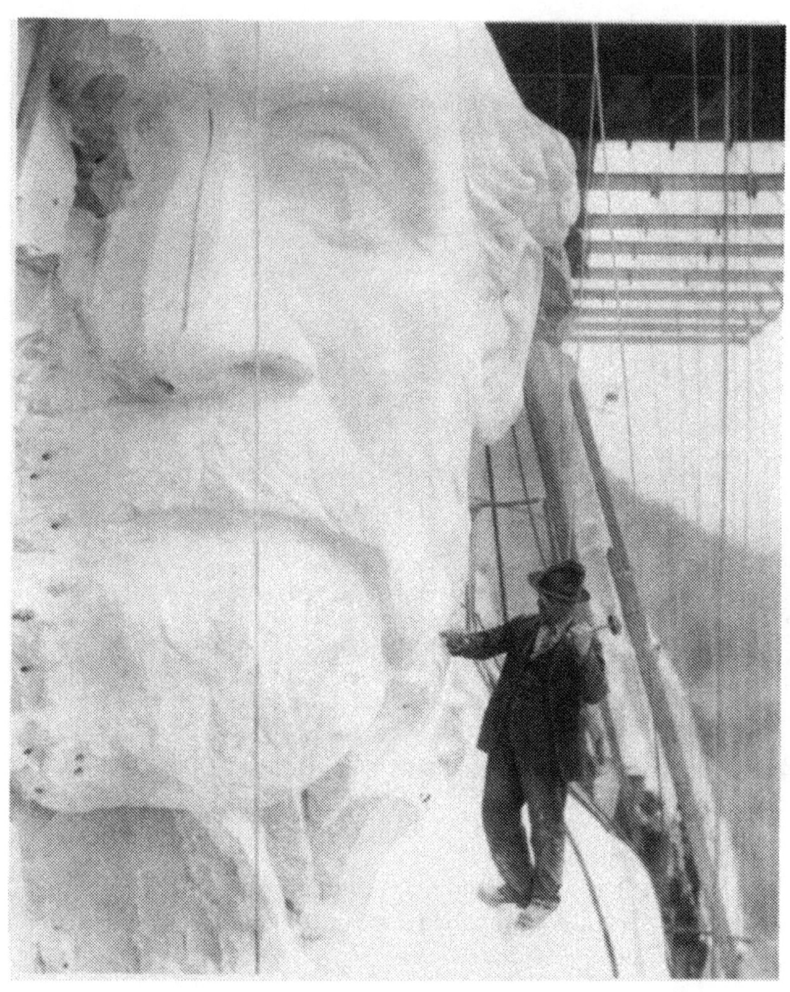

21. Master carver Theodore Bottinelli at work on the figure of General Lee.

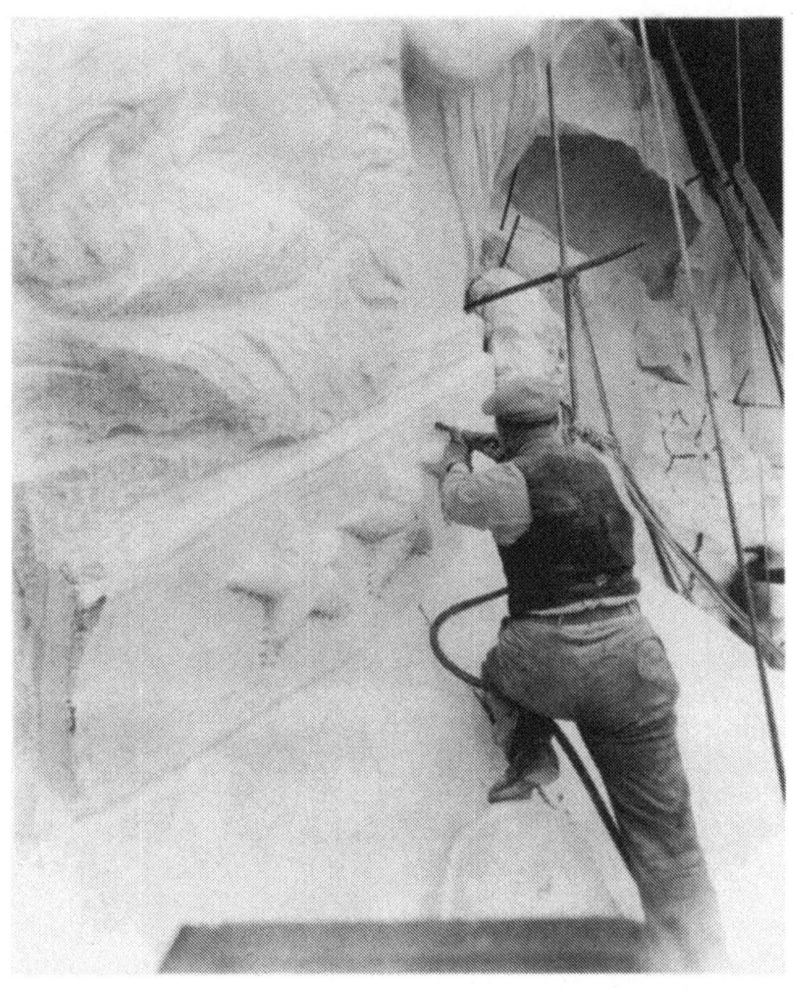

22. Master carver Theodore Bottinelli at work on the figure of General Lee.

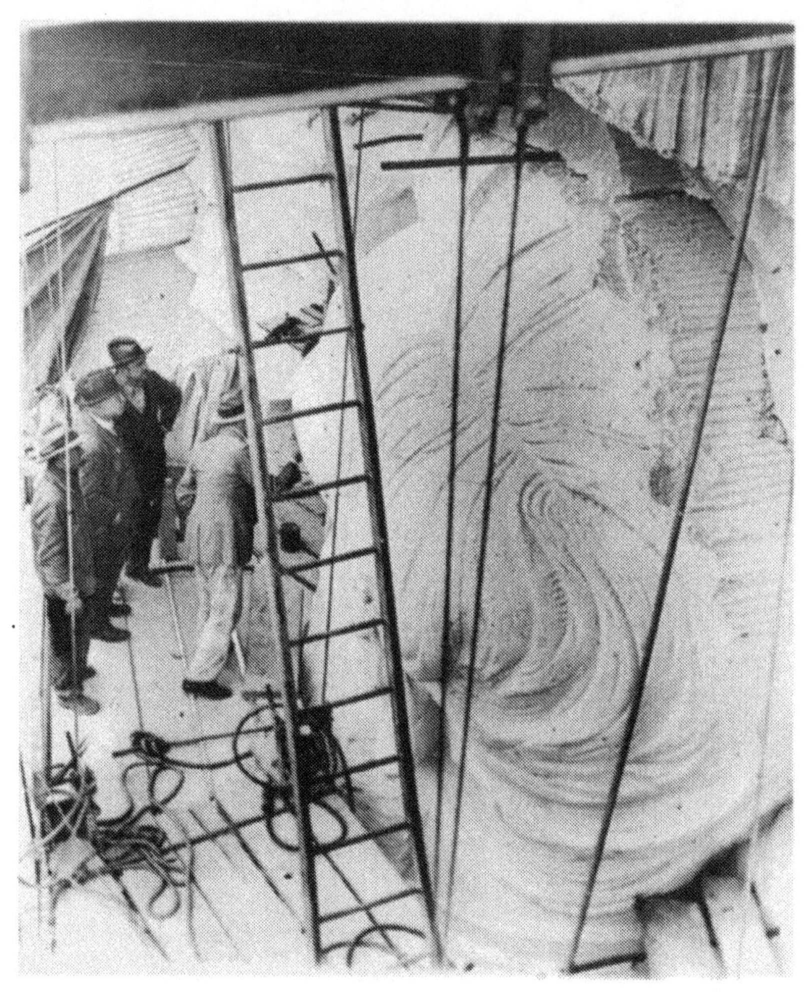

23. Lukeman inspecting the work on Lee's face.

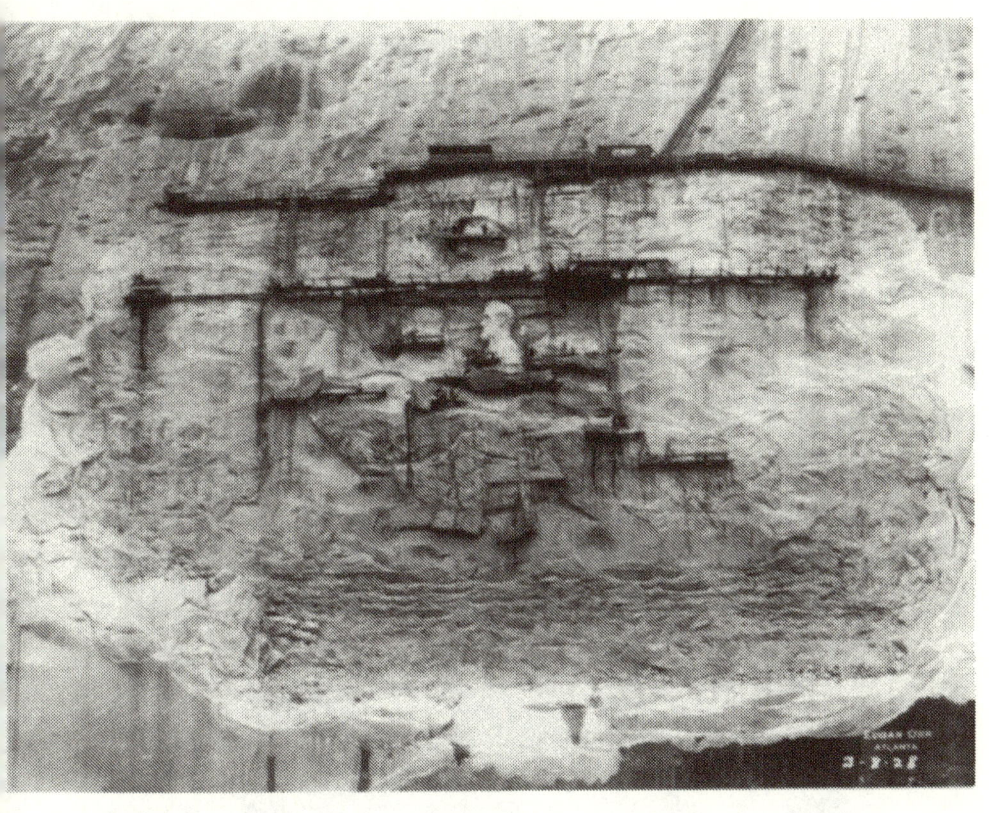

24. The progress of the Confederate memorial in March 1928. Note Borglum's head of Lee above Lukeman's. Borglum's work was destroyed shortly after this photo was taken.

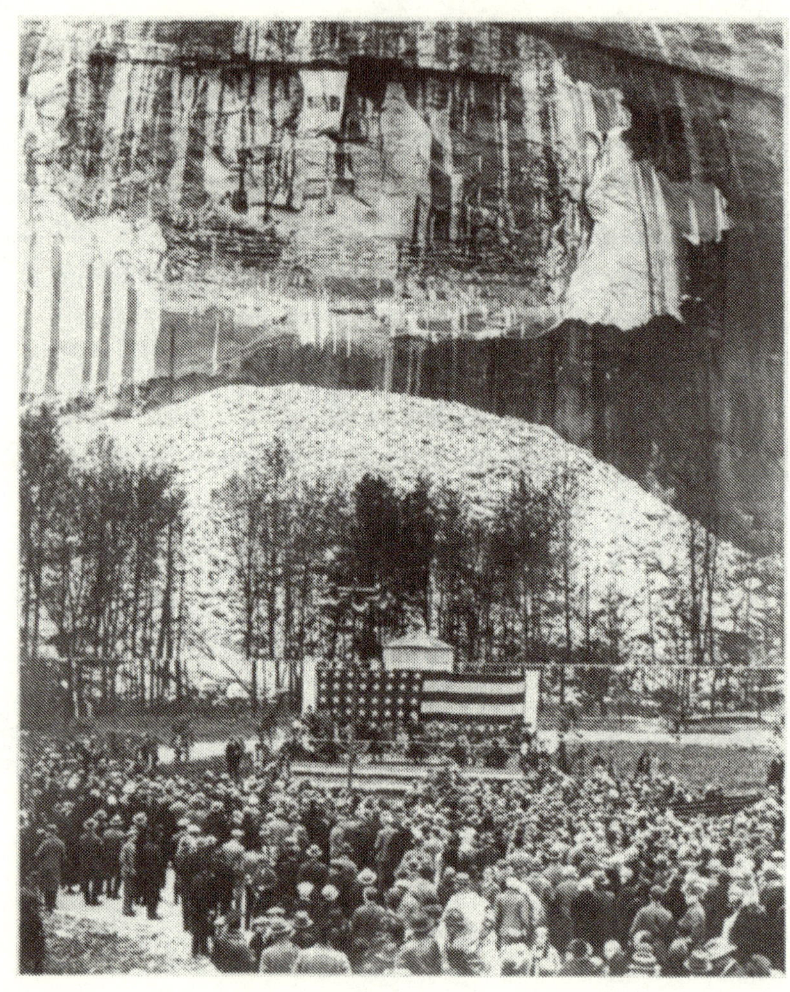

25. The unveiling of Lukeman's figure of Lee in April 1928. Mayor Jimmy Walker of New York was the guest of honor for selling 250,000 stone Mountain half-dollars.

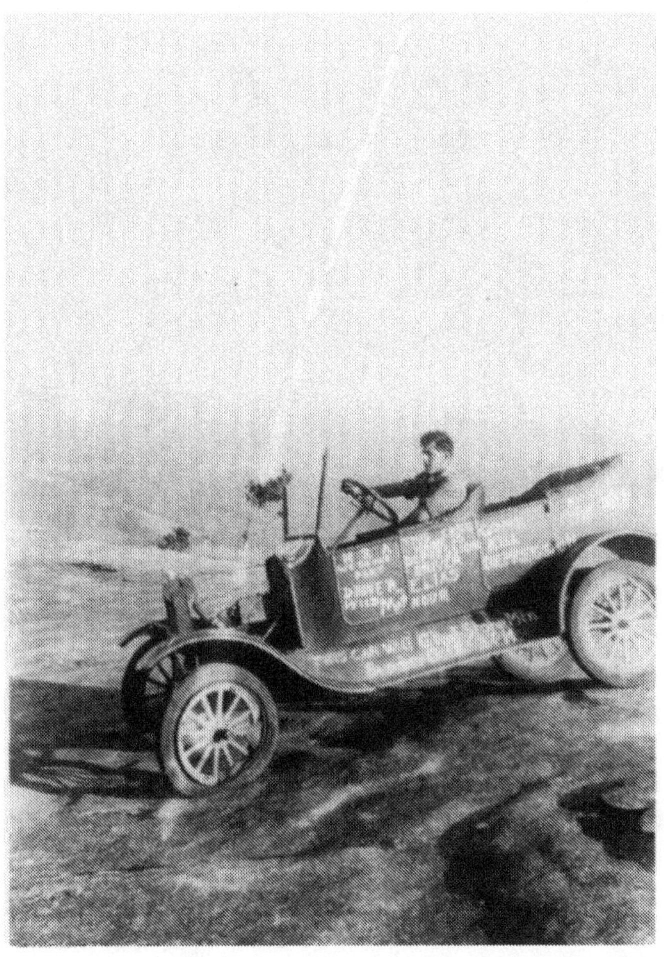

26. Elias Nour of Stone Mountain preparing to drive "Depression" over the side of the mountain in a 1933 NRA stunt.

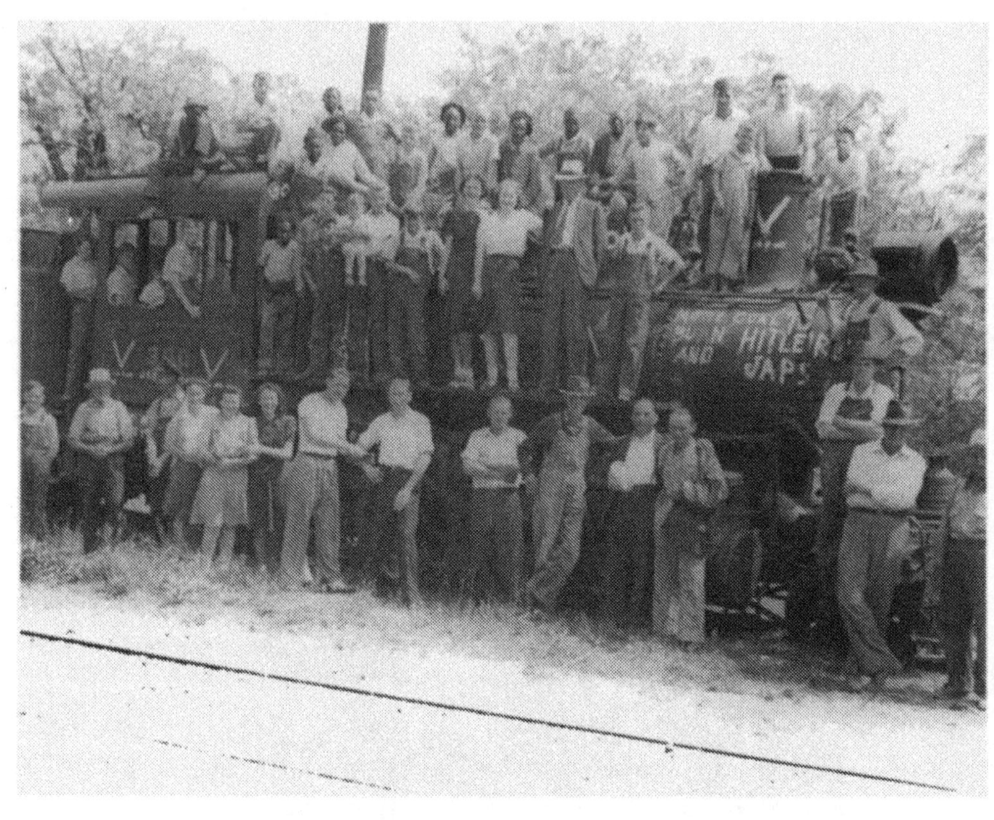

27. Stone Mountain residents posing with the "Dinky" which once pulled tons of granite out of the quarries there. The train was sold to a coal mine in Tennessee.

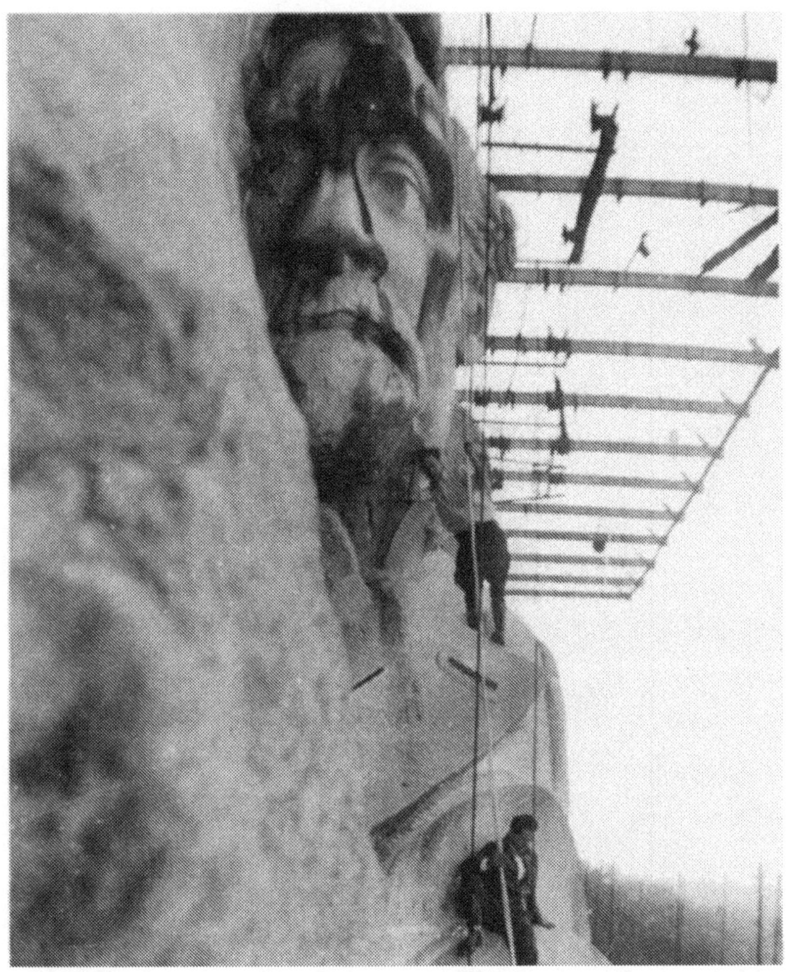

28. Elias Nour (top) and his brother Tony posing with the unfinished bust of General Lee. Many local residents made a sport of climbing down to the old carving site to have their pictures taken prior to state control of the mountain.

Chapter Four

A Mountain of Controversy

Gutzon Borglum's and Jesse Tucker's flight from the law into North Carolina took them to the home of Colonel Beniham Cameron, near Durham. Borglum had many supporters in North Carolina from his previous work in that state, including Governor Angus McLean. By law, McLean had no choice but to have Borglum arrested, but with that formality out of the way, the Governor ordered him released on his own recognizance and invited him to stay awhile at the governor's mansion. He also made the state fairgrounds available for Borglum to set up a temporary studio to remake his Stone Mountain models.

Upon learning of Borglum's whereabouts, E. "Pete" Rivers, on behalf of the Monumental Association, filed for the sculptor's extradition. When Rivers learned that Borglum could not be extradited for a misdemeanor charge of malicious mischief, he had the felony charges of larceny and larceny from the house added to the warrant, and filed a $50,000 damage suit. Governor McLean, however, refused to extradite and the state of Georgia was not eager to press matters. With his wry sense of humor, McLean, joked that he would surround the fairgrounds with the state militia if Georgia tried to take Borglum by force--an unlikely scenario at best.

Georgia Governor Clifford Walker believed that continued ineffectual demands would only make the state look ridiculous. On March 16, he sent a telegram to Hollins Randolph suggesting that the Monumental Association drop its application for extradition to avoid further bad publicity.[1]

Borglum's attorney tried to have the indictments against him dropped but to no avail. For the time being the sculptor was in limbo--in no danger of pursuit, but unable to return to Georgia without risking arrest. He had, in effect, been banished. He spent most of his time at the fairgrounds with Tucker and Villa, who had joined them, remaking the master model for the

---

[1]Gov. Clifford Walker to Hollins Randolph, 16 March 1925. Records of the Stone Mountain Confederate Monumental Association, Emory University Library.

Stone Mountain memorial. He announced that it would be turned over to Governor McLean for safe keeping before he left the South.

Public reaction to Borglum's dismissal was mixed. Most people depended on the newspaper reports to form an opinion, but much of this information consisted of vicious personal attacks on Borglum by the Association. Some readers believed the reports and cheered for the Association; others came to the conclusion that the Association protested too much to be credible and sympathized with the sculptor. The majority simply did not know what to believe. Corra Harris, a noted woman author of the day, gave a reporter her opinion on the matter: "I think it has greatly exalted the quality of gossip in this town. . . . The burning question is no longer shall we or shall we not have the memorial carved on Stone Mountain, but whether Mr. Borglum was or was not justified in destroying his models."[2] She further noted that while Borglum lacked Randoph's hypnotic charm, she thought he was the abler businessmen and psychologist. She also called on Randolph to resign and make a public audit of the Association's books as a "polite confession of incompetency which he owes the UDC."

Among the membership of the Association, most went along with the persuasive Hollins Randolph. A few of the directors resigned right away over the actions of the committee, and a few others decided to decline reappointment at the next annual election. Sam Venable and the members of the UDC continued their strong support of Borglum. They wanted a public audit of the Association's funds and an independent board of arbitration, as called for in the sculptor's contract, to settle the differences between the Association and Borglum so that he could get back to work on the mountain. Their even-tempered appeals were met with flat refusals. They persisted, but Randolph would not relent, stating that, "the re-employment of Borglum is out of the question under any circumstances."[3]

Actually, Randolph had backed himself into a corner through the relentless attacks made against Borglum by the committee. He could not alter his position without losing face before his peers and the public, and by this time the two sides could never have been reconciled. Randolph did

---

[2]"Randolph Is Urged To Resign Position On Memorial Board," *Atlanta Constitution*, 15 March 1925.

[3]As quoted in Howard and Aubrey Shaff, *Six Wars At A Time* (Sioux Falls, SD: Augustana College Center for Western Studies, 1985), 220, citing Associated Press, 7 March 1925.

have an independent audit of the finances done by the firm of Peat Marwick & Associates. He reported that their books were in perfect order, but would not make the details of the audit public, even though they were managing publicly-subscribed funds as a public trust.

For the seven months that Borglum remained in North Carolina, he kept uncharacteristically quiet, stating only that he was innocent of the charges against him and that he was perfectly willing to forget the difficulties of the past to work toward a peaceful solution. Most of the wrangling in the press involved the Association, Sam Venable, and the Atlanta Chapter UDC. In open statements to the press, Venable reminded Randolph that the Association was running out of time to finish the memorial and that they would also need more space on the mountain that originally anticipated. He was willing to grant both if Borglum were brought back.

Randolph had no intention of conceding defeat on this point. Two months earlier, in anticipation of coming events, he had negotiated with Fred Weiblen of the Stone Mountain Granite Company to secure a sublease to the property. Weiblen's lease on the mountain, signed with the Venables in 1911, did not expire until 1951, so Randolph figured the Association had a secure claim on the mountain for another twenty-six years.

Some of Borglum's UDC supporters asked him why he did not take some legal action for breach of contract? His contract called for arbitration to settle disputes, but the Association would not submit to it nor would it allow a hearing before dismissing him. He responded that he did not want to "add to the quarreling" over the memorial. Besides, he was getting much more sympathy playing the part of the persecuted artist. In a letter to Sam Venable, he indicated his intention to wait Randolph out, expecting the project to die in his hands. He further boasted that he alone had the courage, training, and experience needed to find one's way "in that wilderness of granite. . . ."[4]

Borglum's high opinion of himself is typical; no one ever accused him of excessive modesty, and his ego was partly responsible for his fall from grace. He also spoke of "frightful slander" appearing almost daily in newspapers across the country, and repeated in mid-March in the Association's new pamphlet, "A Statement Concerning the Reasons Why It Was Necessary to Dismiss Gutzon Borglum." This statement enlarged upon the

---

[4]Shaff and Shaff, 221, citing Gutzon Borglum to Sam Venable, 31 March 1925, G.B. Papers, Library of Congress, Washington, DC.

original allegations and was widely circulated to the press, veterans' groups, fraternal societies, social clubs, and anyone else who might consider contributing to the memorial. The executive committee took this step in an attempt to justify its position, but the exaggeration and falsehoods in the pamphlet later served as an indictment of the committee itself.

The charges against Gutzon Borglum and the supporting evidence form the basis for his dismissal. The committee first stated that the sculptor was subject to uncontrolled and violent fits of temper leading to fear that he might "run amok and destroy the work on the mountain."[5] As evidence, they pointed to the demolished models and to another instance several years before when he supposedly smashed the sculpted angels he was making for the Cathedral of Saint John the Divine because one of the church leaders criticized his work.

Borglum *was* impetuous by nature and he sometimes exchanged heated words with the executive committee, but his associates at the time and later biographers have shown that he did not throw tantrums and that he never destroyed a piece of art. Eyewitnesses on the mountain said that he displayed only sadness, not hostility. As for the angels, Borglum originally designed them with feminine faces, but when the church committee asked him to make them more masculine, he calmly picked up a hammer, knocked out the model's face, and remade it to the committee's satisfaction. Canon Jones of the Cathedral wired the *Atlanta Constitution* with the real story of what happened and added, "The angels stand serene in their places, where they have stood ever since Borglum put them there. His relations with the committee were always amicable."[6]

Next, the Association charged that Borglum avariciously sought to profit personally from the memorial. He allegedly tried to organize a stock company to operate road houses, drink stands, and other money-making schemes which "would have converted the whole mountain and its environs into a carnival of cheap amusements."[7] Fortunately, they said, the scheme was halted by the refusal of the owners of the mountain to participate.

---

[5]*A Statement By the Executive Committee of the Stone Mountain Confederate Monumental Association Concerning the Reasons Why It Was Necessary to Dismiss Gutzon Borglum*, SMCMA, 14 March 1925.

[6]Mary Borglum, "Answers to a Few of the Statements Made by the Executive Committee of the Stone Mountain Confederate Monumental Association, records of the SMCMA, Emory University Library; and also quoted in Shaff and Shaff, 94., citing W. R. Huntington to Hollins Randolph, Gutzon Borglum Papers, Library of Congress.

[7]*Reasons Why*, 3.

They also claimed that he tried to charge the Association for designing the Children's Roll medal and then went forward without authorization to make arrangements for its manufacture with a company that was going to charge eighteen cents per medal, of which he would receive half as a royalty.

As for the accusation of his scheming to build "cheap amusements" at the mountain, Sam Venable firmly denied that Borglum had ever had such an idea, nor does it particularly accord with the sculptor's high moral standards. The true story of the medal can be found in the records of the Monumental Association. Borglum agreed not to charge for the separate work of designing the medal, and the committee offered to reimburse any expenses he incurred. The Medallic Art Company wrote to E. "Pete" Rivers in March of 1925 stating that the publicized story was "absolutely untrue and entirely unjust" and that "[n]ot one cent was being paid to anyone on this contract."[8] The most damning evidence against the allegation is a letter from Randolph to Rivers in September, 1924:

> I never thought myself that anyone was particularly to blame for the mix-up. . . . I think it is a fact that Mr. Borglum was given authority to close with the Medallic Art Co. . . . I think Mr. Borglum acted on instructions he got from me . . . and went ahead in entire good faith and innocently enough in the transactions. . . . I know I was exceedingly anxious to get the medals and told him to go ahead and have them made, whereas, of course, if I had known how far the office had gone with the Whitehead & Hoag people, I would not have failed to tell Mr. Borglum about that."[9]

It seems that if anyone was responsible for the confusion surrounding the Children's Roll medals, it was Hollins Randolph.

The executive committee further accused Borglum of deliberately delaying the memorial coin to cause embarrassment to the Association. It claimed he could have done the whole thing in four weeks if he had tried. Here again, the Association's own records show that Borglum was doing all he could to expedite matters. Another letter from Randolph to Rivers written in August, 1924, holds the sculptor blameless:

---

[8]Medallic Art Company to E. Rivers, 10 March 1925. Records of the SMCMA.
[9]Hollins Randolph to E. Rivers, 18 September 1924. Records of the SMCMA.

> I seriously doubt whether Borglum could have prevented the delay. . . . In my opinion, [the Grand Army of the Republic] had him blocked insidiously and without his knowledge from the very beginning and would have done anybody the same way.[10]

In the matter of distributing the half-dollars, they charged that he planned to organize a consortium of out-of-state people unknown to the Association to seize control of the whole lot of coins. Borglum offered to have the buyers purchase the coins outright from the government for the Association. One of these buyers was W. W. Fuller, a prominent New York millionaire and the Honorary President of the Stone Mountain Confederate Monumental Association.

The committee also held him responsible for engaging in a publicity war against the Association to discredit its members while he was in Washington in February, 1925. This charge actually has a kernel of truth to it. When Borglum suspected Randolph of planning to divert coin money, he did issue a statement to the press. The innocuous but mostly accurate statement, however, served to embarrass the Association.

Aside from extolling his own part in designing the memorial, he claimed that the Association had no funds (which is what it kept telling him), that the time limit was expiring, and that there was not enough room ceded for the whole memorial. He also accused the Association of having shrunk into a "local habitation," meaning that it did not want anyone outside of Atlanta to have a voice in its affairs, particularly the disbursement of the memorial half-dollars.

His only false statement was that he had no contract with the Association for the work. He later tried to justify this statement by claiming his contract was with the UDC. Why he would take such a stand is a mystery as the document is clearly between him and the Monumental Association. Understandably upset by the release of these disparaging words, the committee accused him of making false statements that he did not in fact make.

The chief charge against Borglum was "gross neglect of his work." Specifically, they said he spent too much time delivering lyceum lectures, breaking business engagements with the Association to keep his ego-boosting speaking dates, engaging in other memorial commissions, spending most of the year 1924 away from the mountain, and otherwise engaging in

---

[10]Hollins Randolph to E. Rivers, 22 August 1925. Records of the SMCMA.

various other activities outside of the Stone Mountain project. The committee claimed that although it had paid Borglum $185,000 of his $250,000 contract, the work was hopelessly behind schedule, with only thirty-four percent of the rough work and five percent of the finish work completed, according to the consulting engineers, L. W. Robert & Company.

This was a rather broad series of accusations, some false and others partly true but misleading. First, it was unreasonable to expect any artist, particularly one of Borglum's stature, to devote his whole attention to a single project to the exclusion of other offered commissions. To criticize him for engaging in more than one work is preposterous. It is true that he was away from the mountain for much of the year, but this is because he was in Washington at Randolph's insistence on the memorial coin business. The records show that he repeatedly asked permission to get back to the mountain, but was denied until the coin design was approved. As it was, he kept in regular contact with Tucker and Villa by telephone and telegram about the progress of the work.

As to the lectures, the Association freely advertised the sculptor's services as a speaker, and they expected him to travel the country promoting the memorial. The records show only one instance of his missing a meeting with Randolph because he was giving a lecture. Possibly, notice of the meeting did not reach him in time. Borglum did not typically miss important meetings, as indicated by records that he canceled several speaking engagements in order to keep appointments with the Association.

The work on the mountain was behind schedule, for reasons already mentioned, but not as hopelessly as the executive committee declared. The roughing out of Jackson's head was almost done, and a considerable amount of roughing out had been done on the head of Davis. Given that it took six weeks for Borglum to do the finish work on Lee's head, one could predict the same time necessary for Jackson and Davis. The two heads probably could have been finished by the June 3 unveiling date announced by Randolph. He had given this date in a press release of 19 January 1925, when he also reported on how well the carving was coming. As people pointed out, either Randolph was lying in January or he was lying in March; there was no way to reconcile the contradictory statements.

Although the Association would not make its financial records available at the time, the information has long since come to light. The audit of 15 March 1925, shows that Borglum received $113,922 under his contract plus $23,341 in reimbursements for expenses prior to the contract, almost

$50,000 less than the Association claimed. The audit also shows that forty-five percent of the Association's income was spent on overhead.

Finally, the pamphlet stated that "those who speak in defense of Borglum are far removed from the scene of his operation in connection with this memorial. They know nothing or care nothing about the facts. Few, if any, of them have contributed any money to the Association."[11] This statement incensed the Venables, the members of the Atlanta UDC, and numerous other local people who were intimately acquainted with and who had contributed generously to the project.

With the circulation of such inflammatory and patently false statements, it is no wonder that the Venable family, the UDC, and other Borglum supporters barraged the Association with angry letters of protest and published rebuttals to the Association's charges. These people knew the truth, but without the documentation from the executive committee's own files, they could only give their word against Randolph's, and the people on the outside remained very much confused as to whom to believe.

As Corra Harris observed, most people were more interested in whether or not Borglum had the right to smash the models. Borglum claimed they were his property and were copyrighted under his name, but the Association pointed to a paragraph in his contract that clearly stated that the models and designs were the property of the Association. The *Literary Digest* of 21 March 1925 ran a lengthy article devoted to this question. For this article, the magazine solicited the opinions of artists across the country. Nearly all of the artists who responded shared the opinion that as an artist Borglum owned the models and had the right to use them as he saw fit. Further, any attempt to turn the models over to a successor would, in their view, be "futile and stupid." By ordering their destruction, they argued, Borglum was merely "protecting his integrity as an artist."

The *Digest* article also sampled editorial opinions from newspapers across the country. Most of these were sympathetic toward the sculptor. The *Times-Dispatch* of Richmond wrote that while the outside world could not evaluate Randolph's criticism of Borglum, it did know that it was the latter who was "stirring the flames of enthusiasm for the Stone Mountain project." Rather than replace the sculptor, the *Dispatch* suggested that it would be "far better, in the interest of ultimate results, to get a new Association, if that is possible." The *Dallas News* editorialized that whether

---

[11]Ibid., 7.

the Association intended it or not, the Stone Mountain memorial was already a monument to Borglum himself, and would remain so "unless the folly of changing the design is engaged in after it is already under way."

While certainly not every artist and editorial was in support of Borglum, the vast majority seemed to be. His peers all seemed to agree that, regardless of anything else, Borglum was a great sculptor, having "shown amazing ability in even beginning the work." Even the 1925 *Encyclopedia Britannica* concurred, referring to him as one of the leading sculptors in America.

He was not, however, the only great sculptor, and at the same time the *Literary Digest* article appeared, the Association was desperately looking for one of these other great sculptors to take over the project. A special subcommittee had the task of finding a new sculptor. It first tried to interest Loredo Taft, but he refused, stating that "no self-respecting artist would take over another man's work."[12] The Association approached Daniel C. French, sculptor of the Lincoln Memorial, as well as sculptors of lesser-known works Charles Shea, Clement Barnhorn, William Sievers, and Vincenzo Miserendino. All of them, however, declined. The National Sculpture Society responded to an inquiry from the committee indicating that their body was not interested in discussing the Stone Mountain matter.[13]

Despite these rebuffs, the Association received letters of interest from across the country. Plenty of sculptors were apparently willing to set aside the ethical concerns of taking over Borglum's work. The committee eventually settled on Henry Augustus Lukeman of New York. Originally from Virginia, the fifty-four-year-old Lukeman met the criterion of many supporters for a sculptor from the South. He was also the exact opposite of Borglum in temperament. At its meeting of 16 April 1925, the executive committee rejected a motion to delay hiring the new sculptor to allow time to "harmonize Sam Venable with the Association." Randolph declared that nothing they could do would please him and to delay further would be to add to the embarrassment of their situation. On the following day the committee publicly announced their selection of Lukeman to carry the memorial project forward.

---

[12]Shaff and Shaff, 220.

[13]A. M. Simpson, Assistant Secretary National Sculpture Society to Stone Mountain Confederate Memorial Association, 16 May 1925. Records of the SMCMA.

A week after the announcement, Helen Plane, then ninety-six years of age, passed away. She never issued a statement on the turmoil surrounding Borglum's dismissal, but privately she expressed profound disappointment in what had become of her great dream. The death of her only son, William F. Plane, Jr., in March 1925, compounded her sorrows. Sources close to her say she became depressed, took to her bed, and died.

After their experiences with Borglum, Randolph and the others established a much more restrictive contract with Lukeman. In terms of his responsibilities and powers, Lukeman's contract concerned only the design and execution of a central group of three to seven figures, consisting of Lee, Jackson, Davis, and others selected by the committee. This design was to conform to the topography of the mountain. For making the models of the design, the Association would pay the sculptor $25,000 and the models would then become the property of the Memorial Association.

The second part of the contract called for Lukeman to supervise the execution of his design, making on-site inspections at least once a month. For his services he would be paid a flat $10,000 per year, out of which he would pay his own expenses. The equipment, supplies and labor were to be arranged for and paid by the Association rather than the sculptor as had been the case under Borglum. Lukeman was to have no part in fundraising or any other aspect of the over-all memorial project. The engineering firm of Robert & Company would work with Lukeman and the carving contractor to aid in the construction of the monument.

Originally, the Association planned to have the new sculptor remake the Borglum models from the file photographs in order to complete the carving. Randolph publicly scoffed at the sculptor's ethic that prohibited the taking over of a living man's work by another, but the taboo was genuine. Neither Lukeman nor any other reputable sculptor would have undertaken to finish Borglum's design; they could, however, take over the monument project and use their own design. The plan to finish the incomplete work was quietly dropped and Lukeman went back to New York to work up a new concept for the carving.

With the services of a new sculptor secured, the executive committee turned its attention to the distribution of the Stone Mountain memorial coins. Hollins Randolph had been at the mint in Philadelphia on January 21, "Stonewall" Jackson's birthday, when the first coins were stamped. He noted at the time how appropriate it was to mint the coin honoring the valor of Southern soldiers simultaneously with the minting of the new Peace dollar.

The first one thousand Stone Mountain coins were placed in separate envelopes and individually numbered. Randolph personally paid the director of the mint $500 in gold for the initial batch of 1,000 coins. The other coins were shipped to the Federal Reserve Bank in Atlanta, which paid for the coins on behalf of the Monumental Association. Altogether, 2,314,000 of these coins were struck at the Philadelphia mint. Beginning on 3 July they were distributed to approximately 3,000 banks across the country, going on sale for one dollar, the premium being set in a special account for the Association.

The one thousand coins purchased by the Association were to be used as gifts to people who had contributed to the minting of the coins or to the memorial in general. The first coin to come off the line was into an engraved plaque made of Georgia gold and reserved for President Calvin Coolidge. Randolph wished to make a personal presentation at the White House in hopes that a photograph of a supportive President would counter some of the negative publicity surrounding Borglum's dismissal. Coolidge, however, kept his distance from the Association, suggesting that "no good purpose would be served by a formal presentation."[14]

The number two coin was presented to Secretary of the Treasury Andrew Mellon in a silver plaque. The remainder of the first fifty-two coins were distributed to the Under-Secretary of the Treasury, the Director of the mint, to the governors of all the Southern states, to various leaders of Confederate heritage groups, to the officers of the Association, and to members of the Venable family.[15]

The names of Gutzon and C. Helen Plane were conspicuously absent from the list of recipients. Not surprisingly, Randolph refused to recognize Borglum, and he was chagrined that it was Borglum's design he was handing out. He tried to pretend otherwise by publicly taking the position that the coin was actually designed by the Fine Arts Commission. Helen Plane had originally been scheduled to receive coin number five, but she died before Randolph made the presentation. Instead of honoring her posthumously by presenting a coin to her heirs, he simply dropped her from the list.

The 1925 annual meeting of the Association was a closed affair because of the simmering controversy over Borglum's dismissal. The officers of the

---

[14]William Hyder and R.W. Colbert, "The Selling of the Stone Mountain Half Dollar," *The Numismatist* (Np., nd.), citing Coolidge Papers at Library of Congress. [Reprint edition in the Stone Mountain Collection, Atlanta History Center, Atlanta, Georgia.]

[15]*Custodians of Imperishable Glory*, SMCMA, 1926, 27-28.

Atlanta UDC had been so vocal about their demands for a public accounting of the Association's funds that Randolph was afraid they might try to attend the meeting. He was right, and when the UDC members tried to enter the meeting room they found the way barred by five policemen who would not let them in, despite the fact that some of them, such as Elizabeth Mason, were members of the Association. They created such a ruckus that executive committee member Eugene Black finally obtained permission for them to enter. Randolph, however, refused to address them or to let them speak.

In his president's report, Randolph condemned Borglum, praised Lukeman, and painted a rosy picture of the Association's future financial situation. Since the 1924 annual meeting, the executive committee had revised its by-laws to enlarge the board of directors to one hundred twenty and invited those sympathetic to the committee to become directors. The committee also declared the governors of the Southern states to be members of the board. At the 1925 meeting, the remaining "Borglumites" among the directors and on the executive board were purged, including Sam Venable, Elizabeth Mason, Mrs. John Purdue, president of the Atlanta UDC, and Mrs. Walter Grace, president of the Georgia Division UDC, among others.

In discussing plans for the near future, Randolph outlined the basics of the Harvest Campaign, the Association's scheme for promoting the Stone Mountain coins. The kick-off for the campaign came at the Conference of Southern Governors in Atlanta on 20 July 1925. This conference was called by Gov. Clifford Walker of Georgia at the request of the Association. The premise of the Harvest Campaign was for each governor to accept responsibility for a promotional blitz to sell his state's quota of coins, calculated on the basis of white population and bank deposits. While the governors chaired the campaigns in their respective states, the actual work was given over to assistants and publicity agents secured by the governors. Promotional materials and salaries of $200 per week for the agents were supplied by the Monumental Association.

Governor Walker, in an appeal to his fellow governors, declared that the "South would be eternally disgraced if it failed to accept the challenge" of absorbing its collective quota of two and a half million coins. In reality, however, governors are busy people with little time for such matters. The campaign got off to a shaky start, with some states beginning sooner or being better organized than others, depending upon how soon the governors arranged to hire agents and how efficient the agents were.

Rogers Winter, publicity director for the Association, kept in touch with the field agents. He reported in September that every Southern governor except Angus McLean of North Carolina was giving full co-operation. Undoubtedly Borglum had something to do with McLean's resistance.

While the governors were overseeing the Harvest Campaign in the South, the North and West were turned over to three professional publicists. The Association paid each of them $500 per week plus expenses to boost coin sales. As an additional gimmick, the bulk of the serially numbered coins were auctioned off at the rate of one a week. Bids for these coins sometimes reached as high as $150 to $200.

As the Harvest Campaign was getting underway in August, Lukeman returned to Atlanta to present his preliminary sketches and model to a special meeting of the directors. Lukeman's design differed from his predecessor's on several points. Instead of the naturalistic positions and arrangements of Borglum, Lukeman's figures were posed in stylized heroic stance and lined up in a frieze. His rationale was that the Civil War was the last traditional war, before armies began firing poison gas at one another from trenches miles apart, and the subjects should be treated in a classical fashion.

The new design featured two groups: Davis, Lee and Jackson followed by another group of four generals. Two color bearers separated the groups and Davis and Lee were depicted without hats. Lukeman explained that he showed them this way because they had just saluted the colors as they rode by. It was also better, he said, to portray Lee without a hat because "of the wonderful beauty and majesty of his head," adding that most portraits show him bare-headed. Randolph later said it was because Lee was too much of a gentleman to wear a hat in the presence of ladies who would be viewing the memorial.

Lukeman's plans for Memorial Hall were very similar to Borglum's, but smaller in size. The hall was to be only 150 feet long and 50 feet deep. For the giant seated figure in the center of the hall to represent the women of the Confederacy, he planned to make it in the likeness of the late Helen Plane. He added a reflecting pool in the front of the colonnade and an urn for burning incense. The naval memorial planned by Borglum was apparently scuttled in the new design.

The directors were very much impressed with what they saw, and authorized Lukeman to make a plaster model of his sketch. Recognizing the need to keep public interest stimulated for the sake of coin sales, Rogers Winter had photos of the model published in newspapers across the country. The Association received numerous letters concerning the new design, mostly complimentary, but with a few consistent critical comments.

The most often repeated remark was that the likeness of Jackson was not very good, and that he always wore a kepi, never a hat as depicted. About half the respondents felt that the figure of Lee left something to be desired, and everyone thought Davis was superbly done. A few veterans of the Army of Northern Virginia pointed out some other mistakes: generals rode with a single bridle rein, not two; Lee wore a cavalry saber, not a straight sword; and real flag bearers wore shell jackets that buttoned up to the neck and had no lapels, and wore kepis instead of slouch hats. One old horseman wrote that the poses of the horses were all unnatural--the head, ears, neck, and limbs of Davis' horse represented one angrily resisting the bit, which was not in keeping with the leisurely pace of the scene, and the extreme curvature of Traveler's neck was not even physically possible.

A few respondents approved of Lukeman's overall design, but still thought Borglum should finish what he had started. The Association emphatically denied the possibility of reinstatement, but also claimed his work would be utilized by Lukeman. This statement was, of course, absolute nonsense. The scale of Lukeman's design was about thirty percent smaller and totally incompatible with Borglum's concept. Despite the press releases, Borglum's work was doomed from the moment he was dismissed.

By the time the Lukeman model was being shown across the country, Borglum had just finished remaking his master model at the North Carolina fairgrounds. In his first public statement in several months, he predicted that the memorial would fail under its present management. He announced plans to start a new Confederate memorial at Chimney Rock, North Carolina, but that project never got past the talking stage. Borglum soon moved west with his family to San Antonio, Texas, to work on commissions there. He sent Jesse Tucker to South Dakota to become superintendent of the Mount Rushmore monument he was planning to carve. From Texas, Borglum continued to issue occasional statements on his shoddy treatment by the management of the Association and call for investigations into its finances.

In the fall of 1925, as the Association was pushing ahead with its plans, the officers of the Atlanta Chapter UDC sent to other UDC chapters around the country a pamphlet entitled *Reasons Why the UDC Should With Hold Funds From the Stone Mountain Memorial Association*. This circular was intended to mimic the one distributed by the Association concerning Borglum's dismissal, but the chapter's small budget never allowed it to have so wide a circulation.

In the pamphlet, Mrs. Walter Grace, President of the Georgia Division, stated five main points: the Association lacked enough room for the monument, it could not be done in the time remaining, the Association was deeply in debt, the UDC had been cut out of the affairs of the Association, and they had no assurance as to what would be done with the coin money. She railed against the libelous propaganda churned out by the Association against Borglum, its ruthless and bitter attacks on Sam Venable, and its high-handed treatment of the UDC, and charged the Association with failing to carve the promised design. She encouraged the other Daughters not to assist with the coin sales because they could not ask the public to contribute money to such an enterprise. She warned the Association that the UDC would not "act as mere puppets in its hands and to pull its chestnuts out of the fire," referring to the slower than expected sale of half-dollars.[16]

Randolph answered these charges by claiming that because the new design was one-third smaller, it could be completed within the time and space allowed, and that the Association had paid off its debt and had ample funds for the carving. He made no response to Grace's criticisms of the executive committee's actions, but did state that the UDC organization was well represented on the board of directors by twelve or fifteen Daughters.

A list of the directors after the 1925 elections showed 120 people on the board. Of these, thirteen were women, and at least one of those was not a UDC member. At most, one-tenth of the board were Daughters, and those who were on the board were friendly to the Association and to Randolph. Their ability to influence the actions of the Association was nil. As Randolph stated at the director's meeting in April, 1925, it was only a mere matter of form to submit matters before the directors because the executive committee had full power to act. It should be added that there were no Daughters on the executive committee. Although still technically represented as Randolph said, the UDC had in actuality long before lost any voice in the Association.

The UDC itself was not by any means a unified body on the subject of Stone Mountain. Several members of the Atlanta and other chapters of the division criticized the officers for purporting to speak for all the Daughters. As with the public in general, many of them no longer cared who was right with regard to the Borglum controversy; they just wanted to see the

---

[16]*Reasons Why the United Daughters of the Confederacy Should With Hold Funds From the Stone Mountain Memorial Association*, Atlanta Chapter UDC, October 1925, 11.

memorial finished and they took exception to their leader's attempts to halt the role of the UDC in its funding.

From the Association's point of view, the UDC pamphlet came out at an inopportune time. Although a few hundred thousand coins had been sold through the Harvest Campaign, the results thus far were disappointing. To encourage northern banks to push the coins more vigorously, the Association offered to pay them a seven cents per coin commission. There is no record of any of the banks having accepted this proposition, and they probably would not or could not have anyway, but it aptly demonstrates the committee's desperation

To increase positive publicity for the Monumental Association, Hollins Randolph, and Rogers Winter put together a very fancy and widely-distributed magazine entitled *Custodians of Imperishable Glory*. This publication served mainly to introduce Augustus Lukeman and his designs to those in the best position to help the Association financially. It included numerous full-page photographs of Lukeman's past works and quoted several letters praising his abilities as a sculptor. The magazine also recapped the overall plan for the memorial, the history of the carving effort, the major activities of the Association, and even managed to give glowing vitae of the officers. As propaganda it was a beautiful bit of work, assiduously avoiding any mention of Borglum or his ten-year labor to make mountain carving a reality. Indicating merely that plans halted "[o]n account of the World War *and other adverse circumstances*," the magazine gave credit to no one prior to the election of Hollins Randolph in 1923. [Emphasis mine.]

William Terrell, mentioned in the magazine as having suggested the idea, wrote to Randolph with his opinion of the sanitized text:

> I do not think that your seeming efforts to belittle and ignore the accomplishments of those who preceded you in the work of constructing the Stone Mountain Memorial is any aid whatever to the attainment of the end so much desired by all of us . . . .[17]

Another curious point about the magazine was the phrase, "were nothing else carved on Stone Mountain but these three figures . . . they would stand supreme above all the monuments of the ages." This phrase, in various ways, was repeated several times throughout the text as if the Association expected it was all that would ever get done. This view is

---

[17]William Terrell to Hollins Randolph, 4 October 1926. Records of the SMCMA.

substantiated by a later statement that the central group would be the extent of the carving, all extra funds being reserved for future purposes and intents of the Association.[18]

By December, 1925, the Association had accumulated enough money to pay off its debts and to resume work on the memorial. Another dedication ceremony was held at the mountain on December 10 to mark the second beginning. This was a small affair compared to the previous Virginia Day festivities of 1923 and attendance was poor. It was mainly for show since Lukeman was not yet ready to start work. The only work going on at the mountain that winter was done by a crew of day laborers hired by the construction committee to renovate the studio and add a store.

Previously the Association had collected donations at the studio and had gotten perhaps twenty dollars per week. The new studio store would not only accept donations, but would also sell postcards, memorial coins, and other sorts of merchandise. A telescope was also installed at the studio for visitors to look through at the rate of five cents a minute. Virginia Milmow and Nettie Ashby wrote a special Stone Mountain song and march about the memorial which the Association published and sold in the store for fifty cents. The store produced an extra income of between $100 and $200 per week for the Association.

In April, 1926, Augustus Lukeman returned to Atlanta from his New York studio to show the directors the finished master model. The greatest change from the preliminary model was the figure of Jackson which had received so much criticism. The new Jackson bore a much closer resemblance to the famous general, and he was bare-headed like the other, with appropriate kepi in hand. The directors approved the master model, and Lukeman went back north to begin work on the one-quarter size models.

The following month, the executive committee opened bids for the contract to do the actual carving, advertising through newspapers in Atlanta and New York, and through the *Manufacturer's Record*. Over the course of the next three months the committee entertained bids from numerous companies, most of which were much higher than anticipated. One company bid $900,000 to do the carving work. The committee finally reached an agreement with Albert Weiblen and the Stone Mountain Granite Company to do the work at cost plus ten percent. The Association closed the contract with the Weiblens on August 17, with actual work starting in September.

---

[18]Casey and Borglum, 210.

Albert Weiblen was a German immigrant who came to America in 1885 to start his own stone business in New Orleans. He had three sons, John, Fred and George, who learned the trade and moved up in the family business, which eventually employed nearly 300 craftsmen. John Weiblen operated the main New Orleans facility, while Fred ran the Stone Mountain branch. When Fred died suddenly in March 1927, George took charge of the operation. Albert Weiblen constantly traveled between the two plants.

To get the mountain ready for Lukeman's design, they began blasting rock from the side of the mountain to form a vertical wall 300 feet long and 190 feet high. Although the north face of the mountain appears to rise almost straight up, it really has a slope of about eighty-five degrees. This meant that cutting into the rock to make a straight wall produced a bottom ledge about forty-two feet wide. The blasting removed in excess of one million cubic feet of rock, or more than 85,000 tons.

The next stage of construction was the installation of new scaffolding. The work crew imbedded twenty-one steel I-beams into the mountain at the top of the cut area. These beams extended outward thirty feet from the wall. The scaffolds were suspended from these beams by steel cables, with winches to raise and lower them from the main platform above.

While work was once again progressing on the mountain, the Association's fund raising was in decline. The Harvest Campaign was stalled to the point that one of the field agents wrote to suggest that the coins be sold for two dollars apiece rather than one dollar so that the profit would be much greater even if sales slacked off.[19]

The Harvest Campaign had brought in more than $430,000 in seven months, but three-quarters of this was spent on the campaign and in overhead at the office. The executive committee apparently agreed with the field agent that too little was being collected for the cost involved and called an end to the campaign on 31 March 1926. It requested that all banks return remaining Stone Mountain coins to the Federal Reserve Bank of Atlanta and remit to the Association all premiums held to its credit. Beginning April 15 coins could be purchased either from the Federal Reserve or the Association for two dollars each. Not surprisingly, sales of coins plummeted.

The exception to this was a special campaign organized in New York City during 1926. With the personal backing of Mayor Jimmy Walker, the Association hoped to sell 250,000 coins in this city. It eventually achieved

---

[19]A. W. McKeand to H. N. Wells, 26 February 1926. Records of the SMCMA.

Association hoped to sell 250,000 coins in this city. It eventually achieved this goal, with wealthy businessmen and large companies buying most of the coins in lots of five or ten thousand. For the New York campaign the cost of the coins remained one dollar.

With coin sales outside of New York at a virtual standstill, the Association began once again to push Founder's Roll and Children's Founder's Roll subscriptions. In the latter part of 1926, the executive committee extended the concept to create the Living Veteran's Roll and the Gold Star Roll, with the subscription cost for each of these being five dollars.

The first campaign was naturally designed for living Confederate veterans, and the publicity for it was full of misty-eyed appeals to "bestow upon these grand old warriors one last tribute" while there was still time. There were approximately 35,000 living Confederate veterans in 1926, and the Association was making its big push for the upcoming reunion of these soldiers in April, 1927. Most of the publicity was aimed at the UDC and SCV chapters to enroll all the veterans in their communities.

The Gold Star Roll was the name given to another subscription campaign open to all adults. For each of these campaigns, the Association promised to inscribe the donor's name or honored veteran's name in a special book to be kept in Memorial Hall. Each five-dollar subscription bought a gold-dipped medal, and the veterans were encouraged to wear them with their Confederate Crosses of Honor.

The medals for the Living Veteran's Roll, the Gold Star Roll, and the new medal for the Children's Roll, were designed by Augustus Lukeman for a fee of $1,000. All three medals featured Davis, Lee, and Jackson as they appeared in his model and had on them the appropriate inscription for each roll. Interestingly enough, when it came time to have the medals made, the Association turned to the Medallic Art Company for the job.

Throughout 1926 Borglum supporters continued to exchange occasional barbs with the Association. Randolph blamed Borglum's published attacks for the poor coin sales, but in actuality they probably did not have a great influence; the GAR was a much more outspoken opponent of the coins. Borglum himself made relatively few statements concerning Stone Mountain--he was too busy tackling Mount Rushmore and other smaller projects. He did, however, write one card commenting on Lukeman's design, which he described as a "hackneyed architectural motif . . . composed with no relationship to the mountain."[20] He also reiterated the charge that the Association had no money with which to "complete the outrage." He was either unaware of the Association's income since his hasty departure or was unwilling to admit to it.

One of the smaller commissions keeping Borglum busy at this time was a marble statue of Alexander H. Stephens, Vice-President of the Confederacy, ordered by the state of Georgia for placement in the Hall of Fame in the U.S. Capitol. The awarding of this commission to Borglum infuriated Randolph, Winter, and their cronies. In a letter to Randolph, Winter referred to Borglum as their "arch enemy" and suggested:

> It is of the greatest importance from our standpoint to devise a way to prevent the acceptance of the Stephens statue, inasmuch as it would stand forever in the Hall of Fame in Washington as an official vindication by the state of Georgia of Borglum's conduct, as well as a repudiation of the Memorial Association's treatment of him.[21]

Winter recommended that they move through a third party to block the legislature's acceptance of the statue, while Harry Stillwell Edwards went so far as to suggest hiring a detective to spy on Borglum to see if he was really doing the work. Edwards knew that most of Borglum's work was done in bronze casting and thought Borglum might be taking credit for someone else's work. These two instances illustrate the depth of enmity on the part of Randolph's faction toward Borglum. None of these measures ever came to fruition, however, and the Stephens statue was unveiled in July, 1927.

Back at Stone Mountain, 1927 dawned without the slightest trace of Lukeman's work in evidence. The month of January was nearing its end when Fred Weiblen and Lukeman dusted off Borglum's specially-made projector to flash the new design up onto the cut-out side of the mountain. The figures measured 125 feet high, resulting in an enlargement ratio of 12.5, one inch on the model being equal to twelve and a half inches on the mountain. With the scale determined, the workers proceeded to outline the figures on the vertical wall by use of a graph system. The graph in this case consisted of steel cables hanging down in front of the moun-

---

[20] "Borglum Breaks Silence," *Atlanta Life*, 20 November 1926.

[21] Rogers Winter to Hollins Randolph, 18 October 1926. Records of the SMCMA.

angles to plot the key points and thus outline the figures in exact proportion to the master model.

The mechanics of blocking out the figures was essentially the same as done by Borglum's workers. They used small charges of explosives to remove the large quantities of stone for blocking out the figures; pneumatic drills and jackhammers were used for roughing out work close to the figures so that hairline cracks caused by the explosives would not appear on the figures themselves.

To cut into the vertical face of the carving area, four men were needed for each drill. The front man guided the drill and held the tip in place, two men on either side held a bar under the drill to support its weight, and the operator worked the trigger and pushed forward to press the drill into the rock. With a figure roughed out in this fashion by the quarry workers, skilled carvers came in with hand and air tools to do the finish work.

The day-to-day carving work was overseen by George Weiblen or an Italian sculptor named Theodore Bottinelli, who was sent to Stone Mountain from New Orleans by Albert Weiblen. George Weiblen checked up on the general work and the roughing out, while much of the finish work was done by Bottinelli personally or under his direct supervision.

Augustus Lukeman came down from New York about once a month, as per his contract, to check up on the work of the stone cutters. It has been rumored that Lukeman suffered from acrophobia and would not go up on the mountain, but would instead stand on the ground in front of the carving and look at it through binoculars.

Spectators undoubtedly witnessed him viewing the work in this fashion as it would have been necessary for him to judge the appearance from the ground. Unless the visitor was there on the right day and happened to be looking through the telescope mounted at the studio at the right time, they would not have been able to distinguish the sculptor from the other workers high up on the scaffolding. Photographs of the work in progress plainly show Lukeman standing next to the carving consulting with the crew, acrophobia notwithstanding.

Some residents of Stone Mountain later recalled that Lukeman, to their knowledge, only made a couple of trips to the mountain. The Association's records show, however, that he did come on a regular basis. Never a showman like Borglum, however, Lukeman did not stay for long periods at a time or socialize with the locals. When he came he stayed in a hotel in Atlanta, spent only enough time to inspect the carving and work out any difficulties, and then went home.

One visitor to the mountain wrote that the carving act was the "greatest show of all time." He described standing spellbound for hours as men "looking no bigger than spiders swinging by thin strands of web" chipping away at the mountain with maul and chisel, and the sound of pneumatic drills echoing like "a hundred woodpeckers greatly amplified." Although at dizzying heights, the workers strolled casually along the horse's back and swung nonchalantly out into space to catch their tools being hoisted by steam winches, all to the amazement of the spectators on the ground.[22]

The Weiblen's stonecutters blasted and chipped steadily away at the mountain throughout 1927. Originally Lukeman planned to execute the carving horizontally, exactly as Borglum had done. All the heads would be done first, then the torsos and horses' heads, and finally the horses' bodies as the men worked their way down the wall. The executive committee convinced him instead to do the entire figure of Lee and Traveler, and then work out to the sides from there. It felt that one complete figure would generate more enthusiasm than a series of disembodied heads.

The scheduled unveiling date was 9 April 1928, the sixty-third anniversary of Lee's surrender at Appomattox. The looming deadline put Lukeman under considerable pressure. Whenever Albert Weiblen recalled Bottinelli to New Orleans to do a special job, work on the mountain slowed considerably. This was a source of great irritation to Lukeman, who complained bitterly to the Weiblens. They were, however, unconcerned. They had a business to run and orders to fill. If Bottinelli was needed in New Orleans, then that was where he went. It was not that the Weiblens did not care about the Confederate memorial--they were keenly interested in seeing it completed and were proud to play a part--but it was only a sideline to their main business of providing building stone to their customers.

Throughout the work, Borglum's head of Lee peered down accusingly on Lukeman's crew. Its presence was also a constant reminder of the unpleasantness of the preceding two years, and its much greater size an obvious indicator of the reduced scale of the new design. With the 1927 tourist season approaching, the executive committee ordered Borglum's work covered by canvas tarpaulins to hide it from view.

---

[22]Neal, *The Story of Stone Mountain*, 32.

The situation of having two heads of Lee on the mountain could not last long. Borglum's unfinished work hovering over Lukeman's frieze would have looked ridiculous. Many people recognized that fact and predicted that Borglum's Lee would have to go. The Association announced publicly for two years that it would not damage the work already on the mountain, and it may have initially believed that Borglum's work could be incorporated into the new design, but the evidence of its actions shows that the idea had been abandoned at least by the end of 1925.

In late 1927 it was evident that something would have to be done with the head before the unveiling of the new Lee. The executive committee did not publicly announce it would destroy the head, but word of the order leaked out nonetheless. When Sam Venable heard about it he went to court seeking a restraining order to stop the vandalism. His efforts eventually failed and in March 1928 Borglum's Lee was blasted from the side of the mountain.

The fight over Borglum's unfinished work was not the only one Sam Venable was waging with the Monumental Association in 1927. In late June of that year, Hollins Randolph went before the state legislature seeking passage of a bill to empower the Association to condemn twenty acres of the Venable's property. This tract included a rise on the north side of the public road built the previous year, and was considered the best spot for viewing the carving. Randolph said that it was vital for the Association to have this land as a public park, but the owners would not sell it to them. The Senate judiciary committee gave the bill a favorable report and passage seemed certain until Sam Venable read about it in the newspapers.

Since 1921, when he deeded his entire interest in the mountain to his niece, Elizabeth Mason, Sam Venable had no personal claim to the property, but, acting in behalf of the entire Venable family, he cried foul. He argued that not only had he or any member of his family never been notified of the pending condemnation, but that the Association had never offered to buy the property.

This revelation, passed on to the Senate by the Venable's attorney, caused the judiciary committee to reconsider the matter. It struck a special subcommittee to investigate both sides of the issue. The ensuing controversy lasted for six weeks and was closely followed by the Atlanta press.

The first meeting of the investigatory subcommittee brought together Sam Venable, Hollins Randolph, and their supporters, to reach an agreement on the land in question. Through its questioning of both parties, the subcommittee discovered that the Monumental Association had sent an agent to inquire of Venable's niece, Mrs. Roper, her willingness to sell the Flat Rock property, but he had never identified himself as an agent of the Association. The subcommittee found that the Association had not made a good faith effort to buy the land before seeking condemnation. When asked if his family would agree to sell the land, Venable replied that they were not eager to sell, but would entertain an offer of $1,000 per acre. At Randolph's request he put the offer in writing.

The matter did not end there, however. Randolph persuaded some members of the judiciary committee to draw up a substitute bill calling for the creation of a Georgia State Parks Commission. The sole purpose of this was to exercise eminent domain to create a Stone Mountain Confederate Memorial Park. The Commission would then build and operate the Memorial Park at state expense.

When Randolph first pushed for power of eminent domain he opened himself up for attack, and the Venables took full advantage of the opportunity. Amid charges of corruption and mismanagement, and with Randolph's own conduct working against him, the subcommittee, under the prodding of Senator John Kelley, decided to probe deeper into the Association's affairs. Randolph stated that neither he nor any of the other officers had anything to hide, that he would appear before the investigating subcommittee at anytime and would gladly make the financial records of the Association available for audit.

Randolph failed to appear at the next hearing, with his representative explaining that he was out of town and asking for more time to gather the requested records. The hearing was postponed for two weeks, but again neither Randolph nor the Association's records came.

Senator Kelley made an impassioned speech to the judiciary committee about what the Association had failed to accomplished. The Association, he said, had spend hundreds of thousands of dollars with only Borglum's head and an hole in the side of the mountain to show for it. He charged Randolph with willfully deceiving the Senate committee and taking advantage of the fact that the subcommittee was not invested with the authority to compel him to appear. He drafted a resolution that the subcommittee be given full powers to subpoena witnesses and documentary evidence to allow for a complete investigation. Under fire, Randolph agreed voluntarily to appear before the subcommittee, and Senator Kelley dropped his resolution.

At the next hearing, Randolph presented himself to the subcommittee, but without the Association's financial records, stating that he was unable to see how they would serve any useful purpose. He read a prepared statement extolling the patriotic virtues of the executive committee, describing how he had brought the floundering Association back to solid existence, and denying any suggestion of extravagance or misconduct by the officers. When pressed for figures he gave rambling answers that side-stepped the question. He put the blame for any wasteful expenditures on Borglum, whom he said was not dismissed but written a courteous letter allowing him to withdraw from the contract. Under further questioning he stated that the Association's overhead expenses did not run more than $40,000 a year, despite the fact that expenses for 1926 were more than five times that amount.

A reporter covering the hearing wrote that Randolph "won over certain members of the subcommittee with his honeyed words. He condescended to be pleasant to the senators and addressed them as 'You boys.' That the committee had undergone a change of heart was obvious."[23] He noted that some of the senators who had previously been so persistent in the questioning did not push very hard for concrete information this time around.

At the final hearing on 10 August before the judiciary committee. Decatur Mayor Scott Candler represented the Venable family. In his address before the subcommittee he characterized the Monumental Association as

> an unfit associate for the state of Georgia and one with which the state should never go into partnership . . . . This whole thing is a scheme to get the credit of the state of Georgia behind the memorial association, which had about gone fluey . . . . I trust you gentlemen will have nothing further to do with this measure.[24]

He also presented a petition against the condemnation circulated by Sheriff McCurdy and signed by ninety-five percent of the property owners in Stone Mountain.

Senator Kelley was once again ready to push for adoption of his resolution to force Randolph to reveal his hand, but before he could do so,

---

[23]"Randolph Admits Failure As Memorial Director," *Atlanta Journal*, 6 August 1927.
[24]"Memorial Bill Withdrawn on Senate Consent," *Atlanta Journal*, 10 August 1927.

the Association's representative announced that they had nothing more to present to the committee and would retire from the meeting. On this cue, Randolph, Winter, Arnold and other officers of the Association stood up and walked out. Then Senator Lester, who had first introduced the bill, asked that it be withdrawn from consideration. Senator Kelley objected to its immediate withdrawal on the grounds that it was just a ploy to end the probe, but the withdrawal was allowed and the investigation ended.

In a bit of damage control, Randolph released a statement to the press blaming a last minute jam of legislation at the close of the session for the bill's failure to pass. He further claimed that the principle of state ownership of the monument had been firmly established. Of course the principle of state ownership had never been questioned and the reasons for the bill's failure were published in full. Randolph's statement only served to further tarnish his credibility among those who followed the matter.

In a scathing letter, Sam Venable hastened to charge Randolph with "pusillanimous conduct" and "lying braggartism" during the controversy. Many editorials appeared in newspapers across the state condemning the Association's actions. The *Dalton Citizen* said the memorial was being "slaughtered by stupidity," the *Macon News* predicted that the Association was "headed for fiasco" under Randolph, and the *LaGrange Reporter* admonished the Association to "heed the breakers of adverse public opinion." The *Savannah Press* made sport of the controversy by printing: "What a good thing for the safety of all concerned that Stone Mountain is so big . . . they can't throw it at one another."[25]

A minority of papers defended Randolph and the Association. The *Bainbridge Post-Searchlight* accused the UDC of circulating "false and pernicious propaganda" by charging the Association with extravagant expenditures. It reported that Rogers Winter, the publicist and only paid officer of the Association, received a "mere pittance of $6,400 a year."[26] This "pittance" was almost three times the average annual income of the day.

The whole effort to gain control of additional space may have been motivated by a planned lease of the mountain top by R. J. Spiller for a house of entertainment. Winter expressed concern that Spiller would build

---

[25]"Editorials From The Disinterested Press Of Georgia And Other Southern States," unidentified newspaper foldout, paid for by the Atlanta Chapter, UDC. Records of the SMCMA.

[26]Ibid.

"a regular hunky dunky which will be an ever-lasting disgrace to the Stone Mountain memorial."[27] Randolph may have feared commercial development crowding the mountain and made his move as a preemptive measure to ensure that the Association, or even the state, took control of the prime Flat Rock property to preserve the dignity of the memorial.

If this was Randolph's motivation, the way he went about it was a serious misstep. His administration was now in desperate straits. The Association's reputation was badly tarnished by the publicity, income from coin sales and subscriptions was down to a trickle, and public enthusiasm for the whole project waned. In addition, Sam Venable was keeping up the pressure for an accounting of the Association's funds. He hired a man to stand just outside the gate to the carving site and hand out to visitors a circular discouraging them from making any donations until the Association could account for how it had spent some $783,000.[28]

In an effort to boost the Association's image, Randolph needed to entice some nationally prominent people to publicly and officially associate themselves with his regime. He decided to open up the board of directors some more and invited such men as New York City Mayor Jimmy Walker, New York Governor Franklin D. Roosevelt, publisher William Randolph Hearst, and oil magnate John D. Rockefeller to serve. By letter he informed them that the executive committee had honored them by electing them as directors. The responses of all but Roosevelt have been lost. He wrote back thanking Randolph, but declined to serve. Randolph wrote Roosevelt a personal letter assuring him that he would not have to attend any meetings as he would be kept fully apprised of the actions of the Association. All they wanted was his moral support. Roosevelt still refused.

Randolph's last hope was that the scheduled unveiling of Lukeman's work would renew public confidence in the Association and result in increased income. Lukeman, however, was not ready for an unveiling. Normally, there were about two dozen workers on the job, but only a few were carvers. The rest were tool toters, blacksmiths, construction workers, or cutters. As 1927 drew to a close, the George Weiblen put hired more workers to try to meet the Association's deadline.

In November the first fatality of the carving effort occurred. Thomas Kennedy was prying off granite loosened by a dynamite blast when a large slab struck the scaffold platform. The impact literally catapulted the

---

[27]Rogers Winter to Hollins Randolph, 12 January 1926. Records of the SMCMA.
[28]Charles Metz to Hollins Randolph, 26 September 1927. Records of the SMCMA.

twenty-seven-year-old worker over the side of the mountain. Three other men who were with Kennedy managed to save themselves by grabbing onto the cables and framework of the scaffolding.

Despite the tragedy, the work continued without interruption and the figure of Lee began to take recognizable form. In January, 1928, Rogers Winter published that Lee and his horse, Traveler, were eighty-five percent complete, although anyone who visited the site could see for themselves that, while Lee's head might be nearing completion, the total figure was only a quarter finished. Lukeman complained that there was no way to have even Lee finished by the dedication date. Winter responded that it did not have to be completely done, it only needed to look relatively finished from the ground.

The April 9 unveiling went on as scheduled. The workmen had managed to get Lee mostly finished down to the waist. Lee's lower body and the figure of his charger were roughly blocked out, as was the head of Jefferson Davis.

The ceremony was marked by plenty of fanfare, but it somehow lacked the same excitement that had marked the first unveiling. Governors or representatives of governors of thirty-five states attended and several thousand spectators braved the unseasonably cold weather. After music provided by the fife and drum corps of the Governor's Foot Guard, Georgia Supreme Court Judge Marcus W. Beck delivered the address--a very long address accepting the carving for the South. Mayor Walker of New York was invited to accept the work on behalf of the rest of the nation. Augustus Lukeman gave the shortest speech of all, remarking only, "What shall I say? There it is up there. Let that speak for me."[29]

The highlight of the event came when little five-year-old Robert E. Lee, IV, great-grandson of the general, released from a basket on the rostrum thirteen carrier pigeons to signal the unveiling. Up on the side of the mountain a giant American flag and an equally large Confederate flag hung side by side. As the pigeons fluttered skyward, the flags drew up and apart like the curtains of a stage to reveal the fruit of Lukeman's labors. The assembled masses cheered.

A few weeks after the ceremony, the Association held its twelfth annual meeting. The deadline of the twelve-year lease was nearly up, and the Association faced a crisis. Sam Venable had repeatedly stated that he

---

[29]"Addresses Delivered at Stone Mountain Memorial at The Unveiling of the Mounted Statue of General Robert E. Lee on April 9, 1928," pamplet in the records of the SMCMA.

would never allow any more time or space for the carving as long as Randolph was president. His nieces had, in fact, drawn up a new deed giving the site to the Atlanta Chapter of the UDC for fifteen years to finish the memorial. With this in mind, Randolph did the only thing he could do at this point--he resigned as President of the Monumental Association, citing other business pressures. In his place the executive committee elected a reluctant G. F. Willis to the post.

Willis inherited an Association virtually devoid of funds, and at the end of May he ordered the work halted because there was no longer any money left to pay the contractor. The only income was from the sale of goods at the studio, which was not sufficient to cover the expenses of the barely staffed office. Willis suggested charging admission to view the carving as a way to raise money, but Sam Venable strongly objected. He always maintained that the public should not have to pay to see a memorial.[30]

In New York, Lukeman awaited word that the carving would be resumed, but the word never came. The memorial project went into limbo. Both the Atlanta Chapter UDC and the Monumental Association now had deeds granting them the right to carve a Confederate memorial on the side of Stone Mountain, but neither party had the resources to do it.

Shortly before the expiration of the original lease, Venable offered to grant, through his nieces, an extension if Gutzon Borglum were brought back to do another carving next to Lukeman's. Willis responded that this was impossible since Lukeman's contract gave him the right of first refusal for any other carving work done on the mountain and the sculptor would not waive his right. In an effort to overcome the differences between Venable and the Association, Plato Durham, President of Emory University, acted as intermediary to carry on with negotiations. Since the reinstatement of Borglum as sculptor was the sticking point, Durham attempted to get each side to soften its position. The executive committee of the

---

[30]It is interesting to contemplate what the course of events might have been had the Association charged a nominal admission fee. More than a hundred thousand visitors came out to see the sculpture each year, and if properly promoted that number could have easily been doubled. No other fund raising would have been necessary and with little office overhead required, nearly all of the money could have gone to the carving. There would have been no need for a special coin and the whole Borglum controversy might have been avoided.

Association conceded a willingness to consider bringing Borglum back if it had satisfactory assurances of his future conduct and tentatively agreed to dismiss the old 1925 indictments.

During the peace talks supporters had kept Borglum informed of the situation because of the possible implications for his return. The sculptor wrote back to Durham insisting that Lukeman complete his partially-carved figures.[31] Borglum evidently felt strongly enough about his own ethical convictions to refuse taking over Lukeman's work or wishing to see it destroyed as his had been. He still held to his elaborate plan of five groupings of figures and could afford to make this magnanimous gesture.

In a letter to Willis, Borglum expressed his concern over the challenge of dealing diplomatically with Lukeman. He wrote that he was not insensitive to the fact that Lukeman had "consistently and deliberately wronged me as no man ever did and he has suffered ostracism in the art world ever since." Recent events, he added, would make cooperation more difficult for Lukeman than for himself, but he was willing to bear this in mind and be patient.[32] Borglum obviously felt himself to be in the superior position and was willing to act charitably toward Lukeman.

Despite Durham's efforts, Willis was not convinced that Borglum could work harmoniously with the Association, and he was not eager to get into a wrangle with Lukeman. The directors eventually rejected Venable's proposal requiring Borglum's return, and in October efforts at negotiation ceased.

Sam Venable continued to censure the Association in the newspapers and demanded a public explanation for what had become of all the money collected since 1925. Although the Association never consented to having its financial records made known, Venable did obtain a copy of the three-year audit done by Peat Marwick & Associates in March, 1928. It showed an income to the Association in the previous three years of $877,235, and that of this amount $164,352, or nineteen percent, had been spent on the memorial. The remaining $712,883 was spent on overhead, which included $223,806, almost twenty-six percent of the total income, for salaries. Venable decried this as, "a wild orgy of extravagance unparalleled in the

---

[31]Shaff and Shaff, 247, citing Gutzon Borglum to Plato Durham, 17 July 1928, G. B. Papers, Library of Congress, Washington, DC.

[32]Gutzon Borglum to G. F. Willis, 7 August 1928. Stone Mountain Collection, Atlanta History Center.

history of patriotic enterprise." It should, he exclaimed, "bring the blush of shame to the cheek of every true Southerner . . . "[33]

With the termination of negotiations, Sam Venable, Mrs. Mason, Mrs. Orme, and Mrs. Roper filed suit in DeKalb County Superior Court to recover title to their land as stipulated in the original deeds. In the text of the petition, Venable outlined his position in passionate terms. Despite giving unsparingly of his time and money toward the monument, his family had only received heartache as the noble concept dwindled into a mockery and a sham, and an artist's dream turned into a painful nightmare. All there was to show for twelve years time and the expenditure of a million dollars was unsightly scar on the face of the mountain. He concluded that under the circumstances there was nothing left to do but to insist upon a forfeiture of the property in order see the monument completed under proper management.[34]

Two audits of the Association's books were conducted by Peat Marwick & Associates in 1925 and 1928. (See the financial statement on p. 120.) They revealed the financial situation before and after Borglum's dismissal. The surplus of total income over total expenses shown was $113,992. Not reflected in the statement of expenses was $72,862 used to pay off loans made to the Association during the first period. This brought the actual surplus down to $41,130, with accounts payable and other liabilities of $24,789. The small surplus was exhausted in the months following the audits and the Association incurred further debts amounting to $39,000 by the end of 1929.

An analysis of the expenditures reveals that only twenty-seven cents of every dollar went toward actual work on the memorial. This would seem to confirm Sam Venable's accusations of excessive spending on everything but the carving.

---

[33]Public statement by Sam Venable, 26 January 1929. Records of the SMCMA.

[34]"Venable Suit Asks Recovery of Title to Stone Mountain," *Atlanta Constitution*, 27 January 1929.

FINANCIAL STATEMENT OF THE STONE MOUNTAIN CONFEDERATE MONUMENTAL ASSOCIATION 1916--1928

Income	1 April 1916- 31 March 1925	1 April 1925 31 March 1928	Total
Donations	$134,482	106,149	$240,631
Founder's Roll	174,000	17,000	191,000
Children's Roll	15,485	20,671	36,156
Veterans' Roll		18,925	18,925
Gold Star Roll		3,077	3,077
Memorial Coin	683,884	683,884	683,884
Merchandise	1,120	19,545	20,665
Miscellaneous	824	7,979	8,843
Total Income	$325,951	$877,230	$1,203,181
Expenses			
Salaries	$49,570	$223,807	$273,377
Commissions	2,310	35,605	37,915
Campaigns	14,993	81,096	96,089
Printing	18,410	54,462	72,872
Travel	2,929	73,014	75,943
Ceremonies	2,662	12,426	15,088
Office Expenses	16,058	69,635	85,693
Medals	289	10,317	10,606
Write-offs	30,470	30,470	
Miscellaneous	9,709	59,400	69,109
Total Overhead	$116,930	$650,232	$767,162
Carving	157,675	164,352	322,027
Total Spent	$274,605	$814,584	$1,089,189

Chapter Five

The In-Between Years

Three decades passed from the time the memorial project ground to a halt in 1928 to when it recommenced in earnest in 1962. These years were marked by a series of rising hopes and bitter disappointments over the status of the unfinished memorial. The commitment of a few people to persevere in the task despite the many difficulties is as much a testimony to the monument builders as the memorial is to the Southern Cause.

The original effort, as it turned out, was not quite dead when Sam Venable filed suit to reclaim the land. The Monumental Association broke off negotiations with him at the end of September 1928, but when the suit was filed in December, the Association once again became interested in making peace. At the annual meeting in April, 1929, G. F. Willis announced that a special mediation team composed of Philip Alston, President of the Atlanta Chamber of Commerce, Lee Ashcraft, of the Association executive committee, and headed by Plato Durham, had made good progress toward reaching an agreement with Sam Venable.

In enumerating the resources at the Association's disposal, Willis cited 750 serially numbered memorial half-dollars available for auction, 725,000 more coins in the vault of the Federal Reserve Bank to be sold for two dollars apiece, 25,000 Children's Roll medals to be sold for one dollar subscriptions, and $25,000 in unpaid pledges The potential income from these resources exceeded $1.2 million. Willis explained that the committee had held these resources in reserve and would convert them into cash to continue the work when an agreement was reached with Sam Venable. This would avoid any obstructions on his part. The carving, Willis assured them, could be completed within a year at a cost of $125,000.

The two sides finally reached a truce agreement in May 1929 that promised to clear the way for continuing the carving. Venable's proposal, accepted by the Association, called for an extension of the deed for two years, the dismissal of all suits by both parties, and that upon completion of the three figures the Association be "reorganized in a manner mutually satisfactory to the donors and the Association itself for the purposes of completing the remaining work on the mountain."[1] This last part was calculated to invalidate Lukeman's right of first refusal for continued work because the body with which he made the agreement would no longer exist. Lukeman would be allowed to complete the carving already under way.

The Association signed the contract and had the old indictments and $50,000 damage suit against Borglum dismissed. It also elected Sam Venable to the executive committee once again. In return, Venable dropped his suit to recover the property.

For a time the prospect of seeing the carving completed appeared bright, but by late summer the two sides began to lock horns again. Philip Alston proposed turning title to the carving site over to the state of Georgia and have it complete the memorial with convict labor. Venable stated that he had no objection to the Association forming another group to take over the work, but he opposed turning it over to the state. He believed that after so many other states had contributed materially to the enterprise that it would not be fair to their acquired interests to localize the project. Moreover, putting the memorial it in the hands of temporary government officials to be used as a political chess piece would jeopardize the chances of its ever being completed. Besides, he added, the state legislature would not reconvene to accept such a proposal until June 1931, after the present contract expired, and he had no intention of granting another extension. He then suggested that if the Association was incapable of complying with the terms of the contract it should turn the property back over to him so that he could take the necessary actions to carve the memorial with Borglum as sculptor.

Willis countered by offering to do just what Venable asked, but under certain conditions. Those conditions were that Lukeman be retained as the sculptor, that Venable give assurance of his ability to raise the necessary funds, that the grounds always be open to the public free of charge, and that if he could not complete the memorial within two years the property should be given permanently to the Association.

Not surprisingly, Sam Venable flatly refused these terms. In a card to the *Atlanta Journal* in September, 1929, he indicated that he had no intention of being a "financial wetnurse" for the failed Association. He further stated that in light of the $30,000 indebtedness of the Association, he did not know whether Willis's proposal was made "through a spirit of sardonic

[1]"Stone Mountain Truce Agreement Suggests Peace," *Atlanta Journal*, 15 May 1929.

impertinence" or "in the mistaken belief that I was running a home for the friendless." To avoid further misunderstandings, Venable plainly stated that if Lukeman's figures were ever completed Willis and his Association would be responsible for doing it.[2]

The once-promising agreement had failed to bring the two sides together and they were again deadlocked over how to proceed. To make matters worse, the DeKalb County Solicitor's Office had Borglum reindicted on the old charges of larceny, larceny from the house, and malicious mischief in connection with the destruction of the models. Solicitor General Claude Smith stated that the Monumental Association had nothing to do with the reindictment, but Sam Venable was suspicious of the timing of the actions, coming as it did just after he had proposed bringing Borglum back to the mountain instead of Lukeman. He said that since Borglum had been reindicted for destroying his own models, it would be only proper that the Association officers also be indicted for destroying Borglum's head of Lee on the mountain.[3]

The situation appeared hopeless, but Durham proclaimed, "There must be hope when so great a people desire so great an achievement. In some way the people of the South will build the Stone Mountain Memorial notwithstanding the many seemingly insuperable difficulties."[4]

Part of the reason for the breakdown of the new agreement was the Association's inability to raise funds. The potential income so optimistically predicted by Willis remained potential only.[5] In actuality, the Association was deeply in debt with several liens pending against them. In April the furnishings of the Association office were sold at auction to satisfy a levy filed by one of the creditors. Only the intervention of a sympathetic Superior Court judge saved the models and machinery at the mountain from a similar fate.

In a special meeting of the Association's directors in October, Willis recommended turning the memorial over to a joint commission between the city of Atlanta, Fulton County, the city of Decatur, and DeKalb County, The directors approved the suggestion and authorized the conveyance of

---

[2]"Memorial Board to Get Deadlock," *Atlanta Constitution*, 26 September 1929.

[3]"Gutzon Borglum Reindicted By DeKalb Jury," *Atlanta Constitution*, 29 September 1929.

[4]Ibid.

[5]It was once suggested that radium, valued at $70,000 a gram in 1930, could be extracted from the granite to pay for the memorial.

all the Association's rights, title, interests, equity, assets and liabilities to these bodies in joint ownership. In conferring with the State Attorney General, however, Willis discovered that only the city of Atlanta had a clear legal authority to accept title. Thus, on 15 January 1930 the Monumental Association made its offer to the city of Atlanta alone.

The proposal first went to the city finance committee for study. Councilman Wiley Moore, chairman of the committee, enthusiastically favored the idea, but other elements did not. The most vocal group was the Atlanta Women's Civic Council, who filed suit against the city to prevent the expenditure of taxpayer money on the project. Others were concerned about assuming the debt of the Association, then at $39,000. Most members of the finance committee, however, recognized the benefits to the city of completing the memorial. Even unfinished the carving had become a tourist magnet, and the increased revenues of Rapid City, South Dakota, for the Mount Rushmore Memorial were not lost on the Atlanta councilmen. They promised that no tax money would be spent and that some arrangement would be made to avoid burdening the city with the debt.

After months of discussion, Wiley Moore introduced a resolution to authorize Mayor I. N. Ragsdale to appoint a committee to seek title to the Stone Mountain memorial. The resolution outlined the need to remove the memorial from the field of controversy and to place the ownership of the carving site unconditionally with the city of Atlanta. To do this it called upon all parties to take such action as was necessary and to give full cooperation to the committee appointed by the mayor.[6]

Mayor-elect James L. Key was a great enthusiast of the Confederate Memorial and he promised his support to carry out the effort when he took office in January 1931. He concurred with the findings of the committee as expressed in the resolution and declared that Gutzon Borglum was the only man for the job. Key also had his own plans that extended beyond Stone Mountain. He envisioned a great memorial boulevard connecting the mountain with the National Cemetery at Kennesaw Mountain north of Atlanta. Along the route there would be monuments commemorating the pivotal Battle of Atlanta. This scheme was an extension of the Memorial Drive built in 1926 from downtown Atlanta out to Stone Mountain.

---

[6]"Mayor-Elect Key Pledges Support to New Proposal," *Atlanta Constitution*, 18 July 1930.

The signing of the resolution by Mayor Ragsdale was the first positive move toward recommencing the work in over a year. Sam Venable affirmed his support for the plan and Borglum responded that he was very much interested in taking up the work as he wished to make Stone Mountain his finest work of dramatic sculpture. The officers of the Association were less eager to accept the proposed plan of action because they did not want to give up the assets and be left with the liabilities.

An editorial in the *Atlanta Constitution* entitled "The Right and Wrong Way" criticized the Association's recalcitrance for refusing to cooperate with those ready to go about the work, and contrasted the dismal handling of the Stone Mountain memorial with the steady progress of the Mount Rushmore memorial, which was similar in scope and conceived by the same sculptor.[7]

Disposal of the Association's debts was the main sticking point in this phase of the negotiations. J. Lawrence McCord, President of the Atlanta Chamber of Commerce, worked with Mayor-elect Key to persuade Willis to surrender title free of any encumbrances. On 5 September Willis tentatively agreed to a compromise whereby an unconditional deed would be turned over to Key to be held in escrow pending the formation of a bonded commission to take charge of the work and retire the debts of the Association. The city could then accept title without concern for of any liabilities. This agreement hinged on the approval of the board of directors.

This breakthrough compromise came just before Borglum's return to the city to discuss his latest plans for Stone Mountain. There was some concern about the attitude the DeKalb Solicitor General would take, but no effort was made to push the indictments, then or later. No persuasive reason for the reactivation of the original indictments has ever been put forward.

Fifteen years after first outlining his dream before Helen Plane and the UDC, the sculptor addressed a rally of interested citizens at the Fox Theater in Atlanta. He said that one thing he learned from carving Mount Rushmore was that the figures should be twice as large as he first planned. The unfinished Lukeman work did not figure into his plans at all; it could be finished by Lukeman at a later date if the commission so desired.

As part of the expanded memorial concept espoused by Mayor-elect Key, Borglum suggested the creation of a park system embracing Kennesaw Mountain Battlefield, Peachtree Creek Battlefield, and Stone Mountain. This

---

[7] "The Right and Wrong Way," *Atlanta Constitution*, 24 August 1930.

last unit in the system would be known as Venable Park. He pointed out that the federal government had begun a program of marking historic battlefields, and the creation of such a park system might draw federal funds.

The commission suggested by Borglum to guide the work of the memorial would be a permanent one. Half of the commission members would be from Georgia and the others would be persons of national prominence. Seats on the executive committee of the commission would be filled by the Georgia residents.

Everything seemed to be on track for resumption of the work, but at the 12 September 1930 meeting of the Monumental Association board of directors, old controversies erupted into heated debate. The meeting was called to order to get final approval of the Willis-Key agreement of the previous week. At issue were the Association's obligations, including its debts and the unfulfilled contract with Augustus Lukeman. The meeting, attended by Mayor-elect Key, Councilman Wiley Moore, and J. L. McCord, resulted in an impasse until Willis suddenly resigned as president of the Association. He said he did not do this in a fit of pique, but instead because his doctor had suggested that he give up civic activities and their associated stresses. He recommended that the vice-president fill his position, but L. W. Robert, consulting engineer for the project, moved that James Key be named the new president.

At first the motion was regarded as a joke, even by the mayor-elect, who responded, "I already have all the jobs I want." Robert, however, was quite serious and delivered a short speech about how Key was the principal figure in the renewed effort and he urged full support and cooperation with his plans. John Ashby Jones said he would only cooperate if the Lukeman contract was carried out and that he did not want to have anything to do with Borglum. "Then my dear man," Key responded, "you won't be named on the commission."

After this rejoinder most of the directors pledged their support to Key and elected him president. Having been confirmed to this post, the mayor-elect Key bluntly laid down the course ahead:

> It is no use to kid ourselves. To revive and bring the memorial to pass will take a tremendous effort. I am, therefore, asking you to remove every impediment out of the way. You have no right to

ask me to take hold of this matter otherwise. The public has lost confidence and we've got to win it back to complete the job.[8]

He made it plain that the city must get the property free of debt as he had no right to assume any. The new organization would have no paid officers, but every dollar would be put to work on the mountain and Atlanta must do its part before going out to the rest of the country. Nor would he accept any deed that made further consideration of Lukeman as the sculptor.

In response to the matter of accumulated debts, Wiley Moore volunteered to void what the Association owed his company as a contribution. He urged the others to go out and speak with other creditors about reducing or canceling outstanding debts and to drum up funds in the business community to clear any remaining obligations. This suggestion met with some opposition initially, but by the end of the meeting the Moore plan was unanimously adopted. As a final piece of business, President Key appointed a committee of five to carry out a resolution to return the carving site to the Venable family so that the Venables could make out an unconditional deed to the city.

There was one person who was not very happy with the Stone Mountain situation, and that was Augustus Lukeman. The month before, he had sent letters to the thirteen Southern governors urging them to put pressure on the city of Atlanta to retain him instead of bringing back Borglum. He also wrote letters to the Atlanta newspapers accusing Borglum of planning to carve the likeness of General U. S. Grant on the mountain. He further accused Sam Venable of using the memorial for his own advantage, and claimed his work would be destroyed. These letters accomplished nothing, leading Lukeman to file suit against the Association for breach of contract and seeking $17,000 for money he claimed to have put into the project when the Association's treasury ran dry. His suit did him no good since the Association was insolvent and no longer had control of the memorial effort. Lukeman was bitter, but was powerless to alter the course of events.

Strangely enough, the renewed memorial effort was derailed by the Venable family. At first Sam Venable wanted to stipulate that the memorial commission be headed by J. L. McCord, but Key was adamant that the deed be unconditional. In April 1931 Venable relented and he and his sister,

---

[8]"Key Elected Head of Memorial Body," *Atlanta Constitution*, 13 September 1930.

Elizabeth Venable Mason, handed over the deed to her half-interest in the seventy-five-acre park site. Mayor Key held the deed until the two remaining heirs deeded their interests, after which the deeds would be turned over to the city of Atlanta and recorded.

The problem was that Mrs. Coribel Orme and Mrs. Robert Roper, the other owners, would not deed the land without a twenty-year reversionary clause in the deed. Mayor Key frowned on this because he preferred an unconditional deed, which he believed would have a greater effect on the morale of movement supporters. In an April 1931 letter he said that putting the project in the hands of the city of Atlanta "would guarantee that a great Confederate Memorial would be faithfully executed," and promised that if for some reason the monument could not be completed the property would be returned.[9]

The sisters replied that they would gladly drop the twenty-year proviso and comply with his request for an unconditional deed just as soon as the city made a legally-binding guarantee to complete the memorial. Mayor Key said he had not intended to convey the impression that the city could absolutely guarantee the memorial would be built, but that every effort would be made to carry the project to its conclusion. He could not construe their demand for a written guarantee as an unconditional offering and declined to accept.

Having been betrayed by the Monumental Association, the sisters felt their request for some assurance was justified and would not relent. Mayor Key could not make any such legally binding guarantee on behalf of the city, so the project languished after three years of toil and effort, just as it was poised to become a reality. Public excitement for the project, which had been growing, faded away to be replaced by frustration and despair.

Through the efforts of Gutzon Borglum, the federal Civil Works Administration pledged its aid by offering to supply the labor necessary to finish the memorial, amounting to a cost of approximately $50,000 a year. This offer, however, depended upon the city having full title to the property and raising funds for materials. In May 1934 after waiting for three years for the city to do its part, the CWA withdrew the offer. The loss of government aid signaled the end of any carving plans. To the general public, the memorial appeared to be as lost as the cause it was to commemorate.

Of course life in the town of Stone Mountain did go on apart from the memorial. Most days went by quietly, but there were a few out-of-the-

---

[9]"Remaining Heirs Assure Atlanta Title to Tract," *Atlanta Constitution*, 25 April 1931.

ordinary events deserving of mention. One of these was the testing of the Ruckstell Axle in a 1925 publicity stunt orchestrated by the Ford Motor Company. Prior to this, most cars were not powerful enough to climb a slope as steep as Stone Mountain, but the new axle design made this possible. The designers field tested their invention by driving up the west side of the mountain parallel to the walk-up trail.

The Ford Model-T, driven by a Tom Sewell, maintained a speed of about ten miles an hour up the slope that sometimes exceeded forty-five degrees, and did so "with an ease which made the most hardened spectator gasp." The newspaper also noted that the descent was "one of the most thrilling episodes of the performance, where a slip meant death and where human strength was added to mechanical excellence."[10] The car was carefully held in check by several men with long ropes as it went down the mountain. The mechanical brakes, it seems, were not as advanced as the axle.

The feat was repeated by another auto maker in 1929 when veteran race car driver Peter De Paolo drove an Atlanta-made Reo Flying Cloud up the mountain. To show the superiority of the car, De Paolo stopped it on the steepest part of the slope, just below the summit, to take on four passengers and then proceeded to the top. As commercials today often show vehicles in high, inaccessible places for dramatic effect, auto makers for decades ran their cars over Stone Mountain for ad campaigns.

Another odd encounter between mountain and machine came in 1928, shortly after the inauguration of night air mail service from Atlanta. Small, single-seat biplanes carried the mail at a time when instruments for night flying were virtually nonexistent. Stone Mountain lay in the direct path of flight to Atlanta's Candler Field and greatly concerned the pilots. For that reason a beacon light was erected on top of the mountain. The contractor carried out every detail of the plans given to him and dutifully turned on the electricity. A few weeks later, on a particularly dark night, pilot Johnny Kytle smashed his plane against the side of the mountain just above Buzzard's Roost. Fortunately, the pilot was not seriously hurt, and several people who heard the crash rushed up the mountain to help get Johnny and his nine bags of mail back down.

Naturally, the Civil Aeronautic Authority launched an investigation to determine why the beacon on the mountain had failed. The job foreman

---

[10]Unidentified newspaper clippings, Stone Mountain file, Special Collections, Hargrett Library, University of Georgia, Athens, Georgia.

brought out his work sheet showing that he had checked off each item. Since, however, the list did not specify installing a light bulb, he had not put one in.

The 1929 stock market crash and the ensuing Depression made the decade of the 1930s one of hardship for most of the country. The Stone Mountain industry that suffered the most during this period was the granite business. A virtual freeze on the demand for cut stone forced several companies to fold. The small operation at the Flat Rock quarry, run by James New and Sam Medlock, went under in 1933, and the much larger Weiblen granite concern declared bankruptcy in 1935. Many of the quarry workers and stonecutters thrown out of work hoped to get employment on the renewed carving, but this never materialized. Still, many found work with the CWA or WPA programs.

President Franklin D. Roosevelt, who took office in March, 1933, instituted several of these "alphabet agencies" to help the nation through its worst depression ever. His rapid response to the economic instability and his homey fireside chats via radio helped to boost national morale. Many Americans trusted that under Roosevelt things would improve.

The citizens of Stone Mountain planned a special rally in October 1933, as an affirmation of their optimism for better times. This was tied to the hype surrounding the inauguration of the National Recovery Administration, whose purpose was to enforce fair competition in business. The town planned a spectacular event to draw people out to the mountain, and nineteen-year-old Elias Nour volunteered to execute the stunt. He drove an old Ford Model-T, christened "Depression" and painted with anti-depression slogans, up to the top of the mountain. He then lit a pile of oil-soaked rags in the back seat and shoved it over the side. To the cheers of spectators below, the blazing flivver careened down the steep north face of the mountain trailing flame and smoke before crashing into a pile of rocks at the base.

Through this and other stunts, Elias Nour proved to be the twentieth-century daredevil of Stone Mountain. Nour was born in Atlanta of Lebanese immigrant parents. The family moved to Stone Mountain in 1924 and opened a restaurant. At first, as immigrants they were not welcomed into the community. Elias and his brother Tony were often taunted by the other boys for their city suits and violin lessons. For the Nour boys the mountain became their playground and refuge. Elias spent the most time exploring the great rock that his family lived next to and soon knew the mountain better than anyone else.

Over the years he gained a reputation for rescuing stranded mountain climbers. He performed his first errand of mercy in 1927 at the age of thirteen. The Nour family diner was located at the foot of the walk-up trail to take best advantage of the tourist traffic. One day word came that a boy had slipped and was stuck on the steep face of the mountain, and Elias volunteered to be lowered down on a rope to bring him back up.

After this his reputation as the unofficial rescuer of Stone Mountain was secure. He saved thirty-six people and six dogs between 1927 and 1963, when the state erected a fence around the summit. He received so much attention from the press that his name almost became synonymous with Stone Mountain. By the 1950s he was referred to as the "Old Man of the Mountain," even though he was only in his late thirties.

Nour's most famous act of heroism occurred in 1953 when he saved a Georgia Tech student trapped above the carving. With dusk falling, he had to lengthen his usual rope with a length of frayed rope that he had taken along only as a last resort. For taking such an extraordinary risk to save a life, Nour received the prestigious Carnegie Medal of Heroism.

The peculiar thing about the rescue business, he noted, was that hardly any of the people he saved ever bothered to thank him. Most seemed so embarrassed and frightened that they disappeared as quickly as possible, not even hanging around long enough to thank the rescue team. The succored canines, on the other hand, showed immediate and uninhibited gratitude.

Nour also participated in what must be counted as the most bizarre stunt ever performed at the mountain, the "Suicide Derby." The object of the derby was for the participants to race from the top of the mountain down the steep side to the judges booth at the base in as short a time as possible. The first race in September 1934 was won by Elias Nour with a time of four minutes and seventeen seconds. He descended part of the way on the steel cables hanging in front of the unfinished carving of Robert E. Lee.

A second derby was held the next month, with Nour beating his old record by two seconds. He said his pace was speeded up somewhat when he ran into a wasp nest. After winning the race, Nour went back up to assist a female contestant who had gotten stuck on the mountain. DeKalb police estimated that more than one thousand people came out to watch each of these derbies.

Despite the Depression, the tourist-oriented businesses in Stone Mountain benefitted from the popularity of the mountain as a recreation spot and from the unfinished Confederate memorial that drew a steady stream of curious visitors. Every once in a while the spirit of tower-builder Aaron Cloud would stir at the mountain as some eager entrepreneur would recognize its profit potential and propose big plans, but because of prevailing economic conditions nothing ever materialized.

The grandest proposal came from Rell J. Spiller, an experienced purveyor of fun and amusement. Spiller had owned the Atlanta Crackers baseball team and operated a resort at Lithia Springs, in Douglas County, west of Atlanta. In 1935 he got the idea, probably inspired by stories of Aaron Cloud, to build an entertainment facility on top of the mountain. He secured a lease to the top of the mountain from the Venable family, and with great fanfare announced the details of his scheme. His concept called for a spiraling road to the top where there would be a hotel and casino, with verandas fringing the cliffs and an observation tower.

Spiller met with a storm of protest from citizens all over the state who felt that his plans would butcher the beauty of the mountain and desecrate the lofty ideals of the Confederate memorial, should it ever be finished. Public tastes had apparently changed since the days of Aaron Cloud. These protests, coupled with the huge cash outlay required, forced Spiller to abandon the resort idea.

Despite appearances, the Confederate Memorial was not quite dead and several attempts were made to revive the effort. About once a year Borglum would visit Atlanta and announce, to no avail, that he was ready to begin work. The Memorial Commission created in 1931 to oversee the project conducted an investigation in 1936 to determine the feasibility of completing the memorial. The investigating committee reported that the new central group planned by Borglum, twice the size of the original plan, would require three years time and $550,000. The entire memorial would probably take ten years and cost $1,750,000. The Venable heirs were still willing to deed the space necessary if a sound program could be developed that would ensure the completion of the memorial. The economic conditions of the time, however, made this nearly impossible and the memorial continued to languish.

In 1940 there was another serious revival of interest in the memorial, spurred by the motion picture *Gone With The Wind*. One of the chief proponents of the memorial was Scott Candler, the newly-elected Commissioner for DeKalb County. Candler was from one of the most prominent families in DeKalb County and was a long-time friend of the Venables. As sole county administrator, he began to put into action a plan to develop Stone Mountain as a park.

Sam Venable having died the year before, Candler spoke with the Venable heirs about donating the land that had created such a stumbling block. To bypass their demand for a guarantee of completion, he offered to buy the land from them and they agreed. The Venable family agreed to give Commissioner Candler a ten-year option on the mountain and 1,700 surrounding acres at a purchase price of $650,000 in exchange for his canceling the county property taxes on the land for the period of the option.

Several Atlanta business leaders once again became excited at the prospect of finishing the memorial and invited Borglum back to Atlanta. Governor Eugene Talmadge also became interested in the project and offered to do what he could to help. The huge purchase price of the land, however, constituted a major obstacle. They would have to create an entirely new plan of action.

Discussions continued for several months into 1941 when Borglum suddenly died. The loss of the sculptor was a blow, but not a mortal one for the project. Borglum had been replaced before and he could be replaced again, but his grand designs were forever abandoned.

Through the efforts of Governor Talmadge, the state legislature passed an Act to create a State Park Authority to construct and operate parks, recreation areas, lakes and other facilities including the completion of the Confederate Memorial. Talmadge approved the Act on 27 March 1941, and the following month appointed State Senator Pat Campbell, representing DeKalb County, Mrs. A. McD. Wilson, president of the Atlanta Chapter UDC, and Douglas McCurdy, an attorney from Stone Mountain, to be the Stone Mountain Memorial Commission, charged with directing plans for completion of the memorial.

The group began to work up tentative proposals, which included building an amphitheater, lake, picnic grounds, and a scenic highway around the mountain that would be a toll road to help pay for the project. As the new sculptor they selected thirty-five-year-old Julian Harris, a native of Carroll County, Georgia, known by most as "Judy."

Harris proposed completing the Lukeman design, but doing so in low-relief. The figures would be outlined by a V-cut line to make them distinct from one another and adjacent surfaces. Less expensive than high-relief, this method of sculpture was frequently referred to as the "WPA style" because the governmental agency preferred its economy. In addition to the leaders of the Confederacy, Harris planned to include a foot soldier beside them as a tribute to the thousands of unsung heroes who fought and died.

He would also prepare a special panel at the base to carve in the names of the old Founder's Roll contributors to fulfill this long-ignored obligation.

The Commission announced in June that the Works Progress Administration would provide the labor as soon as the Park Authority acquired title to the property, and the Reconstruction Finance Corporation (RFC) was considering a petition for a loan of $1,250,000 to start the project. The RFC notified them in September that although it approved of the memorial and was satisfied with the financial arrangements worked out by the Park Authority, the government was presently mobilizing every agency for the national defense program. Non-defense projects, regardless of their merit, were a low priority.

Senator Campbell suggested that the park would serve the national defense interests by providing recreational facilities for servicemen stationed around Atlanta. It would even be available for overnight bivouacs for troops out on training maneuvers. The RFC considered the proposal, tentatively agreeing to raise the priority status of the memorial park, but after the Japanese attack on Pearl Harbor the RFC changed its position. The necessity of all available funds for military purposes made it necessary to abandon memorial plans for the duration.

As the nation geared up for the war effort, the people of Stone Mountain stood ready to do their part. Since the granite quarries had not operated in seven years, the owners decided to contribute the iron rails of the spur track running around the mountain to the scrap metal drive. Many young men of the town clambered aboard the old Dinky train engine to accompany it on the last trip around the mountain. The Dinky and a lone car were pulled along the track by a winch truck as 500 tons of rails were pulled up behind. For many who had worked in the quarries it was a day of sadness that signaled the end of an era. The rails were sent back to the mill to be melted down and the Dinky was sold to a company in Tennessee to be reconditioned for use in the mines.

In June 1942 Elias Nour organized a scrap rubber drive that was conducted in a way that only he could. He sought the donation of an old Model A Ford from Nash Motors, drove it to the top of the mountain, stripped the tires off and sent it rolling down the scarp in a repeat of his 1933 exploit. This time, however, the doomed auto was loaded with effigies of Hitler, Mussolini, and Tojo. Charged a piece of scrap rubber for admission to see the old car take the plunge, eager spectators contributed about a ton to government stockpiles. Nour also intended this stunt as a farewell party since he had just enlisted in the army.

In February 1945, with the end of the war in sight, the Georgia Division of the UDC and Atlanta Mayor William B. Hartsfield appealed to Governor Ellis Arnall to reactivate the memorial commission. Hartsfield argued, "The South owes a debt of honor to the living and revered dead to make Stone Mountain an appropriate shrine to the Confederacy. Thousands of schoolchildren now grown remember giving their pennies more than two decades ago to see that dream come true."[11] Soon after, a bill went before the legislature to authorize the issuance of $5,000,000 worth of revenue bonds. This effort, however, was premature. Sculptor Julian Harris was not available to do any work because he had gone into the Army Intelligence Department and there was still a war to be won. The mountain could wait; it was not going anywhere.

There was more talk in 1946 and the State Highway Department pledged its cooperation in rerouting the Atlanta-Athens Highway, but still nothing was done. Though receptive to the project, Governor Arnall preferred to focus more on progressive reforms for the future than on nostalgia for the past.

Three years later, in January 1949, the option that DeKalb County Commissioner Scott Candler had secured from the Venable heirs was soon to expire, so he paid them $5,000 to renew the option for five more years. This act apparently revived some interest in the project. The Sons of Confederate Veterans soon after appealed to Governor Herman Talmadge, son of former Governor Eugene Talmadge, to reactivate the State Park Authority, which he did.

At first there was some concern that Arnall, a political rival of the Talmadges, might have had the statute repealed, but this was not so. According to the law, any member of the Authority must remain in office until a successor was appointed. Of the three members appointed by Eugene Talmadge, only Douglas McCurdy was still available. The other two were incapacitated by age and illness. Governor Herman Talmadge appointed Scott Candler and Murray Howard, State Commander of the SCV, as replacements. The governor assigned one of his executive aides to work with the Authority with specific instructions to "push it through to completion."[12]

---

[11]"Stone Mountain Authority Bill Introduced in House," *Atlanta Journal*, 21 February 1945.

[12]"Talmadge Revives Stone Mountain Plan," *Atlanta Journal*, 5 April 1949.

The Authority again selected Julian Harris as sculptor in August 1949 and drew up new plans for the park with fishing lakes, horseback riding trails, cabins, camping areas, a golf course, and a Confederate museum, among other attractions. As part of the Confederate memorial, the Authority also planned to erect a special monument to Margaret Mitchell, author of *Gone With The Wind,* who had recently been killed in an automobile accident.

The Authority next commissioned the Joseph K. Heyman Company to prepare an economic feasibility study of building the park, which was used in conjunction with an engineering survey prepared by Robert & Company as a starting point for planning and development. The Heyman study showed that an average of 619 cars stopped at the mountain each day with an average of three visitors per car getting out to view the incomplete carving. It predicted that this annual visitation of 677,000 people could easily be doubled if the memorial were finished. It suggested a minimum income of $338,000 based on each visitor spending an average of fifty cents.

By comparison, one million visitors spent an average of thirty dollars each at Mount Rushmore every year. Since the Black Hills could only be reached by a considerable digression from the main highway, whereas Stone Mountain lay near a heavily-traveled highway for people going to Florida, New York, or the Midwest, the conclusion was obvious.

In presenting the new application to the RFC in 1950 for a $2,500,000 loan, Talmadge emphasized the economic value of the park rather than the glorification of the Confederacy. He noted that seventy percent of the population of the United States lived within an overnight car or train ride from Atlanta, and how many he believed could be induced to stop at Stone Mountain if the memorial were completed. Once again the RFC was on the verge of approving the loan application when the United States became involved in the Korean Conflict and all RFC funds were diverted to military projects.

The Park Authority turned to Talmadge and asked the state to lend $800,000 so it proceed with the purchase of the mountain, which could then be used as security for a $2,500,000 loan proffered by a New York bank to build the park. The debt would be liquidated by gate receipts and concession fees. The General Assembly approved a resolution to make the loan, but the governor refused to act.

Talmadge stated that although he was in favor of the park, paying school teachers and law enforcement officers was more important than buying a mountain. There were numerous meetings between the Park

Authority and the governor in an effort to reach a compromise, but Talmadge held to his position that the state would only buy the mountain only when financial conditions permitted. The mountain, which had once been such an object of controversy, now became a source of endless frustration for proponents of the memorial.

Marvin Griffin was sworn in as governor on 11 January 1955, only to be immediately besieged by the press and community leaders clamoring for him to take up the Stone Mountain project. Griffin needed no encouragement; seeing the Confederate memorial finished had been a desire of his for a long time. A week after his inauguration he proposed that the state buy the mountain and a resolution to this effect was introduced into the House.

Before this effort went very far, however, a rival movement from the private sector took the initiative. In April 1956 Sam Mason, the son of Elizabeth Venable Mason, conveyed his one-fourth interest in the mountain to the other heirs for $125,000, and Mrs. George Hardin, another family member, sold her one-eighth share to the C & S National Bank for $68,500. These Venable heirs lived outside of the state and did not share the same concerns for the property as the local heirs.

To consolidate the various Venable properties in Stone Mountain, the remaining heirs and the C&S Bank transferred their interests to a newly formed holding company called Venable Brothers Contractors, Inc., taking corporate stock in exchange for their shares of land. The directors of this company were Mrs. Leila Venable Ethridge, daughter of Mrs. Mason; Mrs. Robert Venable Roper, niece of Sam Venable; Arthur Kellogg, son of Coribel Kellogg Orme from her first marriage; and Mills B. Lane, President of the C & S Bank. Management of the company was placed in the hands of Lane as the sole voting trustee. The "old homeplace" property where the Venable summer home had once stood and the Flat Rock property were not included in this transfer.

On the same day it was formed, the Venable Brothers Contractors, Inc. conveyed by quit claim deed all interests to the carving site, including forty acres at the base of the mountain, to the Stone Mountain Confederate Memorial, Inc., a nonprofit corporation whose sole purpose was to complete the carving. In the summer of 1956 the memorial group purchased an eighty-eight-acre undeveloped lot between the highway and Hugh Howell Road from several different owners at a total cost of $90,000. To acquire the land, Lane approached each of the owners asking them to name their price. When they told him he said, "You've got a deal." He did this with each of the landowners in a single day so that no one would be able to discuss it with the others before he had gotten an agreement for the entire tract. He was concerned that in collusion they might hold out for more money.

Mills B. Lane and the Confederate Memorial directors planned to develop the park as a private undertaking with as little state involvement as possible. Governor Griffin fully endorsed the effort and promised to help with widening the Atlanta-Athens Highway and other roadwork. Civic and governmental leaders lauded the efforts of Lane, who had a reputation for getting things done.

To make the development work, it was imperative that control of the 140-acre Flat Rock property be obtained by the Memorial group. This parcel, named for the flat expanses of exposed granite, was key for any development plans because it controlled the view of the carving. A few of the Venable heirs had ideas of developing it themselves, which is why it had not been conveyed to Venable Brothers Contractors, Inc. Lane worried that a development incompatible with the ambiance of the park might spring up and ruin the memorial.

The difficulty was that the property was divided into twelve parcels with eight different ownerships. Seven of these were willing to sell, but Lane was unable to reach an agreement with Mrs. Roper, who had complete or partial interests in several of the lots. She apparently wanted a concession to run a cable car to the top of the mountain as part of the purchase price. This was a condition that Lane was unwilling or unable to grant. In June 1957 Lane announced that he had abandoned the venture because he could not get title to the Flat Rock property. He suggested that the state buy the mountain and surrounding land already held by the Venable Brothers and then acquire the Flat Rock properties by eminent domain. Governor Griffin asked the public for its opinion and received an overwhelming response in favor of state acquisition.

A month later, Lane reached a breakthrough with Mrs. Roper so that condemnation would not be necessary. There was, however, a condition. The state would be required to buy the property and make the Confederate Memorial corporation into the state authority in charge of the park development. The press endorsed this scheme as a good way to keep the memorial free of petty politics. Some suggested that the governor and state solicitor be included on the board of the memorial group to represent state interests.

At the time, however, the state's preoccupation with other matters stymied this plan, which was never consummated. For his part, Lane never went any farther with his private development. Even though his effort failed, it stimulated greater interest in the memorial park and paved the way for ultimate state ownership of the mountain the following year.

Chapter Six

A New Start

The thirty years since work on the mountain had ceased were full of false starts and abortive efforts to get it going again. Mills B. Lane's attempt in 1956 was the last link in this chain of struggling efforts leading to state ownership of the mountain. His work to put together the necessary properties simplified the job for the state.

Owing to the distracting political war over school integration, the legislature did not take up the Roper offer of 1957. In his State of the State address in January 1958 Governor Griffin said he was convinced that the completion of the Confederate Memorial by the state would be "an everlasting benefit to the present generation and all future citizens of this state, and the entire Southland." Furthermore, he urged that Stone Mountain "be purchased immediately for public use, and that if necessary, the right of eminent domain be exercised."[1] In the final year of his term Griffin wanted some concrete action on the memorial before he went out of office.

The legislature was very likely to deny support for any proposals of a lame duck governor, but the Stone Mountain acquisition had too much public support for legislators to pose serious opposition. The General Assembly struck a joint committee, five from the House and three from the Senate, to study the cost of purchasing and developing the mountain area.

Representative James A. Mackay, of DeKalb County, chairman of the committee, filed a favorable report. His committee found that the total purchase price would probably amount to $1,454,000, with a breakdown as follows: 1,587.57 acres from Venable Brothers Contractors, Inc., for $1,125,000; the 140.3 acre Flat Rock property for $225,000; the 88.47 acre tract from the Confederate Memorial body at $90,000, and 409.74 acres from DeKalb County for $14,000.[2] (See map on following page.)

---

[1] Kenimer, *The History of Stone Mountain*, 16.
[2] Ibid.

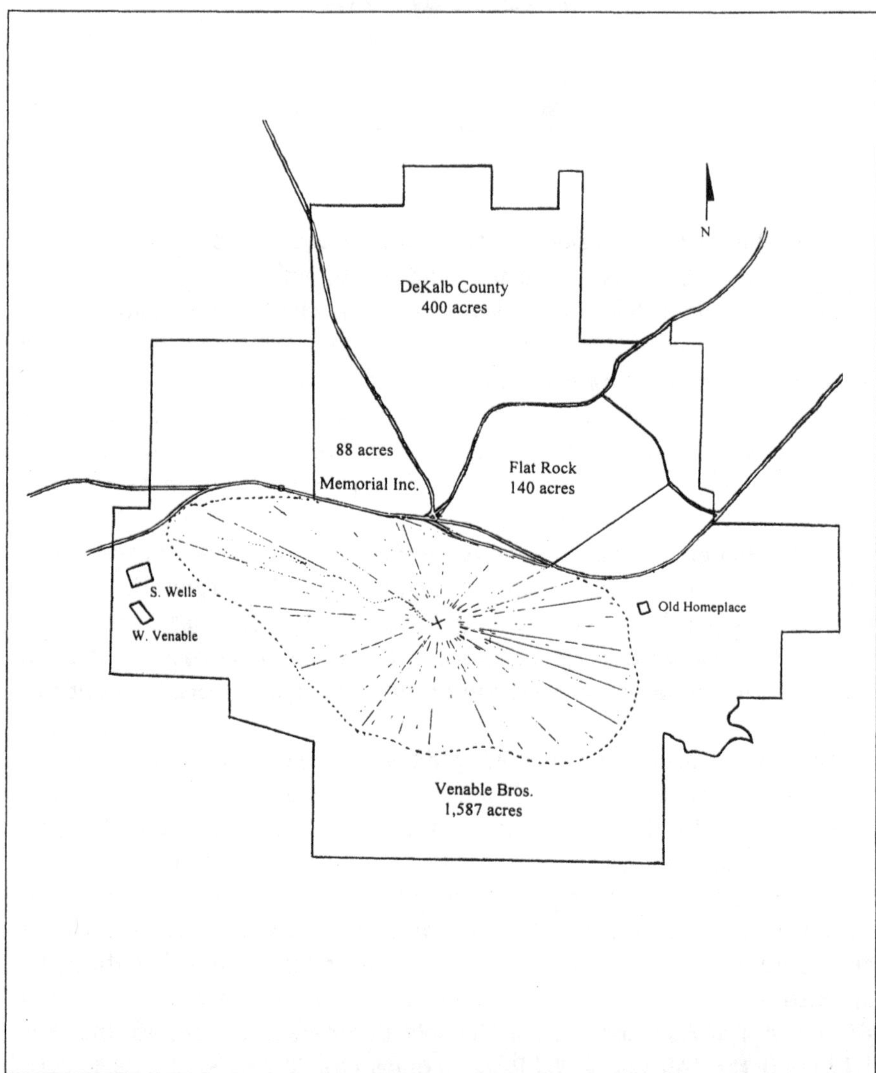

Tracts acquired by the state of Georgia in 1958 for the Stone Mountain Memorial Park. The state's original purchase authority for 2,500 acres was later increased to 3,200 acres.

With gubernatorial backing, the Georgia House passed Bill 946 by a vote of 152 to 41 providing for the creation of a seven-member authority to be known as the Stone Mountain Memorial Association. This body superseded the old three member Authority. The law, designated as Act 57, gave the Association the task of acquiring the mountain and adjacent property for development as a state park. The Association was limited to the purchase of no more than 2,500 acres at a cost not to exceed $1,500,000, or $600 per acre. If necessary land was not for sale, the Association had the power to acquire the acreage by condemnation. It was further authorized to issue up to $2,500,000 in bonds to pay for construction. The Act was amended in 1959 to remove the property restriction and increase bonding authority to five million dollars.

Before the bill passed there was much debate in the Assembly over the make-up of the Association. Griffin favored a mixture of state officers and citizens and Lieutenant Governor Ernest Vandiver suggested that state officers should be in the majority. Other factions thought that there should be only one or two constitutional officers. Senator Peyton Hawes believed that the Governor should be able to appoint all the members so that he could get whatever mix he wanted. In the end, the joint committee established that the Association would be composed of the Secretary of State, the Attorney General, the Commissioner of Agriculture, the Chairman of the Public Service Commission plus three citizens chosen by the Governor.

Governor Griffin signed the bill into law on 21 February 1958 and on March 3 he swore in Secretary of State Ben Fortson, Attorney General Eugene Cook, Secretary of Agriculture Phil Campbell, PSC Chairman Matt L. McWhorter, Secretary of Commerce Scott Candler, Georgia UDC President Mrs. Lee H. Lyle, and retired Vice President of Coca-Cola S. Price Gilbert, Jr. Governor Griffin pronounced it a "red letter day" in Georgia's history and promised to do what he could to facilitate their work.[3]

The Memorial Association first met on the morning of 5 March 1958. The group selected officers and Matt McWhorter was named Chairman. The initial meetings of the Association were devoted to getting organized, writing by-laws, establishing an office in the Department of Agriculture Building, and developing a master plan. Attorney General Cook appointed the Assistant Attorney General and a Deputy Assistant to help the

---

[3]Ibid., 17.

Association with its legal work, while McWhorter requested and received from the governor a $100,000 allocation to begin the work.

The foremost consideration was to acquire title to the land. Mills B. Lane, who had been considered for membership in the Association, was invited to the second meeting to discuss selling the land held by the Venable Brothers, Incorporated and the Stone Mountain Memorial, Incorporated. Lane promised his cooperation and urged Association members to visit with the people of Stone Mountain to generate goodwill toward the new Association. In April 1958 the Association had the land surveyed and requested an appraisal of the more than 1,587-acre tract from the Atlanta Real Estate Board. On 20 June the Real Estate Board submitted its appraisal with an assigned value of $957,000, or $599.83 per acre, just seventeen cents under the Association's budget of $600 per acre. Curiously, the Real Estate Board based its valuation on the land's usage as a residential subdivision, even though the tourist attraction and commercial uses of the land were well established.

The state at long last purchased the Stone Mountain property on 19 September 1958, for $1,125,000, which the heirs divided according to the number of shares they held in Venable Brothers, Inc. This was $168,000 above the appraisal amount, but the larger figure had been expected and more or less agreed to for some time, so the state went ahead and paid the greater amount. In a memo to the other Association members, Chairman McWhorter suggested that the land had a far greater value than that placed on it by the Real Estate Board. He felt that if the state did not pay the $1,125,000 figure and tried to condemn the land, it would end up paying much more in an assessors award.[4]

On the same day that the state purchased the mountain, Mills Lane's Memorial group conveyed as a gift all interest to the carving site to the state, and DeKalb County turned over title to 409-plus acres to the north of the Venable property. The county initially wanted $17,500 as the amount it had invested in the property, but in the end it was deeded for the sum of one dollar. At a ceremony held in the governor's office to receive these deeds for the state, Governor Griffin pronounced it "the happiest day in my whole tenure of office."[5]

---

[4]Matt McWhorter to the Association, 30 June 1958. Files of the Stone Mountain Memorial Association.

[5]As quoted in Kenimer, 18.

With these two large tracts secured, the Association sought to close deals on several smaller parcels. Inside the big Venable conveyance were three small areas not included: the Old Homeplace property of 5.5 acres, the W. H. Venable property of 2.2 acres, and the Steve Wells property of 5.8 acres. These tracts were individually secured in October 1958. In January 1959 Mills Lane's Confederate Memorial group sold its 88-plus acre lot to the state for cost plus interest which totaled $93,879. Other surrounding parcels were later obtained through purchase, gift, or condemnation.

The Flat Rock acreage was one of these parcels acquired by condemnation. It was this key piece of property which had wrecked Lane's attempt since his private corporation did not have power of eminent domain. The Atlanta Real Estate Board appraised the property at $600 an acre, the same as the rest of the property, for a total of $84,000. The DeKalb County Real Estate Board appraised the 140-plus acres at $201,000, which included the land plus the business valuation of Willie Hill Venable's gift shop and museum in the old studio building. The state offered to meet the DeKalb Board figure, but Mrs. Roper would not agree to sell her interest. Unable to reach an agreement with her, the Association filed for condemnation in October 1958. In December the court awarded the Venable heirs $216,400 plus $37,500 to W. H. Venable for the taking of his business.

Roper's share of the award was $38,025. She considered the land to be considerably more valuable than any offer yet made and filed a lawsuit to contest the condemnation action. To appease her Mills B. Lane offered to swap her interests in Flat Rock for a 48-acre parcel on the eastern edge of the city of Stone Mountain that was still owned by Venable Brothers, Inc. She dropped her lawsuit and accepted this land in substitution of the accessor award. After her death in 1967, her executors sold this property for more than two million dollars.

Harkness Kenimer, an Atlanta real estate broker and expert witness who represented Roper during the condemnation hearings, wrote his own account of the state acquisition. According to him, at the time that the $1,125,000 price tag for the Venable property was originally agreed upon, the heirs were to retain ownership of the crucial Flat Rock parcel, which they could then develop themselves. Roper so adamantly refused to sell her interest in Flat Rock because the state offer did not approach the financial benefits she expected to gain from her ownership of the parcel.[6]

---

[6]Ibid., 23.

Over the course of the next two years, the Memorial Association acquired an additional 970-plus acres from two dozen separate owners for approximately half a million dollars. This brought the total size of the park to 3,200 acres at a purchase price of approximately $1.9 million. The additional land was needed to accommodate the rerouting of the highway, the building of the lake, and some of the support facilities of the park. Most of the properties were purchased without trouble while some had to be condemned. Douglas McCurdy donated a tract worth $5,000 and Burton Wilbur made the unusual arrangement of asking for $50 a month for the rest of his and his wife's lives. By the time they both died in the mid-1980's, the Association had paid in excess of $15,000 for their lot.

Most legislators were very pleased with the state's purchase of the mountain and expressed their opinions in the press. Said one, "the state bought a rare jewel at a bargain price," and another happily predicted it would "pay for itself over and over with tourist money." When questioned about the park's money-making potential, one Senator quipped, "A Yankee tourist is worth a bale of cotton and twice as easy to pick."

Once the state gained title to the necessary properties the enormous task of developing the park could begin in earnest. The Association hoped to have the park mostly complete by 1961 for the upcoming centennial of the Civil War. As a starting point it looked at park plans drawn up by Robert & Company in 1950. It then commissioned Robert & Company to do a new engineering survey and to make a detailed topographical model of the property with revised proposals for development.

Because of the different considerations involved in completing the Confederate memorial as opposed to the general park development, Ben Fortson was named chairman of a special monument committee to take on this task. The work of this committee is examined in the next chapter.

Some of the concerns of the Association for park development were the layout of roads, the relocation of Highway 78, the placement of the dam, what buildings were needed and where would they go, landscaping, and what to do with the top of the mountain. Much of the work was to be done by state prisoners, so the Association also had to figure a prison camp into the park plans.

During the planning stages the Association was besieged on every side with advice and suggestions from well-meaning citizens and groups. Most of these non-expert opinions were not very useful or had already been considered. Instead, the Association sought advice from the National Park Service, and the Association members visited Mount Rushmore, Yellowstone, and Yosemite National Parks to study how these attractions were developed and managed.

To oversee the work at the mountain and run the park operations, the Association named Scott Candler as General Manager. Since it would have been inappropriate for the General Manager to be a member of the Association, Candler's seat on the board was given to Brooks Pennington. The "Old Man of the Mountain," Elias Nour, was hired as safety director and vested with the powers of deputy sheriff. Under Nour's direction the park installed a 7,500 foot-long cyclone fence around the top of the mountain, thereby greatly reducing the need for his rescue services.

At this time Candler inquired about having another memorial coin minted, but the Director of the Mint stated that regulations passed since the term of President Hoover prohibited the issuance of memorial coins. With a special act of Congress, the Association could have a bronze medal the size of a fifty-cent piece made by the Mint, if desired.

The first two years after the state acquired the mountain there were few improvements to the property. The Association spent most of this time studying engineering reports, refining its plans, and doing preliminary work such as surveying roads, taking bore samples for the dam, surveying and marking the lake basin, printing promotional materials, and negotiating with concessionaires. Only basic facilities, such as picnic shelters and comfort stations (segregated for white and colored) were built. The Association refurbished the old studio to serve as the park office and souvenir shop. This work, plus the clearing of brush and minor landscaping was done by approximately one hundred state prisoners at the mountain. The prisoners, under the direction of Warden Hoke Smith, also refurbished some old houses and other buildings on the property for their accommodations until permanent facilities could be built.

With the help of Robert & Company, the Association prepared a master plan to guide the park development. The top priority items included a dam and lake, a road around and to the top of the mountain, the main building, the mountain top building, and the selection of a sculptor for the memorial.

By 1960 most of the preliminary work was finished and the contracts sent out for bids, but the schedule for entire project hinged on the rerouting of Highway 78 one mile northward. This was necessary not only to remove a major thoroughfare from the center of the park, but also because the lake threatened to flood a quarter-mile section of the old road.

Until the Highway Department began the project, none of the major construction could go forward.

The Highway Department finally got far enough along on the new road by the end of 1960 for the park to begin work. At ground breaking ceremonies on December 28, 1960, Governor Ernest Vandiver turned the first spade of dirt at the dam site to symbolically begin construction. Bulldozers immediately roared into action as soon as the brief exercises concluded. In his address the governor acknowledged, "This has been a project of dedication by such people as Scott Candler and others, who refused to see the dream die."[7]

The earthen dam, built primarily with prison labor under the supervision of consulting engineers, was sixty-four feet high, 1,175 feet long, and thirty feet at the top to allow for a two-lane road across. It was completed in September, 1961 at a cost of $314,000. The dam backed up Mountain Creek to create a 416-acre lake and, when full, covered the old Highway 78 with sixteen feet of water.

The park development plans called for fourteen miles of roads through the park and around the mountain. Initially designated by letters during construction, the roads were later named after Confederate heroes. Road "A" leading into the park from the east gate became Jefferson Davis Drive, Roads "B," "C" and "D" joined together to encircle the mountain and were named Robert E. Lee Boulevard, Roads "E" and "F" ran along the backside of the lake and became Stonewall Jackson Drive. The little road running behind the plantation complex was named John B. Gordon Drive, and the road leading to the marina was christened Raphael Semmes Drive, in honor of the Confederacy's only Admiral/General. The road and bridge construction cost $1,079,000.[8]

Other park facilities begun at this time included Memorial Hall ($802,000), Confederate Hall ($631,000), the mountain top building and plaza ($922,000), the Stone Acres Plantation ($703,000), the marina ($257,000), Stone Mountain Inn ($2,167,000), campgrounds ($101,000), and the prison camp ($109,000). Utilities cost $564,000, equipment for the park amounted to $970,000, and various other facilities came to a total of $662,000. Most of the major buildings were built of Stone Mountain granite obtained from the King & Kellogg quarry on the east side of the mountain.

---

[7]"Vandiver Pledges Stone Mountain Shrine to Be Completed," *DeKalb New Era*, 29 December 1960.

[8]Ibid.

Money for the construction came from five million dollars worth of revenue bonds issued in 1962, again in 1964, and again in 1967.

As soon as the Association began planning the park, it was bombarded with proposals from prospective concessionaires wanting a piece of the state's action. The Association was of the opinion that all major items should be leased as concessions. Some of the proposals materialized and others, thankfully, did not. The most outlandish proposition came from the Alan Hawes Amusement Company, which wanted to build a 40-acre theme park *a la Disneyland* with an antebellum twist. There would be a Main Street Atlanta 1860, Uncle Remus Land, Old South Land, and various rides. This idea was rejected, but the Association did allow a Mark Twain Land on the east side of the lake. Other failed proposals were to have the Cyclorama, the giant circular painting and diorama telling the story of the Battle of Atlanta, relocated from Grant Park to Stone Mountain; to have the Civil War steam engine *The General* moved from Kennesaw to the park, to build a *Gone With The Wind* museum, and an amphitheater for outdoor dramas.

The *Gone With The Wind* museum started out as a monument to Margaret Mitchell, but expanded into a museum dedicated to her novel and housed in a recreation of Tara. From there the idea combined with another concessionaire's proposal for a modest plantation recreation and grew into the present eighteen-acre plantation complex. The Mitchell memorial aspect was gradually forgotten.

The authentic antebellum structures in the plantation complex were moved to the park from various locations around Georgia and refurbished. The complex was then leased to Kenneth Garcia, an interior decorator, and to Christine Mitchell to furnish and operate. A year later Mrs. Mitchell became Mrs. McWhorter when she married the Chairman of the Memorial Association.

The plantation, originally dubbed Stone Acres Plantation, opened to the public in April 1963. The star attraction was not the plantation itself, but Butterfly McQueen, the actress who played the role of Prissy in the film version of *Gone With The Wind.* McQueen worked there as one of the tour guides on weekends until July 1965, when she ran into conflict with the management. After McQueen's departure all overt references to *Gone With the Wind* disappeared.

Some of the concessionaires did make major capital investments in the park. Herbert Fishler and D.C. Land, of Florida, spent approximately one million dollars to build their cable car sky lift to the top of the mountain. The fifty-person cars were imported from Switzerland, and the dedication of the sky lift in November 1962 was performed by Ambassador August Lindt of that country.

The Stone Mountain Scenic Railroad Company likewise spent one million dollars to construct a four-mile railroad around the mountain. A replica of *The General* pulled antique-styled coaches on a trip around the mountain. At the halfway point of the journey an Indian raid on a mock frontier town greeted the passengers. The Scenic Railroad began operating in April 1962.

Other smaller concessionaires were C. T. Protsman, who leased his collection of vintage automobiles for the Antique Car Museum; G. A. Rilling, operator of a game ranch and petting zoo; the Stone Mountain Riding Academy, which rented horses and maintained a bridle trail; William C.Gibson, operator of the camping sites, and Berlo of Georgia, Incorporated, which held the concession for the sale of all food and novelties in the park.

Although not a concession, the United Daughters of the Confederacy wanted some part in the park development since they still considered the memorial as their brainchild. The Georgia Division petitioned for permission to build a chapel near the lake, but was delicately dissuaded from following through on the idea. The Association suggested instead that the UDC take up the project of putting a flag terrace at the base of the walk-up trail. To raise funds for the terrace, the UDC received permission to sell bricks from the old Confederate Soldier's Home in Atlanta that was slated for demolition. This represented the first material contribution by the UDC to the memorial since Borglum's dismissal. The terrace, which had the American flag flying above the four flags used by the Confederacy, was dedicated in October, 1964.

Ever since Helen Plane envisioned a simple bust of Lee, the Stone Mountain memorial had a reputation for becoming more complicated than originally planned and generating controversy in the process. The 1960s were no exception. The first bit of controversy came in 1962 when Elias Nour lost his job through somewhat mysterious circumstances. He went into the hospital for minor surgery and when he returned to work he was told by the General Manager that he had resigned. Nour insisted that he had not resigned, but that he was being fired. In any case, Nour was no longer employed by the park, and no reason was given for his dismissal. He left Stone Mountain the following year and moved to Orlando, Florida, where he joined his brother in the air conditioning business.

Scott Candler found his own employment as General Manager terminated in May, 1963, when he was demoted to become Chairman McWhorter's assistant. It was rumored that politics was the reason for this action. Candler supported former Governor Marvin Griffin against Governor Carl Sanders in the 1962 primary election, and Candler often disagreed with McWhorter on policy at the park. Rather than accept the demotion, the seventy-six-year-old Candler resigned from the Association and retired from public life.

Candler was succeeded in this post by Harold Maddux, a retired Air Force general. As things turned out, McWhorter was himself replaced as a member of the Association in July of 1963. Someone made an issue of McWhorter's marriage to one of the concessionaires at the park. A DeKalb County grand jury, headed by Zack Cravey, an old political foe of McWhorter's, decided that a conflict of interest existed because the Association Chairman would be benefitting financially from the park's operations vis-a-vis the plantation concession. McWhorter questioned the grand jury's objectivity, but complied with the resignation order. The governor appointed Mills B. Lane to fill the vacancy on the Association board, which elected Agriculture Commissioner Phil Campbell as its new chairman.

The imbroglio over the park development erupted in the spring of 1964 when the building of the Stone Mountain Inn became an issue. Construction on this luxury hotel began in the fall of 1962, but for over a year none of the members of the Association, except Chairman McWhorter, knew anything about it. The hotel was estimated to cost $995,000, but actually cost over two million dollars by the time it was finished in the spring of 1965, two years behind schedule.

The extravagant cost was bad enough, but what the public found most shocking was that seventy-six of the eighty-six double rooms in the hotel had been equipped with bidets--bathroom fixtures designed to bathe the posterior parts of the body. Discreetly referred to as "those things," these fixtures are commonly found in European hotels, but are virtually unknown to most Americans. Harold Maddux, who became General Manager as the bidets were being installed, responded so intensely to the matter that Phil Campbell later commented, "I thought he was going to have a heart attack," when he learned about them. He and other Association members feared that park visitors would not know how to use them or that children might even mistake them for drinking fountains. Or more puritanical types might consider any fixture used for such purposes to be indecent. Eventually

Maddux had the offending fixtures removed from the rooms and put in storage. He tried to get the supplier to take them back, but the company refused stating that these were unpopular items and it did not maintain a stock. Maddux eventually unloaded the bidets by selling them to a Carribean cruise ship.

All the excitement created by the mystery hotel and the titillating news of the bidets sparked a series of reports by the *Atlanta Constitution* entitled "Muddle At the Mountain." The Georgia Press Association had a field day with this and wrote a satirical lyric, "Seventy-six Bidets," to the tune of "Seventy-six Trombones." Reporter Jack Nelson not only looked into matters surrounding the hotel, but also scrutinized the other projects at the park. He commented on the completely empty and very expensive building on top of the mountain, which was about fifty percent over budget, and the reflecting pool with nothing but sky to reflect. The reporter also discovered that the park paid two to three times as much for road work as paid by the state highway department, and that the Association was carrying a two million dollar debt at the time. He lamented that the memorial had become "lost in a campaign to turn the park into a recreation area that would attract out-of-state tourists."[9]

All the while there was a great deal of finger pointing among the Association members. They all said McWhorter did all these things without their knowledge, and McWhorter responded that they had approved the expenditures at the regular meetings. Mills Lane accused everyone on the Association at the time of waste and mismanagement.

The allegations in the *Constitution* reports prompted the state Senate to call for an investigation into the affairs of the Memorial Association. The legislature struck a ten-member joint committee to begin a probe that lasted for six months. In its report, released in December, 1964, the panel assailed many of the actions taken by the Association regarding the letting of contracts and accounting procedures. The committee declared that several major decisions were "made by one or two men rather than by the entire Association membership," and were "based on whim and fancy rather than sound engineering and feasibility principles." It continued to say that although more than $50,000 had been paid to engineers and architects there was "no apparent coordination of design in building construction."[10]

---

[9]Jack Nelson, "How Is Stone Mountain Money Being Spent," *Atlanta Journal Constitution*, 31 May 1964.

[10]Joint Report of the Senate and House Committees, December 1964.

With regard to the Stone Mountain Inn, the committee found that McWhorter had not brought the matter formally before the Association for discussion, but had entered into a contract with an architect and builder on his own initiative. The contract was not counter-signed by the Secretary-Treasurer, rendering it technically invalid. Furthermore, McWhorter did not let the contract out for competitive bid, but gave it on a cost-plus basis to the first contractor who gave an estimate. All of these actions were in violation of the Association by-laws. Execution of the contract was done in a slipshod manner with poor site selection, construction beginning before the engineering specification were complete, and with little cost control. McWhorter explained that everything was done so hastily to make the hotel ready for the formal opening of the park, originally scheduled for the summer of 1963, but the committee did not accept this excuse.

The committee noted that the mountain top facility was likewise constructed without competitive bids or even seeking a second estimate, and that the Association had no specific plans for the expensive structure. It also found several instances where bids were based on an estimated number of units for the job, such as with road work and fill dirt, and after the contract was let the number of units materially increased, thereby increasing the amount of the contract. The contracts had no penalty provision for work done poorly, vastly over budget or finished late.

In analyzing concession agreements, the committee found that most contracts favored the concessionaires much more than the Association and that the twenty-year terms were too long. Other than this, the investigators found no significant problems with any other aspects of the Association's work. The committee did chastise the Association members for not living up to its responsibility to conduct occasional inspections of the property and to be familiar with the major undertakings, but it reported no malfeasance or misappropriation of funds. The members defended themselves by saying their duties as state officers kept them too busy to double check everything being done at the park.

The committee did make several recommendations including reducing the length of time of concession contracts, barring the Association from borrowing money for capital improvements, the establishment of firm construction guidelines for future development, and the removal of the Attorney General from the Association to eliminate any conflict of interest in case he was required at a future time to investigate the Association's operations. The committee noted that under the Chairmanship of Phil Campbell the Association had profited from its mistakes and made many improvements in its management and operations. The committee did not recommend any disciplinary action. The hotel was nearly finished and McWhorter was no longer on the Association board, so the entire question was moot.

Columnist Eugene Patterson lampooned the whole affair with a tongue-in-cheek article for the *Constitution*:

> The muddle at the mountain can have only one redeeming grace at this point: Write what has happened and emblazon it on bronze markers; incredulous world travelers would come flocking to read it and weep, and hail such a monumental mess as the genuine Eighth Wonder of the World.
>
> Snug at the Sitzbath Hilton, served by the Gillis Freeway, the tourist horde would pay and pay to hear guides tell the story. . . .
>
> The Stone Mountain Railroad would chug to a halt and the kids would see, not an Indian fight, but Matt McWhorter and Scott Candler tomohawking each other while Zack Cravey galloped up with a posse of grand jurors.
>
> Besides the reflecting pool that reflects nothing, alongside the mountaintop inn with nothing in it, Memorial Association Chairman Phil Campbell could pack 'em in from far and wide by restaging the development meetings he and board members Cook, Fortson, Pilcher, Lyle and Pennington held, so as to show how they wrought this wonder. . . ."[11]

All the contention surrounding the mountain did not keep people away or hamper their enjoyment of the park. Parkgoers got a bonus when work on the carving resumed during the 1964 season. The carving crew at work on the heights provided an unrivaled attraction at the park for the next six years. To commemorate the 100th anniversary of the Battle of Atlanta, more than four hundred Civil War reenactors staged an action on 25 July 1964, for some four thousand spectators on the hillside in front of the carving. At the height of an artillery barrage, Brigadier General John K. Williams--narrating the event over a loudspeaker--called on the artillery units to cease firing toward Memorial Hall and move the guns further down hill. The huge glass windows in the building were rattling so severely from

---

[11] Eugene Patterson, "Have A Laugh; Its Only $11.2 Million," *Atlanta Constitution*, 1 June 1964.

the concussion of the big guns that he was afraid they would shatter. The climax of the ninety-minute reenactment came with both sides engaged in fierce hand-to-hand combat. Afterward, with weapons at present-arms, the troops and spectators alike joined in singing Dixie and the Star Spangled Banner.

The 1965 season marked the first season with the park fully functional and the new highway opened so that the park was not plagued with traffic congestion. It also marked the first year an entrance fee was imposed. This idea had been considered for some time, but always with stiff opposition. The Association eventually decided that some sort of charge would be necessary if the park was ever going to operate on a self-sustaining basis. It decided that a one-dollar gate fee would be sufficient. For the fee visitors received a permit good for one year, which favored local people who visited frequently. Three years later the annual pass went up to two dollars with the single visit charge remaining at one dollar.

A survey conducted at the park in 1965 by William B. Keeling, director of the Bureau of Business and Economic Research at the University of Georgia, revealed that more than one million visitors passed through the park gates that season. Of the visitors surveyed, seventy-three percent expressed a favorable opinion of the park. Most of the negative comments concerned the prices. "Nice, but expensive," was a common response.[12]

Keeling reported that Stone Mountain was fast becoming "the most significant tourist attraction south of Williamsburg," but more attention should be given to the historical aspects of the park. He suggested having the grist mill actually turn out corn meal, that there should be a working Southern farm producing goods as they did in the nineteenth century, and that there should be more about the history of the Civil War and advances in southern life in the late nineteenth century. "The basic objective of the park," he told the Association, "should be an educational one, in the broadest sense of the term."[13]

The primary focus of the park, however, remained recreational and entertainment. The Coca-Cola Company gave the park a carillon from the 1964-65 New York World's Fair, and the Association spent $127,000 to erect it on a peninsula on the lake. Professional carillonneur Herbie Koch (pronounced Cook) was hired to give concerts for visitors. Added to the

---

[12]"More Than A Million Visited Stone Mountain During 1965," *Atlanta Journal,* 15 December 1965.

[13]Ibid.

park facilities in 1968 were an eighteen-hole golf course costing $600,000 and a beach area, which cost $100,000.[14]

The park continued to draw criticism from various groups with comments ranging from "schmaltzy" to "design squalor." The Polynesian-styled marina was a frequent object of scorn. A landscape architect suggested planting more trees to hide the concession stands and souvenir shops would help reduce the Coney Island effect. One critic lamented, "If the great grey whale would just roll over we could begin again."[15]

Andre Steiner, chief planner for Robert & Company, agreed that sometimes the designer's recommendations were ignored in favor of political and business interests, but added, "In what we've made at Stone Mountain--people like it."[16] Attendance figures seemed to support Steiner's appraisal. By the close of the 1960s approximately three million people were visiting the park each year. Georgia's long-sought Confederate Memorial park was undeniably a huge success.

---

[14] "Campbell Runs Tighter Ship." *Atlanta Journal*, 5 December 1968.
[15] "Stone Mountain Layout Hit As A Coney Island," *Atlanta Constitution*, 1 July 1967.
[16] "Stone Mountain Draws Criticism," *Atlanta Journal*, 30 June 1967.

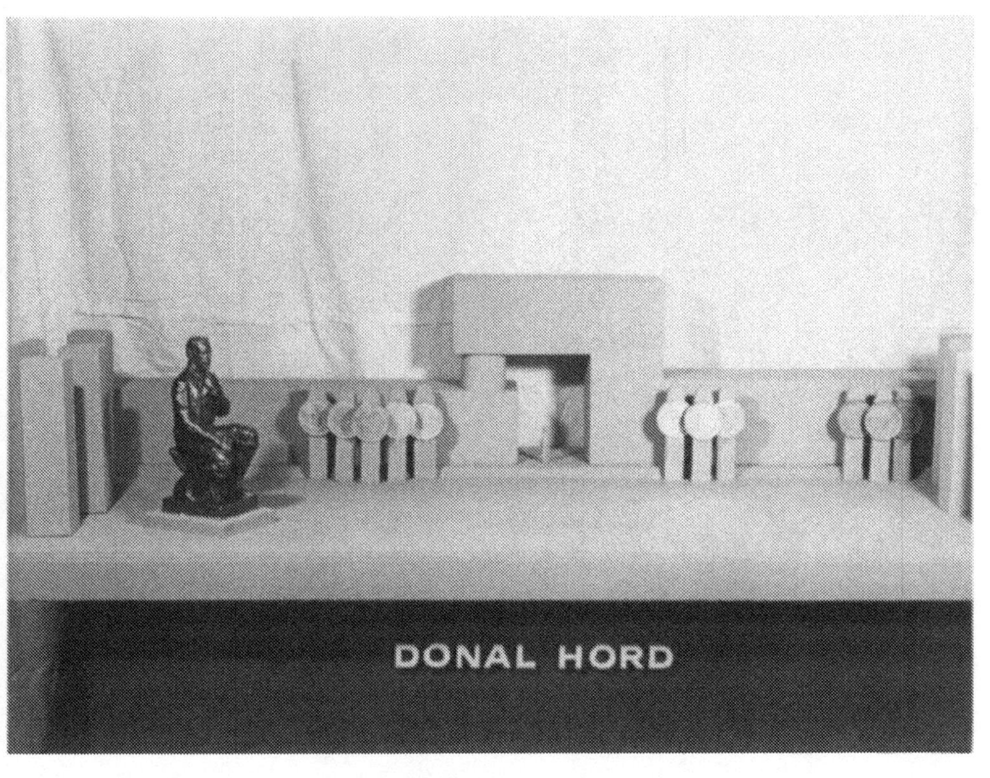

29. Donal Hord's proposed model for the 1962 Confederate memorial.

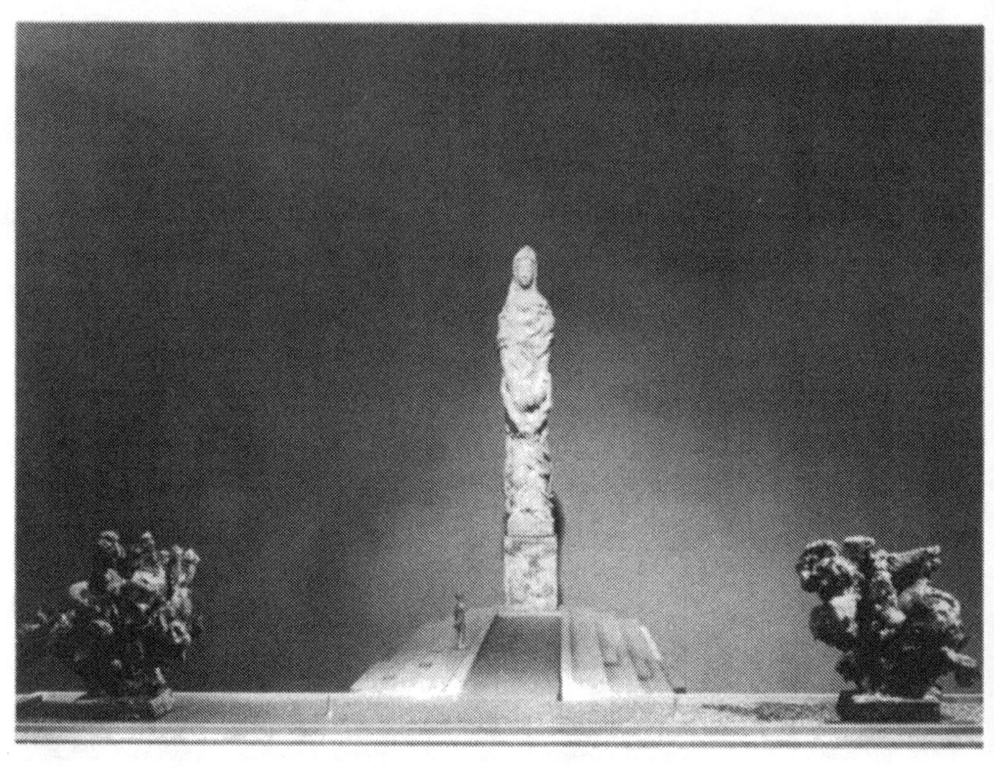

30. Jose de Creeft's proposed model for the 1962 memorial.

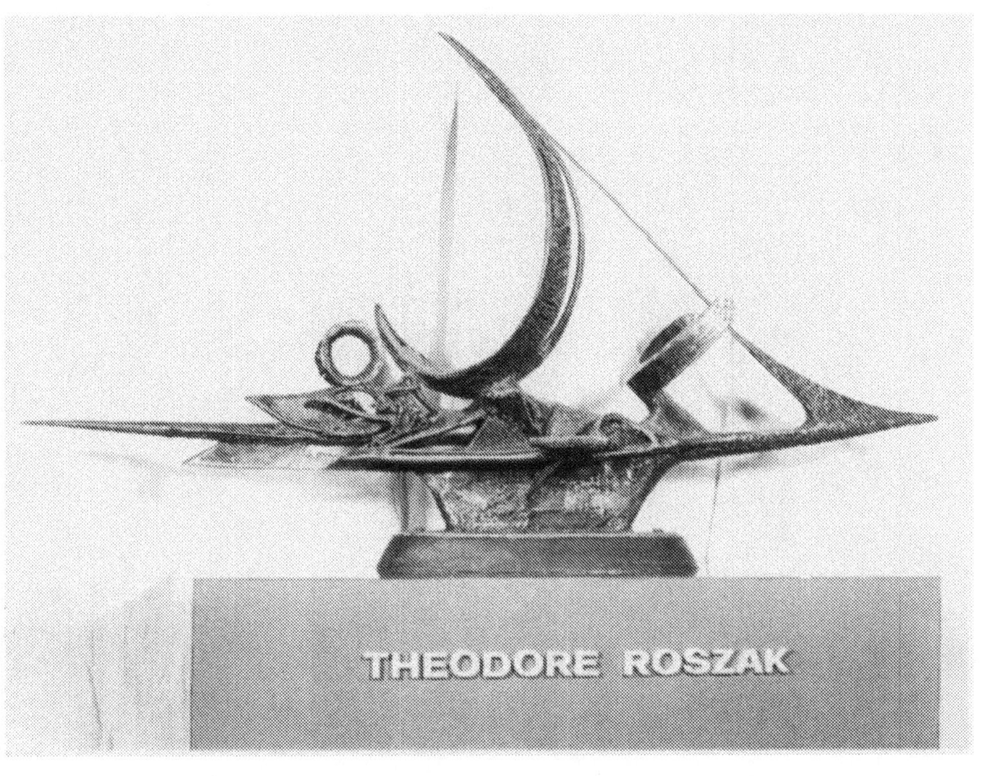

31. Theodore Roszak's proposed model for the 1962 memorial.

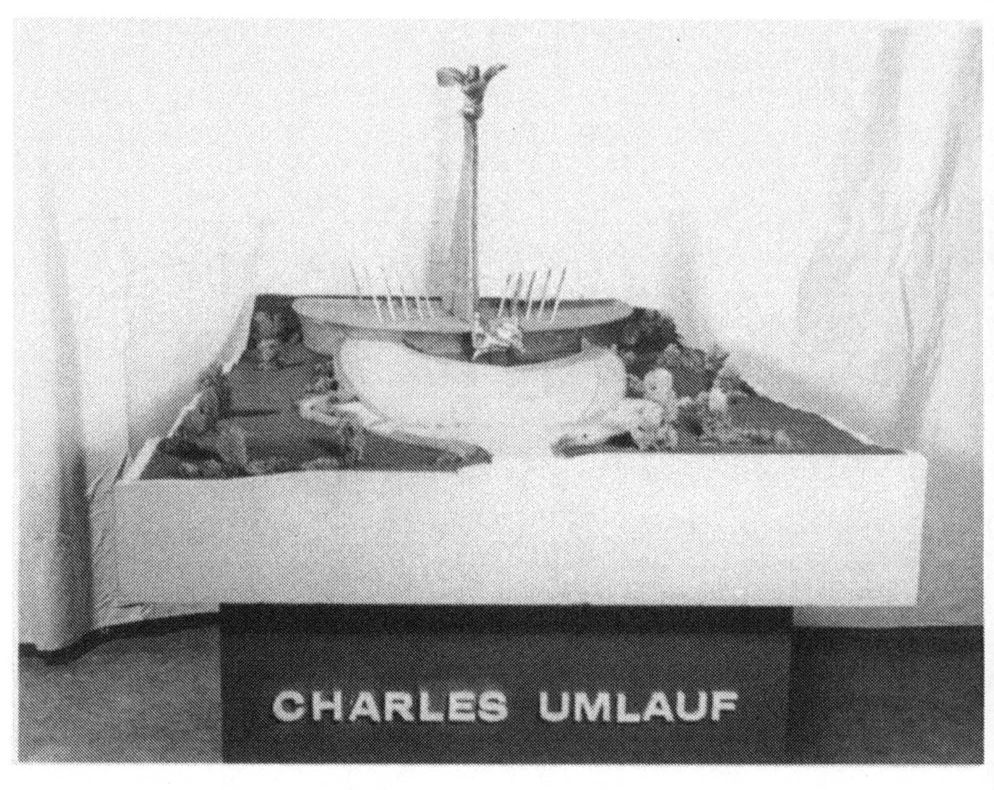

32. Charles Umlauf's proposed model for the 1962 memorial.

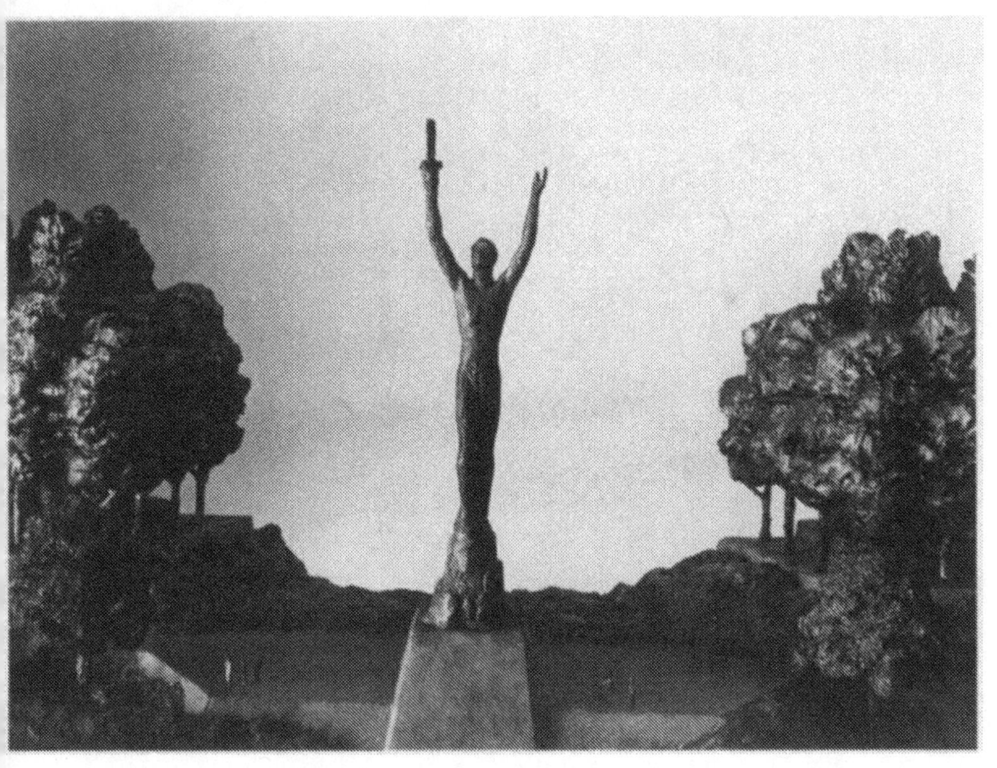

33. Walker Hancock's proposed model for the 1962 memorial.

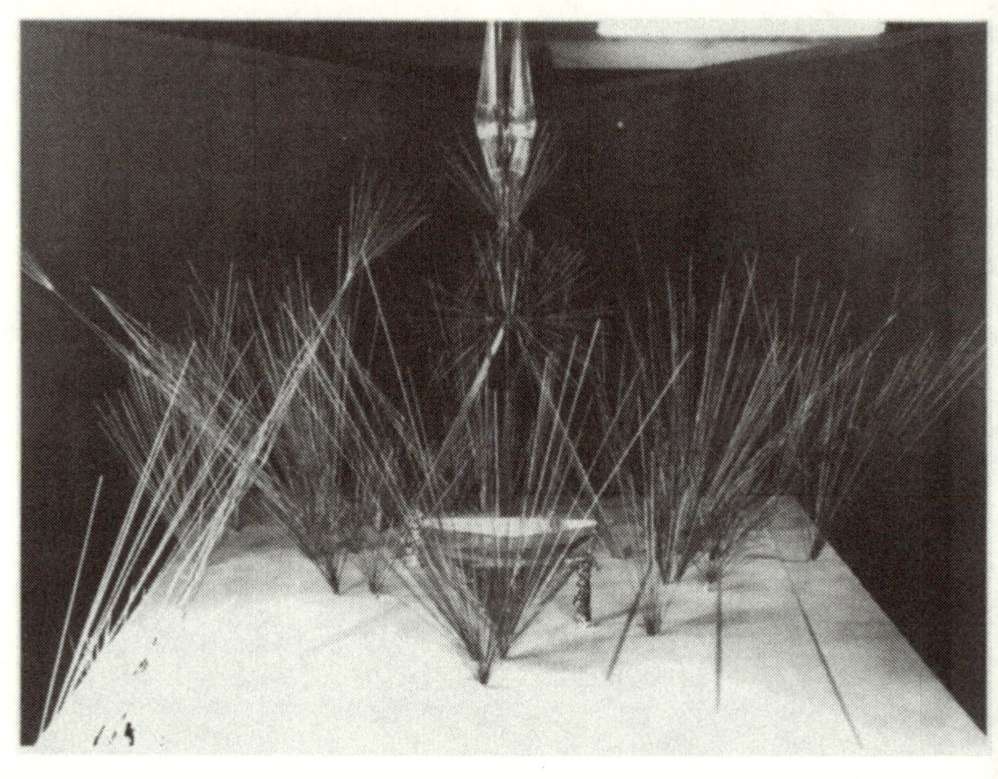

34. Bernard Reder's proposed model for the 1962 memorial.

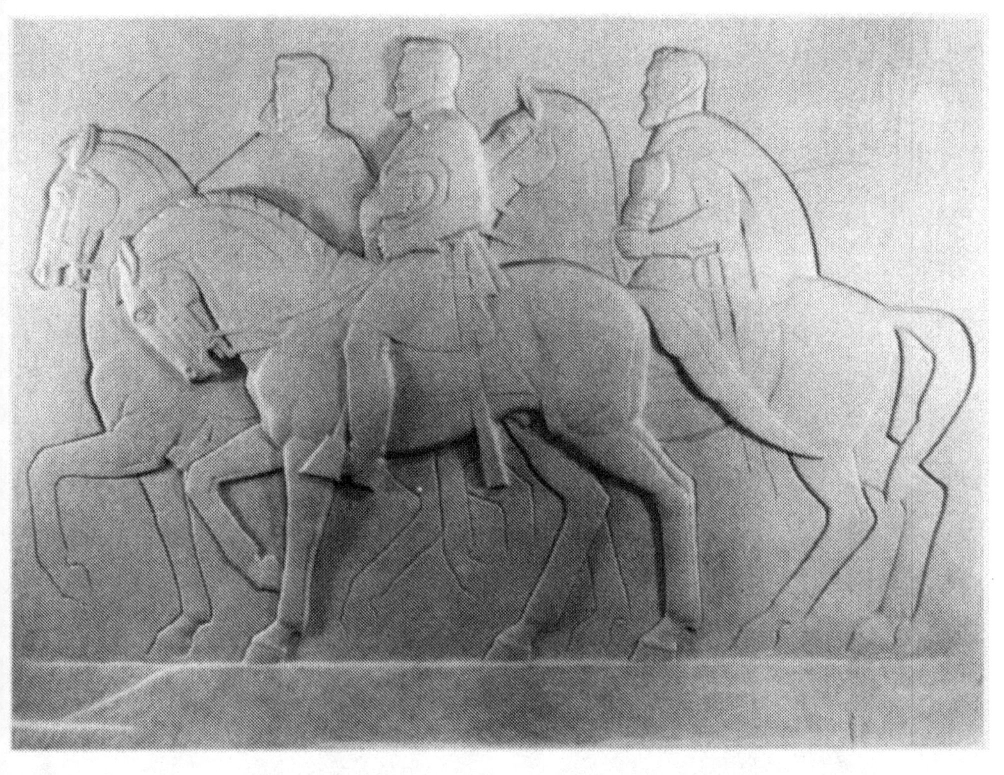

35. Julian Harris's proposed model for the 1962 memorial.

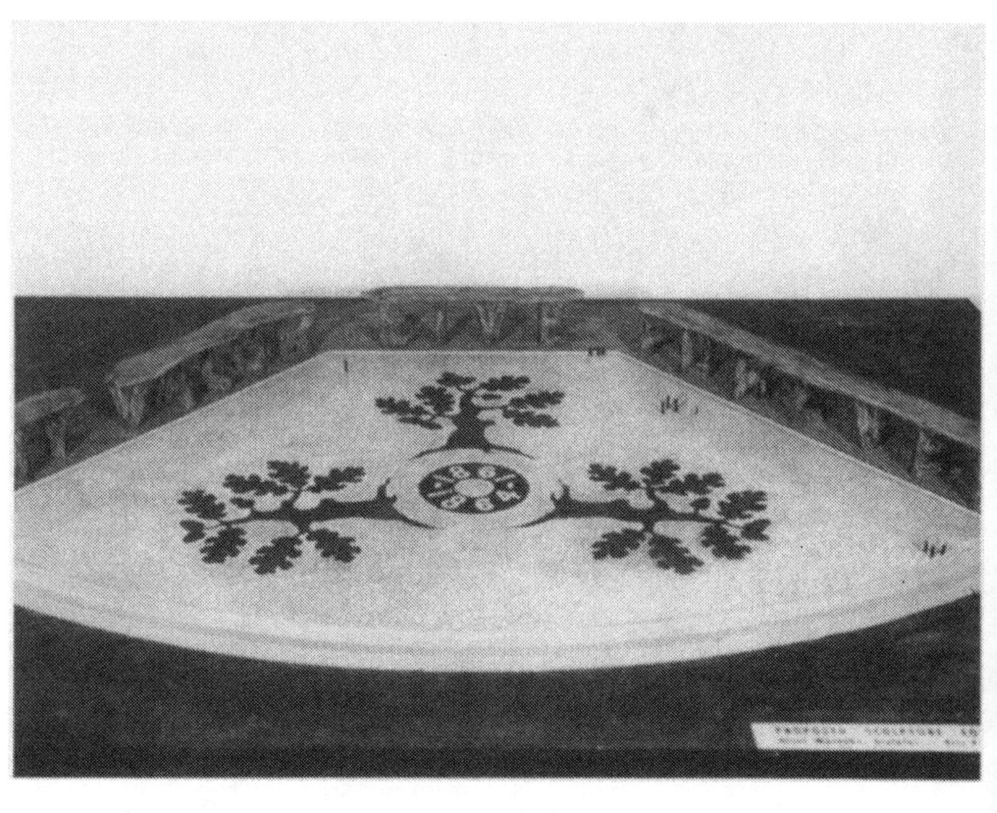

36. Heinze Warneke's proposed model for the 1962 memorial.

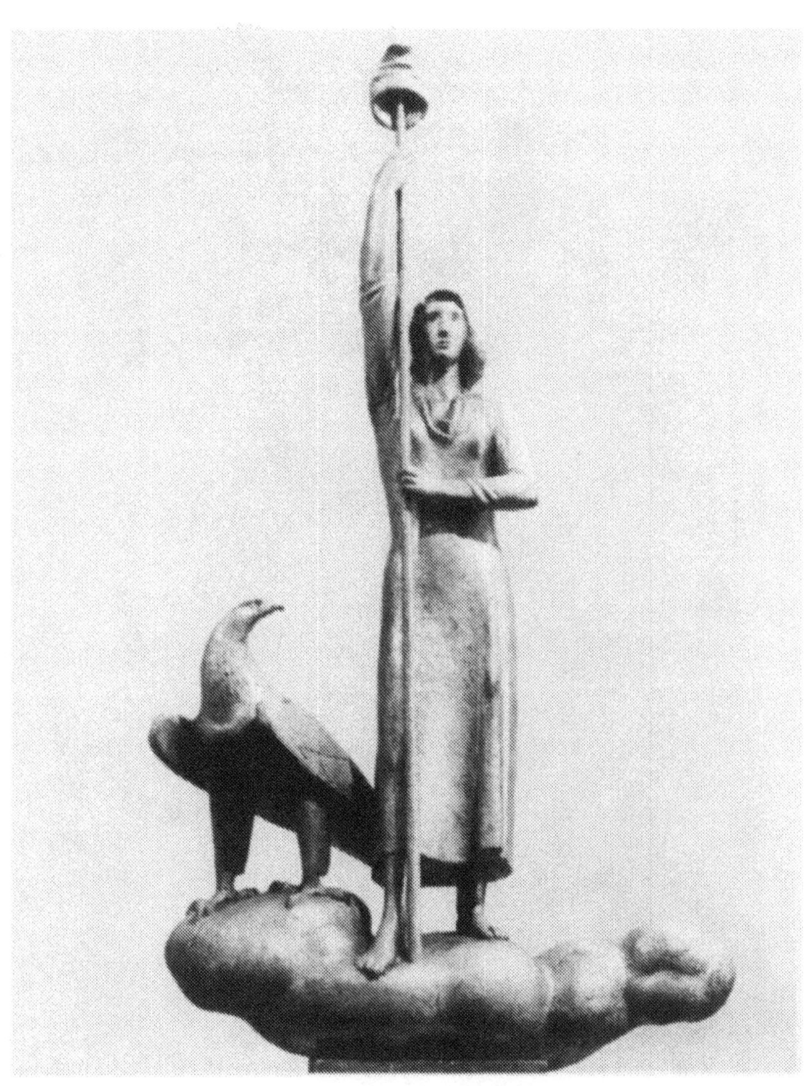

37. Henry Kreis's proposed model for the 1962 memorial.

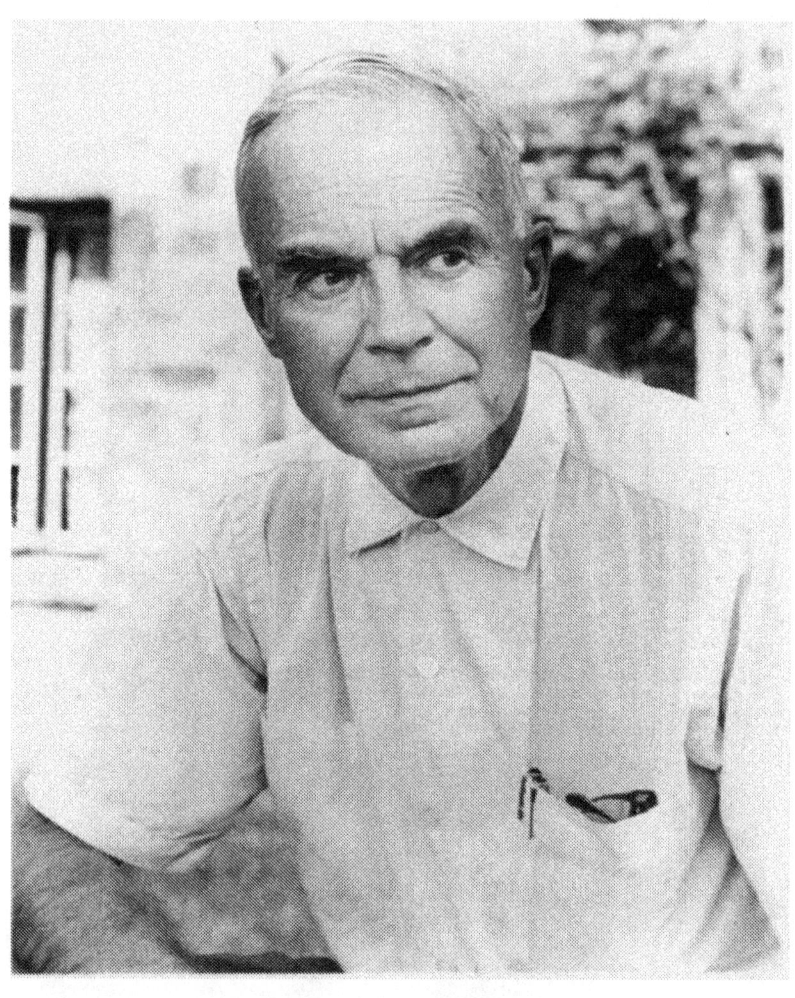

38. Walker Hancock, the sculptor chosen in 1962 to complete the Stone Mountain Confederate Memorial.

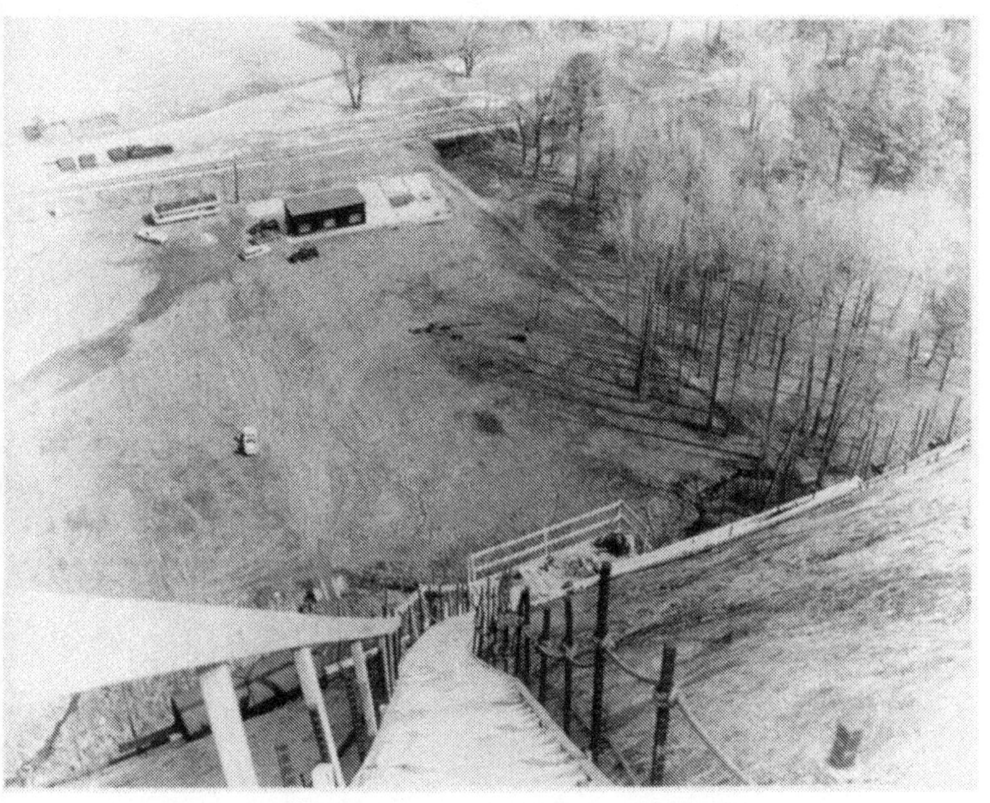

39. A dizzying view from above the carving site. The ground is four hundred feet below. Note the small building sitting on the concrete pad where Borglum's studio once sat. The models for the carving were kept here.

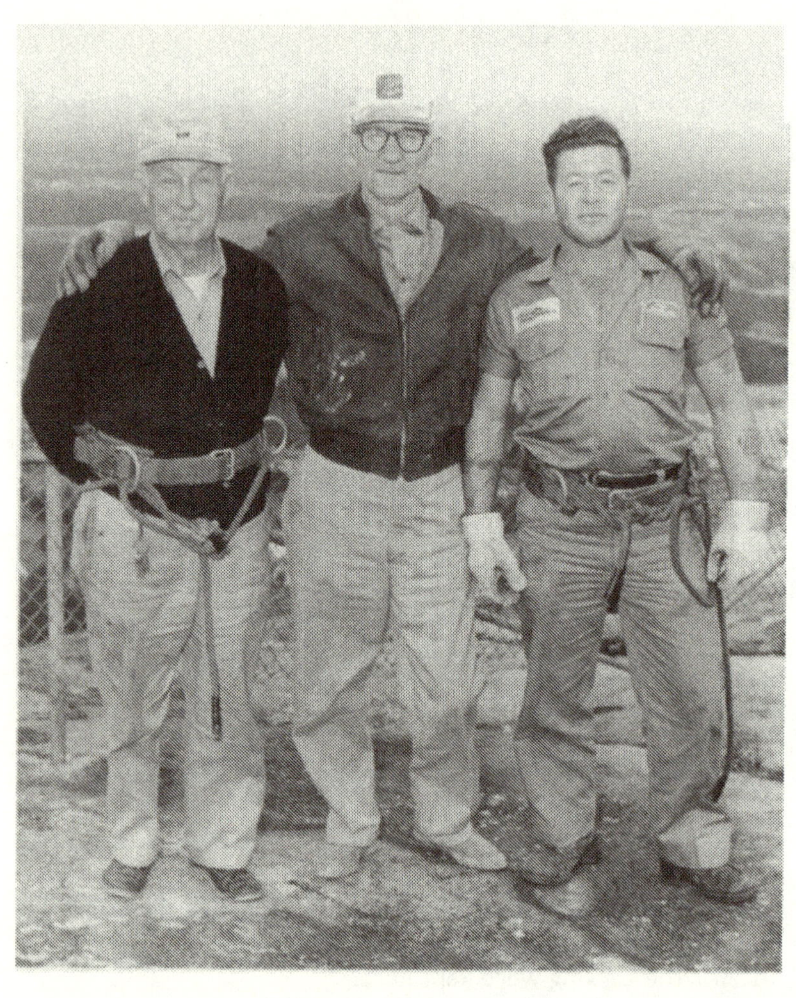

40. Members of the rigging crew. Left to right: Charlie Tucker, Howard "Bollweevil" Williams and Roy Faulkner.

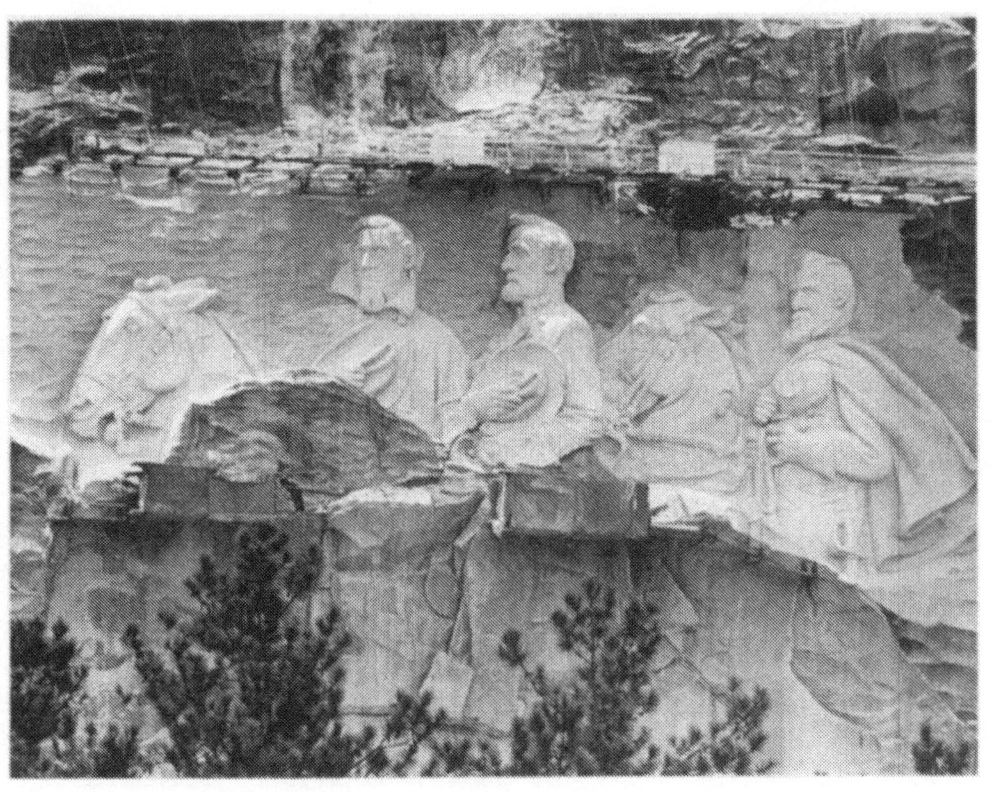

41. Progress on the carving as of 4 July 1966. Note the poorly carved head of Stonewall Jackson (right) and the first hat of Jefferson Davis (left). These features were later corrected.

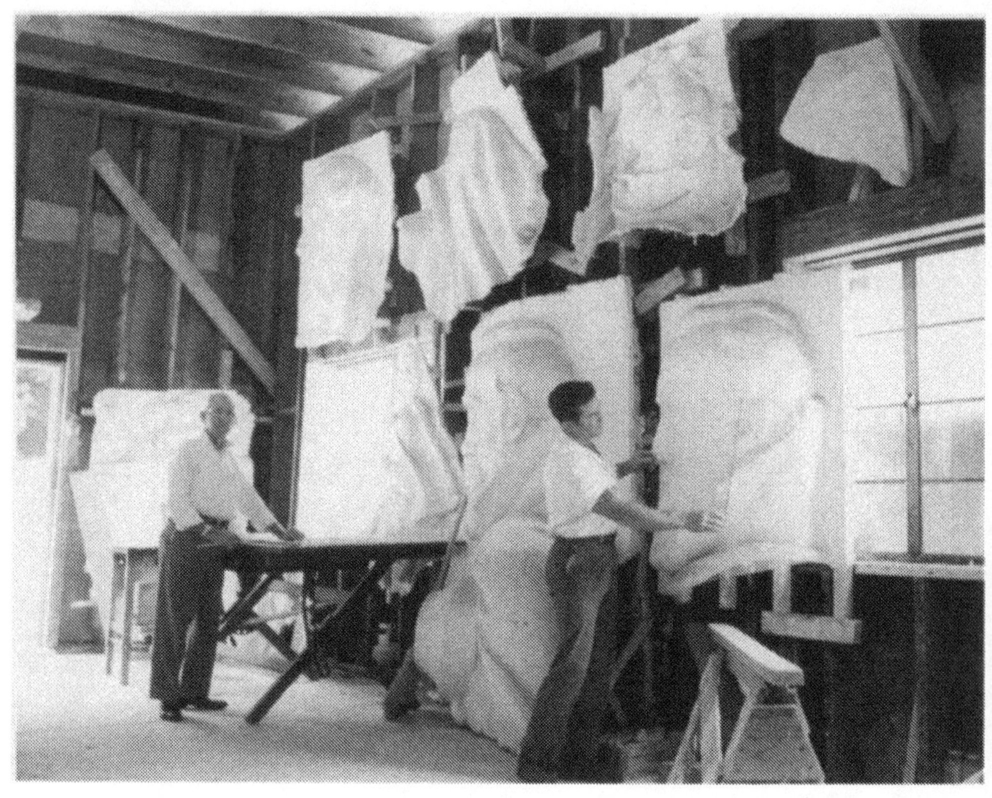

42. Superintendent of the carving George Weiblen and Roy Faulkner taking measurements from models of Stonewall Jackson's head.

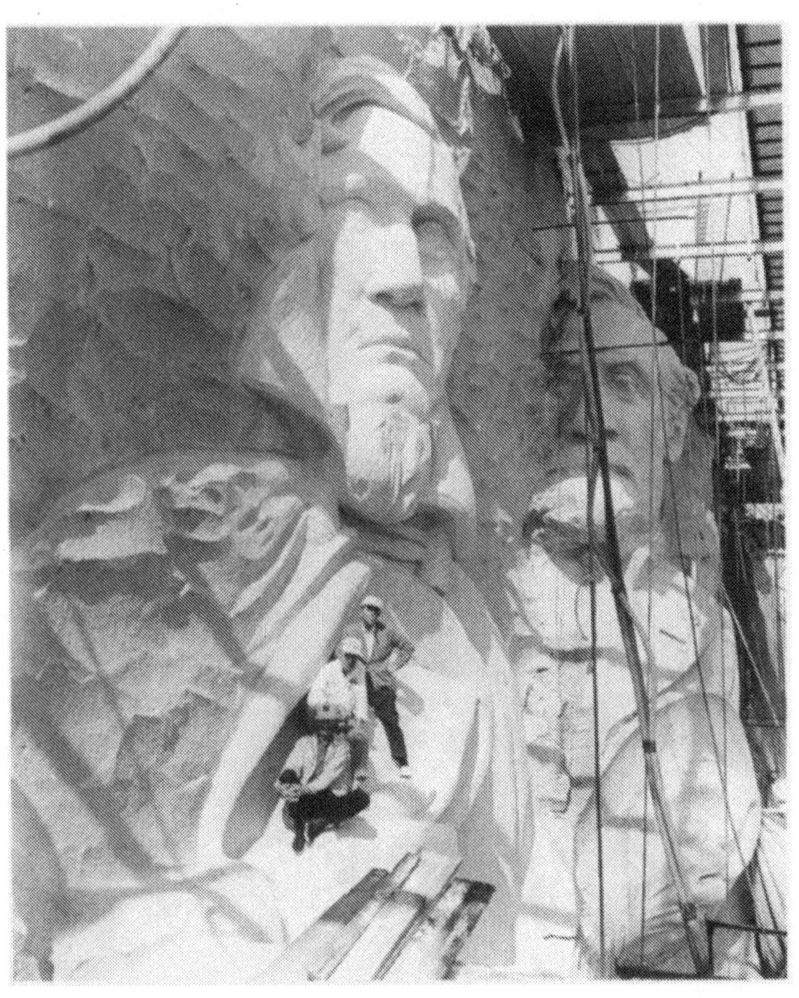

43. Bottom to top: Howard Williams, George Weiblen and Cohen "Dick" Ludwig standing on Davis' hat. Williams fell from the carving three months after this picture was taken.

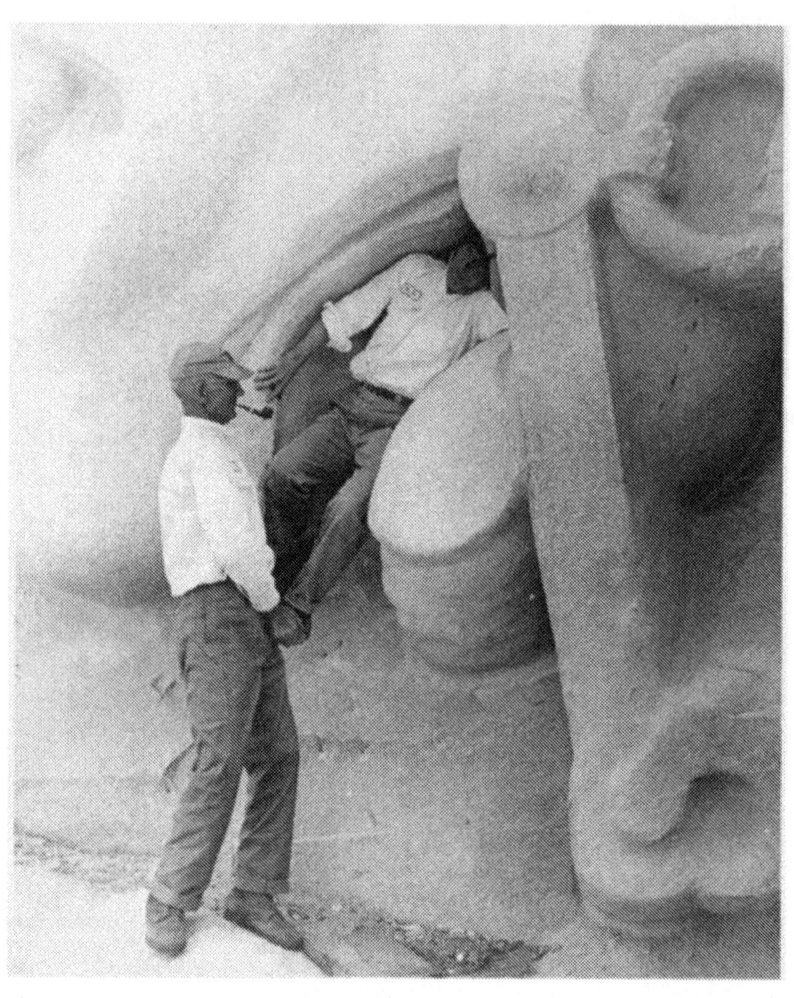

44. George Weiblen and Cohen Ludwig horse around in the mouth of Davis' horse Black Jack.

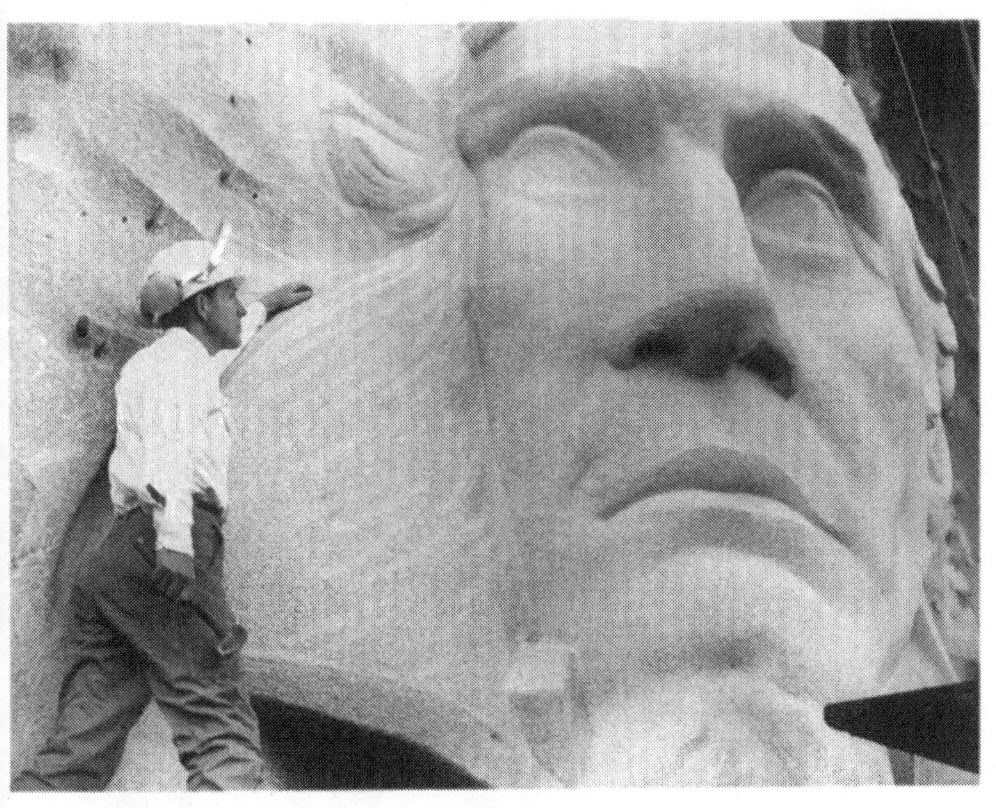

45. Ludwig stepping back to admire his work on the face of Jefferson Davis.

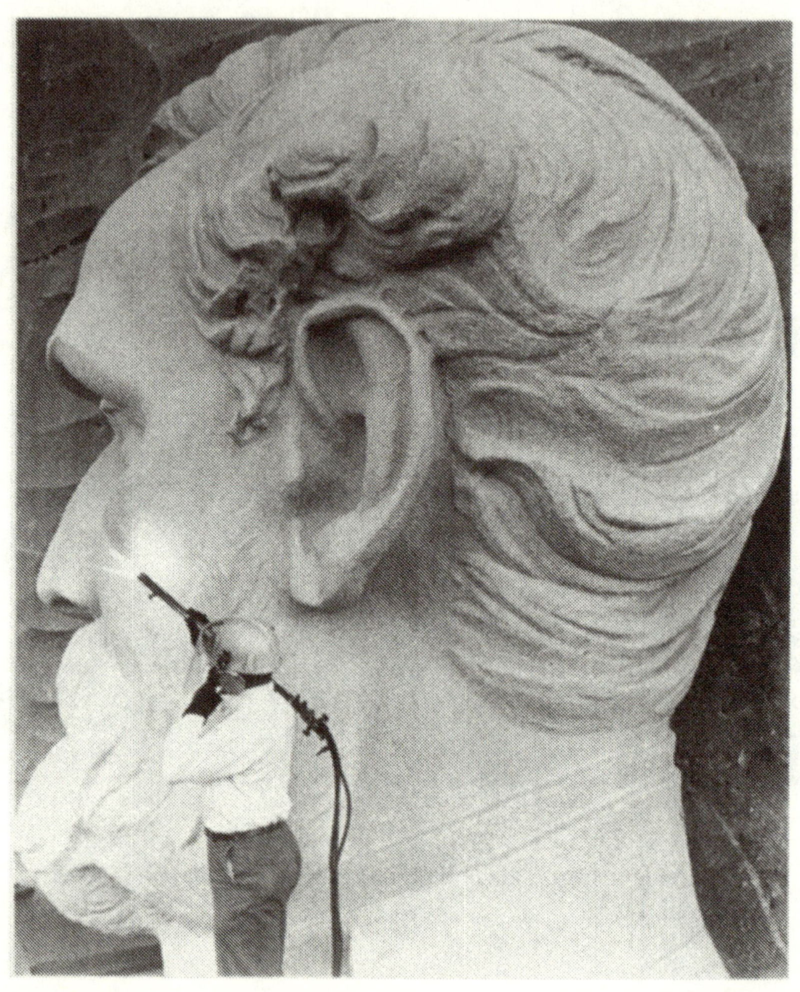

46. Roy Faulkner using a small thermo-jet torch to apply the finishing touches on the sixteen-foot high head of General Lee.

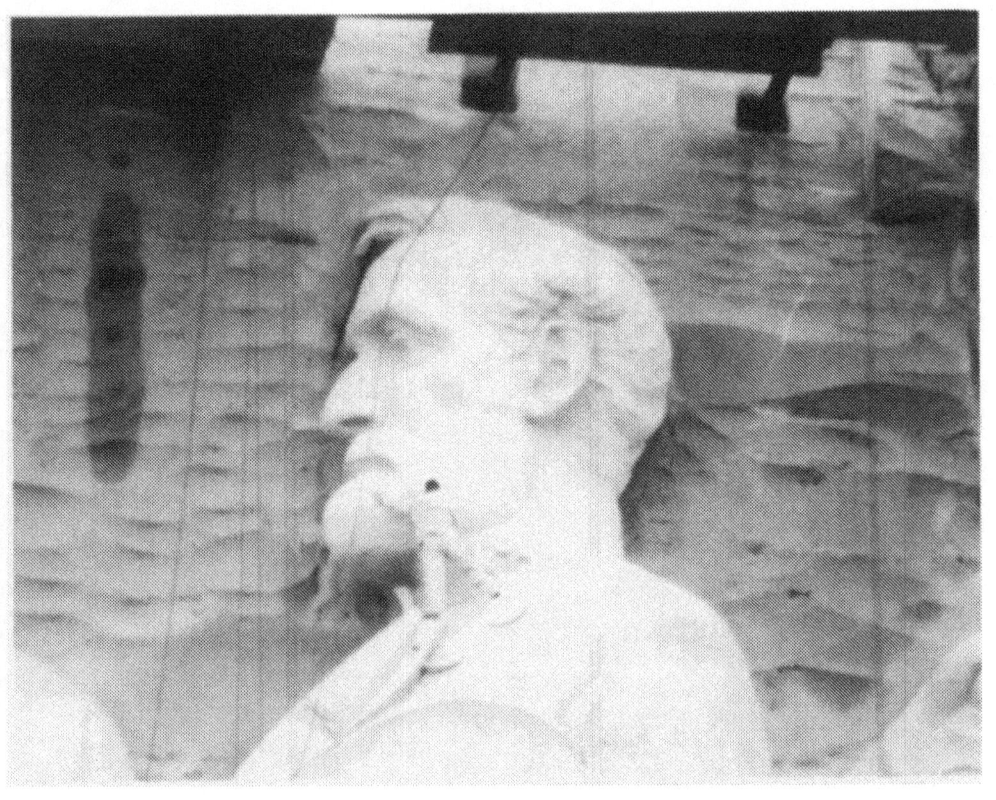

47. Roy Faulkner stands on a uniform button of Robert E. Lee to inspect the detail of the General's beard.

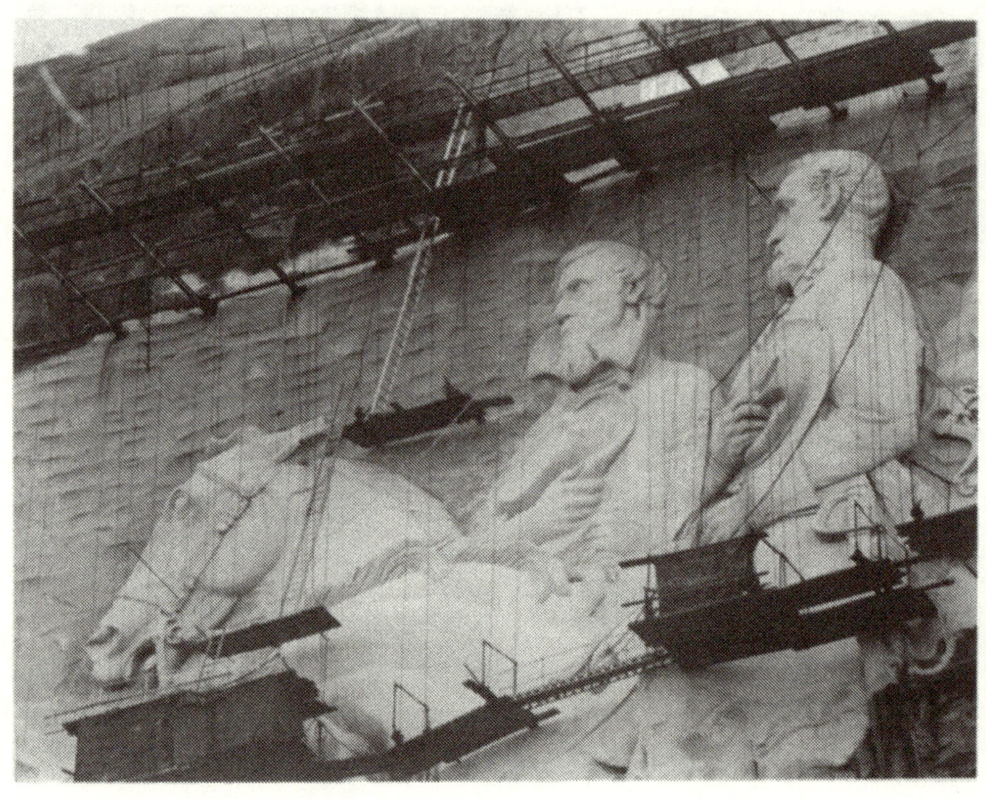

48. The recarved hat of Jefferson Davis shows where a plug has been placed to change the shape. Two dutchmen are also visible on Lee's forearm.

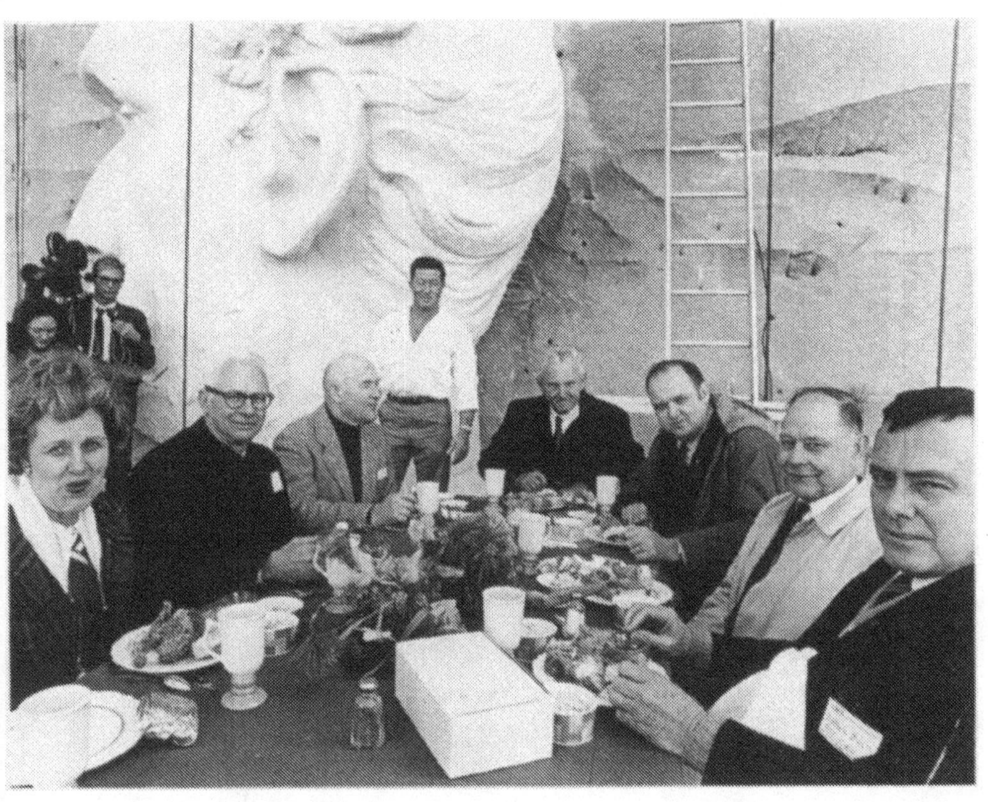

49. Luncheon on the mountain just before the 1970 dedication of the completed carving. Left to right: Mary Payne, Tom Elliott, William Kenny, Roy Faulkner, Ben Fortson, Tommy Irvine, Lane Mitchell and Arthur Bolton.

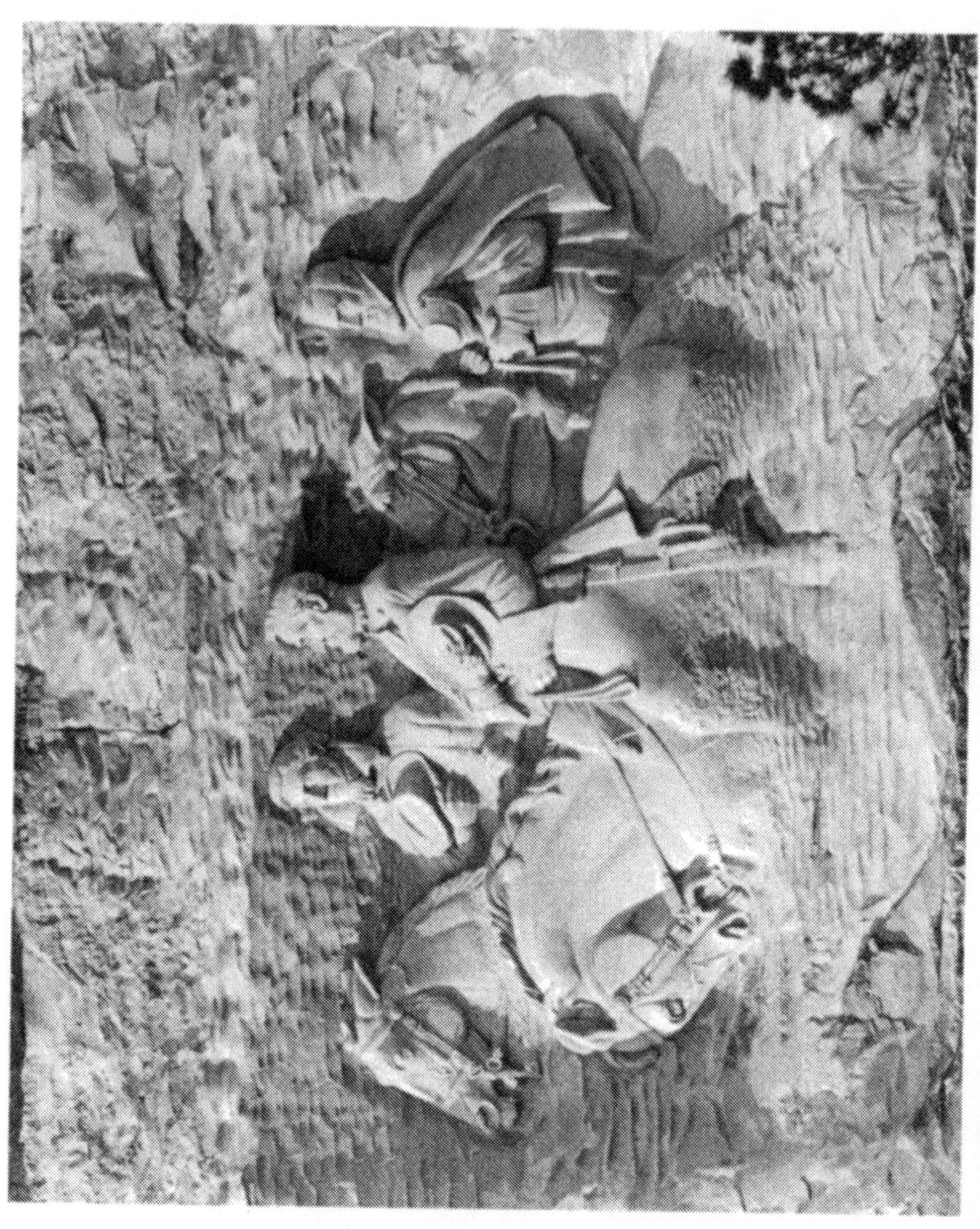

Chapter Seven

It Is Finished

Throughout the development of Stone Mountain Park, it was the Confederate memorial that most interested the public and stirred the strongest passions. Everyone, it seemed, had an opinion on how to complete the memorial. From various quarters during the years preceding the state acquisition, the public suggested many ideas, including adding Union soldiers to the carving. A few people held that General Grant and President Lincoln should be depicted shaking hands with Lee and Davis as a gesture of national unity. Most southern partisans, however, reacted to this suggestion with horror.

Just prior to World War II one faction promoted the construction of a Grecian temple modeled on the Parthenon on top of the Acropolis-like setting of the mountain, with forty-eight columns to represent the states at that time. Larger-than-life-size statues of American heroes could be housed inside the temple with a frieze depicting famous scenes from American history.

At least one person thought that the mountain should be a religious shrine and advocated erecting a hundred-foot high statue of Christ on the mountain's summit in imitation of the Statue of Christ overlooking Rio de Janeiro. To go the Brazilians one better, this person suggested that the statue be placed on a revolving pedestal, enabling it always to face the sun in its course across the sky.

An ambitious plan presented in the early 1950s called for a road up the mountain lined with statues depicting the growth of liberty. The first scenes near the base of the mountain would glorify key battles of the American Revolution. Farther along would come scenes from the Alamo, the Civil War, World Wars I and II, and the Korean War. The climax at the top of the mountain would be a gigantic display representing President Franklin D. Roosevelt's Four Freedoms: freedom of speech, freedom of worship, freedom from want, and freedom from fear.

Then, there was the proposal by an Atlanta architect to polish the granite dome like a giant billiard ball so that it would shine brightly in the

Georgia sun. The rationale behind this idea was never made clear, but it was probably made in jest.

A more sensible suggestion was to leave the carving as it was because it had attained so much fame as an unfinished work of art that it had the same status as Schubert's Unfinished Symphony. Besides, what would better symbolize the unfulfilled ambitions of the Confederacy than the Unfinished Memorial.

Julian Harris was selected in 1941 and again in 1949 as the sculptor to finish the Lukeman work, but those efforts came to naught. Mills B. Lane's attempt in 1956 reopened the question of who was to be the new sculptor. Harris expressed his continued interest in the project, but he was not alone. A Stone Mountain sculptor named Steffen Thomas also vied for the honor.

Thomas's idea was to carve the memorial on the ground in ten-foot square sections and then hoist these granite slabs up to the side of the mountain and secure them with aluminum rods over the unfinished Lukeman work. The panels would be flush with the side of the mountain, eliminating the recessed area and bring the sculpture forward for better natural lighting. Crushed rubble and cement would be used to fill in the void between the carved panels and the surface of the mountain. The design, nearly twice the size of Lukeman's, depicted a frontal view of Lee, Davis, Jackson and several other generals riding toward the viewer.

An alternative scheme was to cast the ten-foot sections in bronze and, like the Statue of Liberty, allow people behind the panels to look out through the eyes of the figures at the surrounding countryside. In either case, Thomas pointed out, bleachers could be erected along the sides of the work area in front of the mountain for spectators. He believed that thousands would willing pay a dollar or two for the opportunity to watch men sculpting the granite panels or making the molds for the bronze castings. In this way, the cost of the memorial would be met as the work progressed.

Mills Lane also received an offer from Lincoln Borglum, who had inherited his father's remade models when the latter died in 1941, to make these models available to the Memorial group. The younger Borglum suggested starting over in a different location as his father had recommended twenty years earlier. Lane, however, never got far enough on his effort to address the issue of a sculptor.

The question of how to complete the memorial arose again two years later. In May 1958, just two months after the creation of the Stone

Mountain Memorial Association, the board formed a special monument committee consisting of Mrs. L. H. Lyle, Price Gilbert, and Ben Fortson as chairman, to handle the memorial aspect of the park development. The committee invited Lamar Dodd, head of the Art Department of the University of Georgia, to discuss some of the problems confronting the committee regarding the completion of the memorial.

After surveying the unfinished carving, examining the Lukeman models and studying the relationship between the memorial and the park, Dodd suggested several possibilities: One was to place some symbolic structure on top of the mountain. Another was to develop a memorial area in front of the unfinished carving. Finally, there was also the option of finishing the carving, either as Lukeman intended or through one of the methods advocated by Harris or Thomas. It was soon evident that the entire problem called for extensive study and Dodd suggested that additional counsel be sought.

At the request of Fortson, Dodd enlisted the interest of several distinguished art authorities, including a sculptor, and invited them to meet in Atlanta for the purpose of serving as an advisory board to the committee. Aside from Dodd, who was selected as chairman, the advisory board included Lloyd Goodrich, Director of the Whitney Museum of American Art in New York; Henri Marceau, Director of the Philadelphia Museum of Art; Andrew C. Ritchie, Director of the Yale Art Gallery; John Walker, Director of the National Gallery of Art; and William Zorach, a sculptor from Brooklyn, New York. In addition, Dodd invited Vernon J. Hurst, a geologist with the state of Georgia and Edward A. Moulthrope, Chairman of the Georgia Art Commission, to participate in the discussions.

Over the next eighteen months the members of the monumental committee and advisory board reviewed all available materials regarding Stone Mountain, including geological studies. They asked hundreds of questions and made an intensive on-the-spot inspection of the mountain. On 12 April 1960, the advisory board met to discuss the possibilities and prepare its recommendations.

The members all agreed that the beauty and uniqueness of the mountain were of paramount importance; any plan would have to be made with the idea of complementing the great massif rather than competing with it. In the opinion of the board, the Borglum-Lukeman concept of a relief carving on the side of the mountain, while a noble one, was not practical because of the lack of direct sunlight necessary to make relief sculpture effective. The small scale of the carving compared to the vastness of the mountain, and the danger posed to any carving work by the exfoliation of loose rock argued against the concept. The board recommended to the monumental committee that a memorial area be constructed at the base of the mountain consisting of one or more pieces of free-standing sculpture with the possibility of a monument of some sort at the top of the mountain.[1]

The board proposed that a small group of sculptors be invited to submit designs to the committee and suggested the names of twenty-five sculptors for initial consideration. The board emphatically recommended that the utmost flexibility be allowed for the interpretation of the Confederate idea in order that the creative ability of the sculptors might not be hampered.

The selection of a sculptor quickly turned political as the Stone Mountain Memorial Association and monumental committee were besieged by different factions, each promoting a favorite sculptor. Julian Harris wrote to reaffirm his interest and many Atlantans voiced their support of his bid. Partisans of Steffen Thomas put him forward as the most able sculptor for the job.

Tommy Tucker, president of the Georgia Granite Company, petitioned repeatedly for the selection of sculptor Felix de Weldon of Washington, DC, creator of the Iwo Jima Monument. Tucker even claimed that he had secured backers who would bear the cost of the monument if De Weldon was chosen. His letters came so frequently that Scott Candler wrote back warning that this continued insistence about De Weldon was damaging any standing he might have had with the Association.[2]

De Weldon's concept differed little from Lukeman's--it featured Davis, Lee, and Jackson heroically posed on horseback--but the scale was much greater. The completed carving would have been 480 feet wide and 336 feet high, extending to within fifteen feet of the ground. His model, created on his own initiative with the hope of getting the Association's attention, was forty feet long and twenty-eight feet high with the figures riding toward the west instead of the east as with Lukeman's.

The sculptor invited each member of the Association to come to Washington, DC and see his model, but Lamar Dodd, believing that Tucker and De Weldon might create another Borglum-type situation, advised the

---

[1]Report to the Committee to Select a Design and Sculptor for the Confederate Memorial Carving on Stone Mountain. Files of the Stone Mountain Memorial Association.

[2]Scott Candler to Tommy Tucker, 28 October 1959. Files of the SMMA.

Association to keep its distance from the pair. He also warned that many of the sculptors contacted about the project were becoming concerned that the selection would become a political issue.[3]

While Dodd and the advisory board were pursued their course, some members of the Association suggested ideas of their own. Price Gilbert suggested removing what had been carved already, then carving a bust of Lee four times as large as the existing figure and cutting into the stone around the figure a Confederate battle flag to serve as a backdrop. This would fill up the recessed area gouged out by Lukeman. On top of the mountain he suggested crowning the summit with a bronze or wrought iron fence. Inside this area would be statues and monuments to individual Confederate leaders and states. Benches for visitors would bear the names and dates of important battles of the war. The flags of the states that had been Confederate would ring the summit. Matt McWhorter and Ben Fortson suggested carving most of the north face as a Confederate battle flag five hundred feet long with Lukeman's Lee taking the place of the center star.[4]

Aghast at these proposals, Lamar Dodd made his feelings known in a lengthy letter to the chairman of the monumental committee. He explained in no uncertain terms that such designs were technically impractical and aesthetically impossible. The McWhorter/Fortson idea was particularly criticized as in poor taste and contrary to the best available advice. Dodd further stated that since the committee had apparently decided to dispense with a dignified solution it should do something with a lighter touch that could make use of "luminous paints and a flickering mechanically operated arrangement of lights." Such a "carnival atmosphere" would undoubtedly receive public approval.[5]

He then implored the committee not to make such a horrible mistake and reminded them that future generations would be the judge of their actions. In a later letter Dodd informed the Association that the seeming lack of commitment to a single course of action was cause for concern among members of the advisory board. Fortunately, these alternate proposals were soon put aside.

As for selecting a sculptor to execute a memorial, the board advised against an open competition because it would not attract the best qualified

---

[3]Lamar Dodd to Ben Fortson, 9 May 1961, 30 March 1961. Files of the SMMA.

[4]Lamar Dodd to Ben Fortson, 27 January 1961. Files of SMMA.

[5]Ibid.

sculptors. The men with the stature and experience desired for the project could only be secured by means of direct invitation.

After much consideration of many different sculptors, taking into account their experience in working in large scale, their ages, and type of work executed, the advisory board selected eleven sculptors for the monumental committee to invite to Atlanta. Of the eleven, the following eight accepted the offer to view the mountain and submit a design:

Jose de Creeft, of Rye, New York
Walker Hancock, of Gloucester, Massachusetts
Donal Hord, of San Diego, California
Henry Kreis, of Essex, Connecticut
Bernard Reder, of New York City
Theodore Roszak, of New York City
Charles Umlauf, of Austin, Texas
Heinz Warneke, of Washington, DC

To these eight the name of Julian Harris was added to satisfy the demand that a local sculptor be given the opportunity to compete.

According to the recommendations of the board, these nine sculptors were asked to produce models of their proposed monuments at a scale of six inches to one hundred feet along with landscape architect's drawings of the area surrounding the memorial and an estimated cost of the project. Each sculptor would receive $10,000 as the fee for his services. The members of the advisory board agreed to Lamar Dodd's request that they serve a jurors to select the best model.

The sculptors were given until September 1962, to deliver their completed scale models to the monumental committee. Of the nine submissions, only Julian Harris took the traditional approach. He proposed finishing the existing carving in low relief, as he had advocated for over twenty years. The other sculptors submitted free-standing works, most of which were modernistic or abstract. These models seemed to represent the individual artist's views of war in general rather than capture the feeling of Southerners toward the Civil War in particular.

Four of the models were for statues in which the symbolism was fairly obvious. Walker Hancock's model was for a sixty-five foot high bronze statue of a man clad only in a breech cloth, his arms reaching to the heavens and a broken sword in his right hand. Henry Kreis proposed a woman standing on a cloud holding a spear with the tip covered by a

Freedom cap and an eagle standing beside her. This 18-foot figure of Liberty would stand on the hill facing the existing carving. Jose de Creeft's entry was a forty-foot-high figure of a mother and child in pink granite representing the suffering of war. Donal Hord's model featured a seated figure of Lee. Behind him along a wall were the current seals of the former Confederate states.

Heinze Warneke's model did not feature any sculpture. Instead it showed a scallop-shaped plaza, with a tile mosaic of three mighty oak trees representing Davis, Lee, and Jackson radiating out from the center of the plaza. Along three sides were the words "MAY VALOR LIVE FOREVER" in thirty-foot-high granite letters akin to a Confederate Stonehenge.

The remaining three entries were more unusual. The model submitted by Charles Umlauf showed an abstract eagle mounted on top of a curved pylon of black welded steel. Theodore Roszak's model was a bizarre-looking design called a solar ship perched on an island in a great circular pool. The ship also functioned as a giant sundial. Bernard Reder proposed five clusters of forty-six-foot-long polished steel shafts projecting in all directions like shell bursts. A powerful light in the center of the shafts would reflect from them. Critics claimed that the resemblance to a collection of lightning rods would call down the wrath of the gods on the memorial.[6]

While the advisory board was considering the models, a local television station, WAII-TV, Channel 11, showed photographs of the models during station identification time, with copy reading, "The Eyes of Atlanta are on a proposal for the Stone Mountain Monument." There were also many editorials in the Atlanta newspapers taking sides and exhorting the Association to make a particular choice, usually for Julian Harris. Few editorial remarks were kind to the other designs.

General Manager Scott Candler put the models on display in the building on top of the mountain and invited the public to express its opinion of the different treatments for the Confederate Memorial. Nine out of ten people cast ballots expressing a preference for the Harris model. Candler privately commented that the other models were ridiculous. As a partisan of Julian Harris since 1941, Candler probably intended to use the pressure of public opinion to influence the decision of the Association in Harris' favor. Lamar Dodd was greatly offended at what he perceived as inappro-

---

[6]Frank Veale, "'Light of the Confederacy' Shines at Stone Mountain, *Atlanta Journal and Constitution*, 21 October 1962.

priate and unfair publicity and the degeneration of an important task into a popularity contest among uninformed people.

Despite the large public outcry in favor of Harris, the advisory board finally decided in January 1963 to recommend the awarding of the contract to Walker Kirtland Hancock, even though his proposed design was turned down as submitted. When the Association announced its choice a month later, letters of protest poured into the office. Several of these were from members of the United Daughters of the Confederacy and one was from Hugh Gordon, grandson of General John B. Gordon. He felt that Hancock's proposed figure, though perhaps a fine piece of abstract art, was too generic and completely without any meaning to the descendants of Confederate veterans who wished to commemorate their fallen ancestors.[7]

Within a few weeks it was apparent to the Association that the public would not stand for a new memorial without the old one being finished first. Publicly the Association remained evasive about what it intended to do with the carving, but privately the monumental committee discussed with Hancock the possibility of his serving as artistic consultant to complete the Lukeman carving from the original models while working on his own design for a memorial area at the base of the mountain. Nothing could be decided for certain until a new geological survey of the carving site declared the rock to be sound for carving.

This was done in September 1963 by geologist Vernon J. Hurst, who pronounced the stone eminently suited to carving, even more suitable than Mount Rushmore. The carving, he explained, was inside the main exfoliation sheets and no part of it had been marred even on a small scale since the work stopped thirty-five years before and no significant changes would occur in the next 200 years. A skeptical newspaper columnist asked why he should believe the memorial would be finished in 200 years.

Hancock's absence from the country for extended periods and procrastination on the part of the Association delay the working out of an acceptable contract until the end of 1963. General Manager Harold Maddux warned the Association that it risked losing Hancock's services if he was to be kept in a stand-by situation for much longer. In a letter to Phil Campbell, the new Association Chairman, Dodd wrote that after all that he had been through in the previous four or five years with the Memorial Association,

---

[7]Hugh Gordon, Jr. to Phil Campbell, 5 March 1963. Files of the SMMA.

and knowing what he did, he personally would never sign a contract with the Association to do that job.[8]

Mills B. Lane became a member of the Association in July 1963, and the following month he invited both Walker Hancock and Lincoln Borglum to come down to Stone Mountain to discuss starting another, larger carving above the old one. The men met on September 5 to talk over the possibilities. Borglum was quite excited about the prospect of working on the Mountain and wrote to Lane: "I think we should go ahead and develop the model, as we talked of the other night. I will start on this next week . . . . You and I will have Stone Mountain as it could be, if we put it in our back yards."[9]

Walker Hancock, sensing a conflict of opinion within the Association, was cautious about taking sides. The issue was finally resolved at the Association meeting of 16 January 1964. At this meeting, the seven members of the Association had a final discussion on the contract with Walker Hancock. Lane opposed the contract because it required Hancock to complete the Lukeman figures, which he did not believe expressed the "true spirit" of the Confederacy. He stated for the record that the Association was making "a very, very serious mistake." It should have, he insisted, given consideration to the Borglum proposal that called for filling in the old carving site with concrete and in a fresh location carving the figures of the Stone Mountain half-dollar.[10] After Lane finished speaking, the Association approved the contract by a vote of six to one.

Chairman Phil Campbell forwarded the contract to Hancock the following week with a $2,000 signing bonus. The contract Hancock signed had two parts. For the first part, the completion of the Lukeman carving, he was to receive $10,000 as a consulting fee plus $200 per day for site visits and $100 per day for work done in his studio on new models, which eventually reached an amount in excess of $40,000. For the second part, the memorial plaza of his own design, he was to receive $25,000.

Controversy surrounded the Association's decision to have Hancock do what Julian Harris had proposed doing all along. Georgia Tech supporters in particular suspected that the long-standing rivalry between the University of Georgia and Georgia Tech had prejudiced Lamar Dodd against

---

[8]Lamar Dodd to Phil Campbell, 1 March 1963. Files of SMMA.

[9]Lincoln Borglum to Mills B. Lane, 12 September 1963. Files of the SMMA.

[10]Memo, Phil Campbell to Harold Maddux, 3 February 1964, regarding statements made at the Association meeting of 16 Janauary 1964. Files of the SMMA.

Harris, a member of the Tech faculty. The answer to this debate is found in some correspondence between Hancock and Harris.

In late 1964, Walker Hancock asked Julian Harris if he would consider being the continuing sculptor for the project to look after the progress of the work while the former was away. Harris politely refused, citing aesthetic convictions. He did not believe that the high relief and very detailed Lukeman design was desirable or practical. He insisted, as he had all along, that his low-relief, stylized version was the only solution. He wrote: "Without the privilege of simplifying and altering the design, I could not with good conscience participate in the execution of the work."[11] Harris' conviction was at odds with the desire of the Association, which was to have the carving finished in the same style as begun. The chosen sculptor, Walker Kirtland Hancock, was a native of St. Louis, Missouri, and was recognized internationally for his work. At the time of his selection he was the resident sculptor at the American Academy in Rome, which necessitated extensive travel between there and his studio in Gloucester, Massachusetts, where he had lived for the previous thirty years.

An unnamed Georgia reporter, apparently unaware of Missouri's status as a Confederate state, questioned Hancock's ancestral credentials for carving General Lee. Hancock responded that both of his grandfathers fought for the Confederacy, his father was a member of the Sons of Confederate Veterans, his mother was a member of the Daughters of the Confederacy, and he himself was a member of the Order of Stars and Bars. This answer seemed to satisfy those disapproving of a Yankee sculptor.

Hancock studied the problems posed by the carving and in the spring of 1963, announced his plan for completion. His goal was to "raise the carving above the level of purely literal illustration." This would be done by "shaping the roughed out areas in such a way that will appear to have been deliberately left in that state . . . to give the emphasis to essential features while avoiding a stark realism where it would be inappropriate."[12]

In simpler terms, he decided not to carve the horses legs, but would blend the carving into the rough background. This would eliminate a great deal of work that would only result in an uninteresting tangle of legs and would keep the focus of the carving on the faces of the men.

---

[11]Julian Harris to Walker Hancock, 28 November 1964. Harris Collection, Special Collections Department, Price Gilbert Library, Georgia Institute of Technology, Atlanta.

[12]Ted Simmons, "Sculptor Reveals Plans for Mountain," *Atlanta Constitution*, 8 March 1963.

According to Scott Candler, this was actually first suggested by Eugene Wyatt of Decatur. In January 1963 Wyatt showed the Association a sketch illustrating how the carving might be completed by using a cloud effect to obscure the horses' legs and to give the figures an ethereal appearance. This was more than two months before Hancock's announcement.

When the Association advertised for a contractor to do the carving work it received just two responses: one from the Georgia Marble Company and the other from George Weiblen, who had been the superintendent of the carving thirty-five years earlier. Weiblen's interest in the job was personal rather than economic, therefore his bid of $600,000 was substantially lower that the other. The Association considered his prior experience an added advantage and awarded him the contract.

Weiblen received authorization in September, 1963, to proceed with the preliminary work. He secured the assistance of Elias Nour to inspect the carving area, bringing him back to the mountain from Florida for the first time since his falling out with the General Manager eighteen months earlier. The men found the steel beams to be in good condition, but the steel cables needed to be replaced, as did nearly all of the wood in the stairs, platforms, and scaffolding.

Nour returned to Florida after the initial survey and Weiblen began mapping out plans for the job ahead and lining up his workers. By January 1964 he had a crew of four men--James DuPree, Roy Faulkner, Charlie Tucker, and Howard "Bollweevil" Williams. Tucker had worked on the carving under Borglum, but was not related to Jesse Tucker. Later, Weiblen added Willie Watson, his son Ricky, and master carver Joseph Canales to the team.

The rigging crew spent the first eight months of 1964 putting the work area in order. This first required rebuilding the more than 600 wooden steps down from the top of the mountain and clearing off a great deal of loose rock from around the area. George Weiblen looked into having a 400-foot-high elevator installed on the side of the mountain. Bids for specially made elevators were too high, so he ordered a prefabricated one and the rigging crew put it up in 28 days.

Assembling the elevator, like so much of the work on the carving, was equal parts skill, ingenuity, and nerve. The elevator shaft was built by stacking one section on top of another, and as it rose straight up it got farther and farther away from the sloping face of the mountain. Roy Faulkner, the foreman of the work crew, had to swing out on a rope Tarzan-style from the elevator shaft to the mountain's surface to anchor the support beams. By the time the shaft was at its full height, the gap between it and the mountain was more than thirty feet. At the time, it was regarded as the world's highest outside elevator.

The elevator made getting to the carving platform much easier, quicker, and safer than using the steps. The next phase was to bring up the metal catwalks, ladders, lumber, cables, winches, hoists, and other equipment to assemble the scaffolding. To aid in this task, the crew used a truck--with a long cable attached to the back and running to a block up on the mountain--to hoist materials to the carving site.

The twenty-one steel beams embedded in the mountain supported the main platform. Suspended from the beams was the scaffolding from which the men worked on the carving. These could be raised and lowered as needed and arranged in any order necessary. At one end of the main platform the men built a shack to serve as a tool shed and lunchroom. Their little cabin was complete with running water, a refrigerator, a hot plate, and a heater.

Advances in technology in the previous four decades promised to make the carving job much easier this time around. The Jet Age brought with it the thermo-jet torch, a tool developed for use in the granite quarries that would revolutionize mountain carving. Described as a miniature jet engine, the torch consisted of an eight-foot long tube with a jet nozzle, fed by three hoses carrying oxygen, kerosene, and water, to cool the nozzle. The kerosene and oxygen mixture could produce a flame as hot as 4,000 degrees Fahrenheit.

When such intense heat strikes the rock, moisture within the granite suddenly converts into steam causing flakes the size of dinner plates and a half-inch thick to explode from the surface of the mountain in a continuous stream. Holding a lit torch was compared to firing an automatic shotgun; the operator had to keep himself braced against the backward thrust of the flames. There was also a smaller version for fine work. The flame could be adjusted as thin as that of an acetylene torch and could cut along a pencil line.

The carvers experimented with the torches on what remained of Borglum's old work. They found that the big torch could remove as much stone in a day as twenty men could do in a week with pneumatic drills and wedges. They also learned that carving was a one-person job. Two workers in the same area would pelt each other with hot rocks. The flakes exploded in all directions and ricocheted off the mountain and scaffolding so that even alone one could expect to be peppered with shards. For protection, the operator wore a clear plastic shield over his face, and ear-muffs, similar to those worn by airport ground crews. This was to insulate his ears from the roar of the torch, which could be heard across the north end of the park.

The jet flame had a vitrifying effect on the surface of the exposed stone, leaving a grayish, glassy appearance. This was removed by going over it lightly with a pneumatic bumper, a vibrating tool with a four-point tip, in order to restore the whiteness of the fresh granite.

Work on the Confederate Memorial officially resumed on 11 July 1964. On hand for the occasion was Mrs. Hiller Gammage, President of the Georgia Division UDC, who with Helen Plane in mind described the event as "the final step toward the realization of a woman's dream."[13] Governor Carl Sanders gave the keynote speech at the ceremony, and on his signal--the waving of a Confederate flag--George Weiblen and his crew lit the thermo-jet torches and went to work. They estimated that working eight to ten hours a day, six days a week, the carving could be finished in three years, but in actuality it required six years due to unforeseen complications in the process.

One of the first necessary tasks was to sandblast clean the lichen-stained figures of Lee and Davis so as to convey to the public a sense of immediate progress and to make them match the freshly-carved areas. The next priority was carving the head of Stonewall Jackson. The carvers continued working from Lukeman's one-twelfth master model, with one-quarter size enlargements of crucial and highly detailed areas.[14]

Although the tools for removing stone were new, the method of determining where to cut was the same as before, namely by measuring. In starting a feature, the workers measured the distance from a center line on the master model and distances from other established points. Extrapolating inch measurements on the model to foot measurements on the mountain, the distances were remeasured from the corresponding points on the carving. When all the measurements came out at the same spot, the men painted a black X there. When all the key points were marked they were connected by a dotted line to outline the feature. A hole was drilled at each key point to the depth required for the relief being created.

---

[13]As quoted in Morris Shelton, *Georgia's Piece of the Rock* (n.p., 1981), 34.

[14]For using the Lukeman models, the Association had to pay Willie Hill Venable an extra $15,000 per the sales agreement for his studio property and inventory.

After verifying all the measurements for the feature and all the depth holes were drilled, the carver used the large torch to cut down to within a half-inch of the bottom of the holes. He then switched to the small torch to cut the rest of the way.

Carvers roughed out Stonewall Jackson's head by the end of September and completed two months later. A tarpaulin spread across the scaffolding sheltered the workers from the autumn winds, and blocked the public's view of the work. The public got its first view of the carving when, without any formal unveiling ceremony as in the 1920s, the canvas was taken down on Saturday, 28 November.

There was a problem with the carving, however. The nose as carved looked more like that of comedian Jimmy Durante that of General Jackson. Distortions in the beard, collar, and other parts of the bust also created difficulties. Part of the problem was that Lukeman's model was a poor likeness, but Joseph Canales had also been at fault. Although a talented carver, he was unable to visualize such huge figures at close range and had not been able to see when the work went awry. Fortunately the errors were correctable. Nevertheless, to avoid future problems, Weiblen dismissed Canales in January 1965 and began looking for a replacement.

The work continued on Jackson's torso and the head of his horse, albeit at a slower rate. Much of the torch work was done by Roy Faulkner, a 31-year-old Marine veteran and welder from Covington, Georgia, who discovered that he had a talent for using the torch. Initially assigned to simple tasks, he soon took on a greater share of the carving work while Weiblen looked for a new head carver.

In September 1965 Weiblen hired Cohen "Dick" Ludwig, a stone carver from Faith, North Carolina. He began working on the head and torso of Jefferson Davis and the head of Davis' horse, a task that took over a year to complete. Hancock was very pleased with his work, but Ludwig, a victim of acrophobia, had difficulty adjusting to the heights. Able to work on a platform, he could not manage to work on the ladders, which slowed the pace of the work. Eventually Ludwig's phobia led him to resign in November 1966.

Ludwig's anxiety was exacerbated by a tragic accident that befell a member of the rigging crew on 1 August 1966. Charlie Tucker and Howard Williams were adjusting the height of their scaffold when one of the boards on which the latter was standing slipped out of place. In his fatal fall, Williams struck the top of Stonewall Jackson's head and then tumbled nearly 400 feet to the pile of rubble at the base of the mountain.

This tragedy deeply affected all the workers and all but George Weiblen and Roy Faulkner quit. A new crew, consisting of Carlos Powell, Nelson Wilborn, and Wayne Hall, had to be hired before the work could continue.

On another occasion, Roy Faulkner nearly perished in a fall from the carving while working on Jackson's horse. While he walked across a scaffold a plank that had not been nailed down slipped out of place, causing him to fall some thirty feet. Miraculously he managed to catch his fall by grabbing the torch hoses. Pulling himself back up to the scaffold, Faulkner made the negligent worker regret the oversight.

Walker Hancock was only able to come inspect the carving about two or three times a year, though he discussed problems with George Weiblen and his crew by mail and telephone on a regular basis. Weiblen, of course, submitted monthly progress reports and photographs of the work to Hancock, but the sculptor still felt the need for more regular inspections. In the fall of 1965 Hancock asked the Association to hire Charles Rudy, of York, Pennsylvania, as the continuing sculptor for the carving. Rudy was more readily available to make visits to the mountain and recommend a course of action based on his direct observations. On one occasion he authorized shortening the ears of Davis' horse so that it would not appear that he was riding a mule, but for the most part his trips only confirmed that the work was progressing well. As the continuing sculptor, Rudy would have taken over as sculptor for the project in the event of Hancock's death.

In his Gloucester studio, Hancock worked on duplicates of the Lukeman models to make corrections. He would then have a one-quarter size model made of the revised detail and send it down to Stone Mountain. One of the errors found in the Lukeman models was that all the harness buckles on the horses were backward, so that a hard pull on the reins would have caused the bridles to come apart. Hancock corrected this mistake on his new models. Then there were such matters as eliminating the billowing expanse of Davis' cape, which was so long that had he stood up it would have dragged the ground, and lowering the profile of Traveler's head and neck to give the neck a more natural curve. By doing this, Hancock exposed more of Davis and his horse, making it necessary to create a new model of this area to fill in the missing parts that would now be visible. Hancock also remodeled Jackson's head so that it looked more like the general than did Lukeman's rendition.

Hancock discerned a more serious flaw in Lee's head--which turned to be some ten percent larger than appropriate for his body. His arm was also three feet too short of normal proportions. Hancock studied these problems for several months before finally deciding to build up Lee's chest and lengthen his arm by adding granite "dutchmen." This process, called patching, became one of the greatest challenges of the whole carving.

To accomplish this, workers cut a roughly shaped block of granite from the side of the mountain near where the dutchman was to be installed. They then built a track with railroad rails running from where the block was to where it needed to go. With this in place they broke the block free from the mountain (called plugging), guided it carefully down the track, and slid it into a socket cut to receive it. The dutchman was secured in place with a mortar-like substance called Porok and five-foot-long pins of case-hardened steel. Then workers carved it in accordance with the revised models to blend with the rest of the figure.

The dutchman for Lee's chest was installed first in September 1966, and weighed four and a half tons. Two smaller blocks of stone were added to Lee's elbow and forearm the following May. This job was even trickier than the first because the dutchmen had to be installed under a projecting ledge so that gravity was working against rather than for them. Hancock informed the Association that Roy Faulkner was to be especially congratulated for his skill in handling the difficult and dangerous job, and he predicted they were now over the highest hurdles. Hancock also wrote to Weiblen's crew that they not be discouraged by such difficulties, even if there seemed to have been wasted effort. He informed them:

> A great deal is being said about the vastness of this carving -- as if that were the amazing thing about it. Few will realize that the real achievement will be to bring a creditable result out of the really unparalleled situation that was left us nearly forty years ago.[15]

Additional dutchmen were later added to Traveler's head, to Jackson's beard and collar, and to Davis's hat.

The patching sparked rumors of plastering to cover a botched carving job. *Atlanta Journal* reporter Morris Shelton got permission to go up on the mountain to investigate these accusations. The carving crew candidly explained the patching technique and told him why it was necessary. Shelton published his findings and put an end to the unfounded stories.

---

[15]Walker Hancock to George Weiblen, 19 August 1966. Files of the SMMA.

Cohen Ludwig was no longer working when the first dutchman was put in place, but he returned in time to see Faulkner install the second one. Ludwig recarved the head of Jackson according to Hancock's new model, putting the nose in proper shape and reworking the hairline so that it did not cast distorting shadows. He also worked on the head of Davis's horse. Ludwig remained on the job until September 1967, when again he left.

George Weiblen enticed him to come back in early 1968, but in April of that year he quit for the third and final time. He wanted very much to finish, but he could not overcome his instinctive fear of heights. He did leave behind, however, some magnificent work. In an interview with *Southern Living* magazine, Weiblen referred to Ludwig as a genius and credited him with salvaging the head of Jackson.

After Ludwig left for the last time, most of the carving work fell to Roy Faulkner. Hancock initially expressed some trepidation at Faulkner's obvious ambition for a greater role in the carving. He was concerned that Faulkner might attempt to be innovative and work himself into a situation beyond his skill level. The sculptor expressed his opinion to the memorial committee that Faulkner would be able to complete some details if given "frequent and precise criticism," but the practicality of continuing the project without an experienced carver was "still an open question."[16]

Still viewed as a beginner by Hancock, Faulkner had nonetheless developed a respectable degree of proficiency and he was extremely careful in making the measurements. He eventually gained Hancock's full confidence, leading George Weiblen to name Faulkner as the new chief carver.

Faulkner once related that after completing the measurements he could sometimes look at the stone and envision the feature he was about to carve. Then as he was working he would get the feeling that was the wrong shape or the wrong size or in the wrong place. There was no place on the scaffold to step back for a better view, so he endured the nagging doubt until he came down in the evening and could see it in the proper perspective. It was always a relief to see that everything was as it should be.[17]

With only one carver and two assistants, work from 1968 to 1970 continued at a slower but steady rate. From time to time project leaders discussed hiring a second carver, but never took any action on this matter. Some of the work during these last years included recarving Jackson's arm to lower the relief, removing an awkward ear from Little Sorrel (Jackson's

---

[16]Walker Hancock to Ben Fortson, 19 February 1969. Files of the SMMA.
[17]Neal, 13.

horse), carving the lower portion of Lee and, of course, carving Traveler. Lowering the horse's neck and head required adding another dutchman to fill in the jaw. There were also a dozen refinements and corrections to make, such as lowering the relief of Jackson's sword, horses' reins and other details, and softening some of the outlines.

Faulkner's greatest challenge was the recarving of Jefferson Davis's hat during the latter part of 1968. This alteration came about when Hancock was musing over how to relieve the sameness of the hats and hands of Davis and Lee. Critics had pointed out that Davis, as President of the Confederacy, should have a civilian hat, not a military one as depicted by Lukeman. The sculptor decided to solve his problem by using this suggestion. He remodeled the hat, removing some parts and building up others to achieve the desired headgear. This major task, universally regarded as the most painstaking part of the project, took many weeks to accomplish and required the addition of another large dutchman.

The problem of blending the carving into the rock background was a vexing one since the transition from rough to finished surfaces had to appear gradual and authentic. Hancock explained his desired effect to Faulkner, who experimented with different techniques until he learned how to make the feathered cuts to fade the figures away.

Faulkner and his crew stayed on the job year-round regardless of the weather. Keeping one's footing on the scaffolding while facing a driving rain or forty-mile-an-hour winds was not a task for the timid. Canvas tarpaulins could sometimes offer a little protection from the elements, but not always. In the case of thunderstorms, the men took refuge in the shack until the storm passed. According to Faulkner, the wind was their worst enemy because it could change direction with no warning, but he estimated the they lost no more than forty days during eight-and-a-half years due to bad weather. In interviews with the press, Faulkner expressed a closeness with the three men whose likenesses he had worked on for so long and a heightened appreciation for nature. Quite naturally, he also regarded his work on the largest piece of sculpture in the world with great pride. "You could hardly," he proclaimed, "do anything more satisfying than that."[18]

George Weiblen retired from the mountain in March 1969, much to the relief of his wife, Sara. He remained a consultant for the project and gave his opinion from time to time. Of the work drawing to a close he said that he would miss it because it was part of his life for so long, but took

---

[18]Willard Neal, "Men On the Mountain," *Atlanta Constitution Magazine*, 9 May 1970, 42.

comfort in imagining that people a thousand years in the future would still be coming to look up at the carving.[19]

The carving was eventually completed in the spring of 1970. Prior to the dedication, the Stone Mountain Memorial Association hosted what newspapers dubbed the "luncheon in the sky" for officials of the Association and members of the press. Nearly seventy people braved the heights on March 23 to partake of a fried chicken dinner in imitation of the 1924 luncheon orchestrated by Gutzon Borglum. Participants in the aerial repast on that chilly, blustery day included Commissioner of Agriculture and Chairman of the Association Tommy Irvine, Attorney General Arthur K. Bolton, Secretary of State Ben Fortson, and Association member Lane Mitchell. Seated with members of the governing body were some of the top officials at the park: General Manager Tom Elliott (who replaced Harold Maddux in 1968), Assistant General Manager William Kenney, and Executive Assistant Mary Payne.

More than a few of the reporters experienced some apprehensions at the prospect of ascending to the carving, but the sight of Ben Fortson confidently negotiating his wheelchair around the scaffolding shamed them into boarding the elevator for the trip up. Roy Faulkner told them to speak up if they felt at all uncomfortable and he would gladly take them back down. One of the reporters noted that two guests took him up on his offer right away, and another had flatly refused beforehand to get into the elevator. No one faulted them, as the other television, radio, and newspaper reporters performed their assignment with the utmost caution.[20]

Atlanta Journal columnist Hugh Park revealed that the ones who lost their nerve were men. The women, he wrote, "were going to stay there and eat that chicken if it killed them so they could tell their grandchildren about it."[21] Actually, only Association and park officials got fried chicken. Everyone else got sweet rolls and coffee.

The banquet was viewed as both a historical reenactment and a tribute to the originators of the Confederate Memorial undertaking. Each participant received as a personalized bronze-plated carving wedge like those used in the early attempt. Shortly afterward, most of the scaffolding came down to give an unobstructed view of the carving for the dedication.

---

[19] John Logue, "The Old Man And the Mountain," *Southern Living*, May 1970.
[20] Shelton, 20.
[21] Hugh Park, "Chickened Out On the Mountain," *Atlanta Journal*, 24 March 1970.

General Manager Elliott scheduled the dedication ceremony for 9 May 1970. The Reverend Billy Graham agreed to give the invocation, and Georgia Senator Herman Talmadge secured President Richard M. Nixon as the keynote speaker. Three days before the dedication date Elliott received word that Graham would be unable to attend due to illness. Then President Nixon backed out citing matters of state revolving around the war in Southeast Asia. In his stead, the President offered to send Vice-President Spiro T. Agnew.

Many spectators were unhappy with this last minute substitution, as Agnew was at that time under a cloud amid charges of income tax evasion and taking bribes during his tenure as governor of Maryland. Also, the selection of the Reverend William Holmes Borders, the well-known black pastor of Atlanta's Wheat Street Baptist Church, to fill in for Billy Graham angered the Ku Klux Klan and Imperial Wizard James R. Venable boycotted the ceremonies.

On the day of the event organizers anticipating a crowd of 100,000 were disappointed when only 10,000 spectators and special guests gathered on the lawn in front of the carving. Admission to the park was free for the day and free shuttle service was provided from the Stone Mountain Industrial Park to ease traffic congestion. The 50,000 expected to ride the shuttles, however, turned out to be 4,067. Likewise, the Wishbone Chicken Company sold only 2,000 of 10,000 boxes of fried chicken prepared for the event.

One of the invited guests, Jesse Tucker, Borglum's superintendent of the carving who had retired to Florida, predicted that because of the great heat applied to it, the rock would eventually crack, causing the carving to fall off. Tucker declined to attend due to poor health.

Music for the two-hour ceremony was provided by the Decatur Civic Chorus, the Third Army Band from Fort McPherson, and the Stone Mountain Park carillon played by Herbie Koch. The audience heard short speeches from U. S. Representative Ben Blackburn, Herman Talmadge, and Governor Lester Maddox prior to the main dedication address by Vice-President Spiro Agnew. The theme for the event was "Unity Through Sacrifice" and all the remarks focused on this ideal.

Governor Maddox, in presenting the carving to the rest of the nation on behalf of the people of Georgia, called the carving an enduring expression of pride in the South's heritage and its contributions to the nation.

Though the Civil War was over, he proclaimed, the lessons learned from it will remain as long as there is a written history.[22]

The Vice President eulogized the three men depicted in the carving--Lee, Davis and Jackson--who "were bonded together in war, and now are bonded together for the ages on a great mountain of granite." In paying tribute, Agnew said Jackson's life exemplified loyalty, that Davis illustrated dignity, and that Lee set the highest example of honor. He called these three principles "the bedrock of idealism that underlies our hopes for future generations."

Turning to what must be done to achieve these principles, Agnew stated that Americans must "overcome the new slavery"--the willingness to become slaves of passions and ideologies, and the evils of sectionalism. He warned that "just as the South cannot afford to discriminate against any of its own people, the rest of the nation cannot afford to discriminate against the South." This statement brought the only sustained applause of his speech.

The Vice President made reference to Lee urging his fellow Southerners after the war to make their sons Americans, and then spoke of the "young men of the South and young men of the North . . . fighting side by side in Vietnam." He closed his speech by alluding to the protests across the country of President Nixon's Cambodia policy, reminding the audience "that we have paid too great a price for being one nation to let ourselves now come apart at the seams."[23]

In conjunction with the dedication, the Association commissioned the making of a commemorative medal in bronze and silver. Designed by New Jersey sculptor Abram Belskie, and struck by the Medallic Art Company of New York, the medal pictured the three figures as carved. The reverse side showed crossed Confederate and United States flags against a silhouette of the mountain and circled by a wreath of wheat straw to symbolize peace. These medals went on sale at the Park.

The medal was not the only commemorative item, however. Gutzon Borglum had said in 1915 that a small carving would look like "a postage

---

[22]Text of remarks prepared for delivery by Governor Lester Maddox during the Stone Mountain Carving Dedication Ceremony, 9 May 1970. Files of the SMMA.

[23]Address by the Vice President of the United States at the Dedication of the Stone Mountain Confederate Memorial, 9 may 1970. Files of the SMMA. Agnew's speech was 1,150 words long and lasted fifteen minutes, while Judge Marcus Beck's speech in 1928 ran some 6,750 words and took ninety minutes to deliver.

stamp on a barn door," but no one at the time realized how prophetic those words would be.[24] The finished carving did look like a postage stamp, not because of its relative size to the mountain, but because the Postal Service created a stamp of the carving.

The idea arose when Fred E. Richards, of the Warner Robins Stamp Club, suggested using the Stone Mountain carving as the central feature of the Warner Robins Philatelic Exhibit (WARPEX) in October 1966, which was to include a display of Confederate stamps. Afterward, he contacted the Memorial Association about having the carving design placed on a stamp. Association Chairman Phil Campbell assisted the Warner Robins Stamp Club in enlisting the support of various government officials.

Postmaster General Winton Blount, an Alabama native, received the idea favorably and sent a copy of the rules for issuance of stamps and criteria used by the Citizen's Stamp Advisory Committee to select designs. Ben Blackburn introduced House Joint Resolution 623 requesting Blount to issue a stamp commemorating the Confederate Memorial carving. The Resolution was adopted by the House on 15 January 1968 and in the Senate on 19 January. Two months later the Citizen's Stamp Advisory Committee considered the proposed design and gave its approval.

General Manager Tom Elliott wanted to tie the release of the stamp to the dedication of the carving, but printing delays made this impossible, making it necessary to postpone the First Day Issue ceremony until 19 September 1970. The six-cent stamp was printed in gray with an initial issue of 32,675,000 stamps. The Stone Mountain Post Office established a special branch on top of the mountain for the day to give the first day issue cancellation.

Even though the carving was essentially finished, Roy Faulkner's work on the mountain was not yet done. Hancock suggested a few last details to be corrected and the background still needed to be finished. To prevent disfiguring streaks on the figures by weathering and the growth of lichens, the carving was then coated with a clear, silicone-based water repellant developed by Union Carbide. Governor Jimmy Carter mounted the high scaffolding in early 1971 to ceremoniously apply the first brush strokes of repellant. Faulkner and his crew brushed on several layers over the next six months, allowing time for one layer sufficiently to dry before adding another.

---

[24]Gerald W. Johnson, *The Undefeated* (New York: Minton, Balch, and Company, 1927), 24.

Once this was completed, the workers had the delicate task of removing the tons of scaffolding, rigging, steel beams, stairs, and elevator equipment accumulated over half a century. During this phase of the work tragedy struck again when another worker, Nelson Wilborn, was killed in a fall from the mountain in 1971 during disassembly of the shack. The final support beams were cut early the next year, giving the public its first uncluttered view of the mountain in fifty-six years.

The Confederate Memorial envisioned by the Association was not finished with the completion of the carving. The second half of the plan called for Walker Hancock to create an original composition at the base of the mountain. Working with the landscaping architects of Griswold, Winters & Swain from Pennsylvania, Hancock designed a memorial plaza that he believed would accentuate the carving as the focal point of the whole memorial.

Hancock's concept called for a broad lawn extending from Memorial Hall sloping downward toward a reflecting pool at the base of the mountain. The pool, which would reflect the giant equestrian carving, was to be flanked by two eighty-foot-high aluminum towers representing the military and civilians of the Confederacy. The cylindrical towers would be of open lattice-like construction that would become increasing lighter toward the top. They would be illuminated from the interior and reflect light onto the carving. Niches at the base of each tower would contain life-size statues representing the ideals of the Confederacy.

The towers would stand on circular bases thirty feet high and 130 feet in diameter connected by a bridge over the water. Visitors would be able to walk up the spiraling ramp to the top of the pedestals and across the bridge to view the reflection of the carving.

The plan also called for walkways extending down both sides of the lawn with thirteen viewing terraces along the walks representing each state of the Confederacy. At the entrance to each terrace the plan called for a large granite paving stone engraved with the outline of the state represented along with the dates of secession and readmission to the Union. A low rock wall would surround each terrace and trees, shrubs, and flowers would beautify the walk.

The Association accepted the proposed design in 1967 and set aside $3.5 million of its bond issue that year to pay for the Memorial Plaza. Hancock said the function of the towers was to provide a visual frame for the carving to keep it from being dwarfed by the bulk of the mountain, and to give greatly needed light for an effective sculptural relief. On a loftier level, the towers would raise the concept of the memorial above the level of simple historic portraiture to one of patriotic inspiration. They symbolized, he explained, "the Light of Confederate Idealism." Opponents, however, thought it represented bad taste.

In announcing the proposed design the Association immediately drew criticism from the Georgia Art Commission, the Georgia chapters of the American Institute of Architects, the American Association of Landscape Architects, and art critics from the High Museum. They believed the design would detract from the carving, would be overwhelmed by the mountain and that it was much too busy. They asked the Association not to accept the design, and when it did they asked the governor to intervene.

The President of the American Institute of Architects requested that Governor Lester Maddox censure the Association for ignoring the Georgia Arts Commission's request to be further heard prior to the awarding of $3.3 million contract for the memorial area, and for approving a plan that, in the opinion of design professional, would detract from the awe-inspiring quality of the mountain. It was unconscionable, he wrote, that the Stone Mountain Memorial Association would so "blatantly disregard professional opinion."[25]

The Association intended to go forward with its plans regardless of such discontent, but in 1970 the park made a discovery that scrapped most of Hancock's design. Everyone had assumed that the side of the mountain came straight down into the ground, but as the prison workers began removing the pile of rubble accumulated from the three carving attempts they found a uncovered a large hill of ancient gneiss (metamorphic rock) protruding from the base of the mountain.

As a result of this unexpected obstacle, Hancock was forced to reconsider his concept. The reflecting pool could be moved further away from the mountain, but the bridge had to be eliminated because moving it would cause it to cut across the reflection of the carving. After examining different options he abandoned the whole tower idea and brought everything down to ground level.

Instead of two towers, he designed two plaza areas, each featuring a bronze statue and linked in front of the two-acre pond by a pathway rather than a bridge. Like the towers, the two statues represented the military and the other the civilian side of the Confederacy. The statue *Valor* depicted a

---

[25]James Hunt, President American Institute of Architects to Governor Lester Maddox, 17 January 1969. Files of the SMMA.

suffering soldier holding aloft a broken sword, and the statue *Sacrifice* portrayed a woman carrying a child on her shoulder. Set around the edge of the circular plaza areas would be fourteen quotes from various American leaders exemplifying the ideals represented by the sculptures.

Hancock modeled the dress of the bronze figures in a very generalized and simplistic fashion. He explained that this work, which aimed to symbolize abstract ideas, should avoid the effect of costumed period pieces. Fixing the figures in a specific time and place, he explained, "would reduce their universal significance and interfere with the allegorical expression of the themes."[26]

Eliminating the towers and bridge lowered the cost of the memorial area to $1.1 million. The Association accepted the new design and work commenced in 1972. This part of the work was conducted first, since the plans for the sixteen-acre lawn and the thirteen state viewing terraces remained unchanged from the original design. Work continued for the next five years on grading and painstakingly reshaping and landscaping the terrain in front of the carving. Most of the work was done by park employees and inmates of the Stone Mountain prison branch.

Walker Hancock sent his two completed full-size models of *Valor* and *Sacrifice* to the Modern Art Foundry of New York City for casting and installed the finished statues at the park in November 1977. *Valor* measures seventeen feet tall and stands on a five-and-a-half-foot high base of pink granite. Carved in the base are the words, "Men who saw the night coming down upon them somehow acted as if they stood at the edge of dawn." This is attributed to a Confederate soldier just before his death. The statue of *Sacrifice* stands fourteen feet high, or over nineteen feet on its granite pedestal. Inscribed in the base is the phrase, "The country come before me," uttered by the wife of General P. G. T. Beauregard.

The park dedicated the completed plaza on 23 April 1978. There were actually two ceremonies on that day. The first was a special Confederate Memorial Day observance organized by the local chapter of the UDC to honor the Confederate dead. Following this was the plaza dedication ceremony with Secretary of State Ben Fortson and Governor George Busbee as speakers. Other guests of honor included Senator Herman Talmadge and former governors Ellis Arnall, Marvin Griffin, Ernest Vandiver, and Lester Maddox.

---

[26]Walker Hancock to Ben Fortson, 21 March 1970. Files of SMMA.

Compared to the dedication of the Confederate Memorial, the one for the plaza was largely ignored. Most people viewed the plaza as a nicely-appointed but ultimately unnecessary expenditure. Nevertheless, the massive undertaking to create a memorial to the Confederacy was finally finished twenty years after Ben Fortson's monument committee took up the task.

Chapter Eight

A Park for All Seasons

Since its founding in 1958 Stone Mountain Park has been many things to many people. Through the park the visitor can learn about and enjoy the varied forms of nature that appear there, from the tiny fairy shrimp that reside in the rain pits on top of the mountain to the rare Georgia Oak, which grows only on granite outcroppings. Thirty species of plants are listed as rare, and many others are so uncommon as to be known to only a few knowledgeable visitors.

The bounty of the mountain's surroundings have been remarked upon as early as 1854 when an English woman named Mrs. Murry visited there. In describing the wonders to those back home she wrote that "certainly I would have walked barefoot through the water rather than to have missed the scene. In my opinion, the Stone Mountain of Georgia is a greater marvel of nature than the caves of Kentucky."[1] Botanists from many of the universities in the region have utilized the mountain as a special laboratory for over a century, and in 1961 the park took on a full-time professional to study and safeguard the mountain's natural treasures.

For the historically-minded, the park attempts to interpret the mountain's historical context. The recreated plantation and the extensive museum in Memorial Hall describe many aspects of the mountain's past. The mountain serves as a place for social events throughout the year, as well as a venue for simple relaxation. For some, it has even been a site for spiritual enlightenment. Throughout its history, the park has continued to expand its offerings and to grow in popularity with the public. Only the Disney theme parks in Orlando, Florida, attract more people each year.

Over the years a number of unusual and noteworthy events have occurred there. For instance, on 14 December 1970, as part of the Park's holiday celebration, Metropolitan Opera star Blanche Thebom sang *Silent Night* from a stage mounted above the carving after lighting a giant wreath

---

[1] *DeKalb New Era*, 28 May 1925. Clipping in the Stone Mountain Collection of the DeKalb Historical Society, Decatur, Georgia.

on the face of the mountain. This was certainly the most unusual performance ever given at the mountain and the only time it has been ever done.

On 18 October 1974, astronaut John Young came to Stone Mountain to unveil a special moon rock on temporary display at Memorial Hall. This four and a half ounce specimen of breccia rock was collected by the crew of Apollo 16, of which Young was the commander, from a hilly area in the moon's Descartes Region they dubbed Stone Mountain. Young said he knew about Georgia's Stone Mountain from his student days at Georgia Tech and the name seemed appropriate. In recognition of Young's visit, Governor Jimmy Carter declared 18 October 1974, as John Young Day in Georgia. The rock sample was later transferred to Warner Robbins Air Force Base near Macon, Georgia, for permanent display.

In addition to an astronaut or two and the occasional governor, Stone Mountain Park has hosted several heads of state, including the Crown Prince of Denmark, the Queen of Norway and, of course, President Jimmy Carter, as well as other dignitaries.

Thus far the park has had six General Managers. Scott Candler and General Harold Maddux oversaw the building of the park, and the carving was finished under Tom Elliott. Elliott was a member of the Georgia Tech faculty who had been lent by that institution to the Memorial Association as a consulting engineer. He was appointed General Manager in 1968, but was still on a loan basis. Georgia Tech paid his salary, for which it was reimbursed by the Association.

In 1975 George Willis became the new General Manager. During his administration, there was a greater emphasis on recreation with the addition of a water slide at the beach and the opening of a sports complex with miniature golf, tennis courts, a roller skating trail, and an ice chalet. The last two attractions did not prove very successful. Trail Skate operated for about four years and was moderately popular, but the park eventually was forced to close it because of the high injury rate. The ice skating chalet was planned and built during Willis' administration, but opened under his successor. It remained open for ten years but was never heavily used and finally closed in 1994.

These new attractions were operated by the park itself, not by concessionaires. After nearly twenty years, the Association concluded that private ownership of the attractions was not in the park's best financial interest. In 1977 the Association bought out the contracts for the concessions held by D. C. Land, the original owner of the skylift concession.

Over the years, however, he had acquired the concessions for operation of the plantation, the inn, the restaurants, and the gift shops.

When Ham McAfee's concession for the scenic railroad expired in 1981 the Association declined to renew it and paid him $900,000 for the railroad cars and other equipment. Art Rilling's concession for a petting zoo ran out three years later and he was likewise refused a renewal. The park hired animal expert Jim Fowler of *Mutual of Omaha's Wild Kingdom* fame, to design the Animal Forest now operated by the park. Tommy Protsman, with the antique auto and music museum, was the only concessionaire allowed to remain.

Larry Allen succeeded George Willis as General Manager in October, 1983. Having previously served as the administrator of the Six Flags Over Georgia theme park, his hiring indicated a conscious decision by the Association that Stone Mountain Park needed the leadership of someone with amusement park experience. Allen brought in others with similar backgrounds to fill key positions.

Soon after Allen's arrival the park began an improvement campaign to upgrade and renovate many of the facilities that had been allowed to deteriorate. Allen had a sidewalk put in along Robert E. Lee Boulevard to accommodate pedestrian traffic and ordered repairs to the Stone Mountain Inn, skylift, railroad, the Top of the Mountain building, and others. In 1987 the wooden train depot was replaced by a larger brick structure modeled after the 1854 Atlanta depot destroyed by Sherman's troops. Allen also initiated a beautification program to plant thousands of dogwood trees and azalea bushes around the park.

To draw more visitors without the expense of adding new attractions, Allen began promoting more festivals and other special events. The park had long been home to the Yellow Daisy Festival,[2] the Highland Games, the DeKalb Sheriff's Posse Rodeo and the Arabian Horse Show, and the Easter Sunrise Services, and Fourth of July fireworks shows were already established traditions. During Allen's administration the number of events multiplied to include Springfest, the Antebellum Jubilee, the Great Miller Lite Chili Cookoff, the South's Largest Garage Sale, the Chicken Wing Fling

[2]This is the park's oldest event. It had its origin from a Decatur Garden Club picnic in 1960 when the Confederate Yellow Daisies were in bloom. Originally conceived as a flower show, it has evolved into one of the largest craft shows in the country. The flower for which the event is named is quite rare, growing only on a few granite outcropping in Georgia. It had no common name until the local residents dubbed it the Confederate Daisy.

Cookoff, A Tour of Southern Ghosts, Taste of the South, Alpenfest, and the Winter Golf Classic, among others. These events have helped boost attendance and revenues, while corporate sponsorships for the events have kept the park's expenses to a minimum.

By far the most popular event at the park is the laser show that plays each night during the summer. First shown in 1982 on a two-week trial basis, it was so well-attended by the public the park added the laser show to the regular schedule the following year. Crowds of 200,000 or more come to see the brilliant multi-colored laser beams projected onto the steep face of the mountain, a natural one-million-square-foot screen, to create dynamic graphic designs and animated stories accompanied by popular music.

The New Georgia Railroad came to the park in 1988 to bring sightseers from downtown Atlanta to Stone Mountain. The train passengers rode in refurbished dining cars out to the park and around the mountain, where they had the option of getting off before the train returned to Atlanta. The park cooperated in the construction of a connecting track between the Georgia Railroad line and the park's scenic railroad. The New Georgia Railroad excursions began running in June 1988, just in time for the Democratic National Convention held in Atlanta that year. Ridership, however, never met the initial expectations and the railroad ceased operation in 1992.

Under Larry Allen's leadership, the park ventured into a new era of endeavor--hosting corporate conferences. The natural beauty of the surroundings and the amenities available at the park made it an ideal place for such events. These functions needed a special facility, of course, and in 1989, after several years of planning and a bond issue of $23 million to pay for it, the Evergreen Conference Center opened on the east shore of Stone Mountain lake. With 250 hotel rooms, nineteen meeting halls, a ballroom, an auditorium, and an exhibit hall, the Evergreen has proven to be a major success and remains booked year-round. The income generated here helps offset costs throughout the park.

At the same time the Evergreen was built, the park expanded the nationally ranked golf course to its present thirty-six holes. A new golf club and pro shop, The Commons, opened in 1994.

These new facilities, although financially favorable for the park, drew a great deal of criticism. The Friends of Stone Mountain, a watchdog group concerned with environmental issues at the mountain, and others decried the over-development of the park and the despoiling of its natural surroundings. Of course, this was not the first time such charges had been leveled against the park administration. Some group or another always seems to be displeased with how the park is managed.

The immense popularity of the park is, in fact, a double-edged sword. The approximately five million visitors each year keep the park financially healthy, but the heavy foot and auto traffic and the tons of litter left behind take their toll on the surroundings. Reconciling the conservation of a great natural asset with abundant human use and balancing the diverse interests of park users--history, recreation and nature--while keeping the operation in the black is a tremendous challenge for the Association. Some critics claim that the park has lost its focus as a Confederate Memorial and others say it needs to broaden its appeal beyond the Confederacy and the management is often caught in the middle of these divergent opinions.

These and other concerns led to the development in the early 1990s of a comprehensive master plan to guide the future development of the park through 2010. Working with Robert and Company, the original designers of the park, the management put together a phased program of facilities improvements and habitat conservation.

The master plan called for dividing the park into four districts: the natural district, the historic district, the recreation district, and the events district. The natural district, comprising sixty-five percent of the park, was designated as a wilderness area and marked off-limits for development. The historic district comprises the center of the park and includes the Memorial area, plantation, railroad, grist mill, and most of the other attractions. The recreational district, located in the eastern third of the park, comprises the golf course, camping area, tennis facility, beach and other leisure activities. The events district, at the north end of the park, provides permanent facilities and plenty of room for the many special events held at the park during the year. A third gate from Hugh Howell Road leading directly into the events area was designed to ease the traffic burden on the other two gates during these events.

The most controversial part of the master plan was the proposal to build an incline railway up the west side of the mountain to eliminate the need for the skylift and thereby get rid of the visual clutter created by the cables and cars. The Friends of Stone Mountain, a group concerned with environmental issues at the mountain, vehemently opposed this suggestion because of the irreparable damage that building an incline railroad would do to the mountain. In the face of very vocal public opposition, the park dropped the railroad from the master plan and decided to build a new skylift with a greater capacity.

The creation of the long-range plan was spurred on by the awarding of the 1996 Summer Olympics to Atlanta and the selection of Stone Mountain Park as one of the sports venues. The need to get the park ready added additional motivation to implement the plan. Projects were identified as Phase One, to be completed before the Olympics, or Phase Two, to be done afterward. The expansion of Memorial Hall to house a comprehensive museum of the area's history, the new skylift, the replacement of the Top of the Mountain building with a smaller structure, construction of a north gate into the park, and road resurfacing were all given Phase One priority. Plans for a new inn, a re-creation of a nineteenth-century Southern town, a working farm, and an expansion of the Evergreen Conference Center received Phase Two status.

The only special construction at the park for the Olympics was the facilities necessary for the events, which included a 12,000-seat tennis arena in the recreation district, a cycling velodrome, and an archery field, the latter two to be removed after the Olympics.

In July 1994 the Memorial Association named Curtis Branscome as the new General Manager to replace Larry Allen, who had resigned two months earlier. Branscome was for twenty years the city manager of Decatur, Georgia, and later was the Executive Assistant to DeKalb County Chief Executive Officer Liane Levetan. Under his administration, work began on the projects called for in the master plan.

During the centennial Olympic Games in July 1996 the Stone Mountain Park venues provided the stage for two Olympic firsts. The U. S. archery team won its first gold medal and the tennis stadium hosted the first professional players allowed to compete in this event. Tennis star André Aggassi won a gold medal for the United States.

As the park faces the challenges of the twenty-first century, more disagreements over its direction are sure to arise. Gutzon Borglum reportedly said long ago that Stone Mountain was too great for human beings to meddle with. Of course he and those who followed were unable to resist meddling with it anyway. With such a precious asset as Georgia has in the mountain, differences of opinion over how it should be managed will be inevitable. Despite all the furor surrounding it through the years, Stone Mountain has taken its place before the nation and the world as a one-of-a-kind masterpiece of art and nature.

BIBLIOGRAPHY

ARCHIVAL MATERIALS

Bond, J. B. *Lithonia and Environs.* Undated manuscript at the DeKalb Historical Society, Decatur, Georgia.

Borglum, Gutzon. Personal Papers, Robert W. Woodruff Library, Emory University, Atlanta, Georgia.

DeKalb Historical Society. *Collections of the DeKalb Historical Society.* Decatur, GA: DeKalb Historical Society, 1952.

Brewster, Gaines. "Rocks to Riches or How Granite Has Benefited DeKalb." Paper presented at the DeKalb Historical Society, Decatur, Georgia, 28 February 1974.

Candler, Charles Murphey. Address At the DeKalb County Centennial Celebration, 9 November 1922, DeKalb Historical Society, Decatur, Georgia.

Georgia Historical Society. *Letters of Benjamin Hawkins 1796-1806.* Spartanburg, SC: The Reprint Company, 1982.

Hanleiter, Cornelius R. Personal Papers. Stone Mountain Collection, Atlanta Historical Society, Atlanta, Georgia.

Harris, Julian. Personal Papers, Julian Harris Collection. Price Gilbert Memorial Library, Georgia Institute of Technology, Atlanta, Georgia.

Minutes and Records of the Stone Mountain Confederate Monumental Association, 1916-1929, Robert W. Woodruff Library, Emory University, Atlanta, Georgia.

Minutes and Records of the Stone Mountain Memorial Association, 1958-1978, Stone Mountain Park.

Minutes of the United Daughters of the Confederacy, Georgia Division, 1914-1919.

Plane, C. Helen. Personal Papers. Robert W. Woodruff Library, Emory University, Atlanta, Georgia.

Plats of Stone Mountain Properties. Report by Patterson and Dewar Engineers, 1958. Files of Stone Mountain Park.

Raffalovich, George. "Stone Mountain Memorial Controversy." Manuscript in the Stone Mountain Collection, Atlanta History Center, Atlanta, Georgia, 1938.

Venable, Samuel. Personal Papers, Robert W. Woodruff Library, Emory University, Atlanta, Georgia.

Willard, Levi. "Early History of Decatur." Manuscript at the DeKalb Historical Society, Decatur, Georgia, 1879.

Winter, Mary Carter. Personal Papers, Georgia Department of Archives and History.

LEGAL DOCUMENTS

DeKalb County Grand Jury Presentments, March Term, 1963.

DeKalb County Land Records. Various deed books, DeKalb County Courthouse.

Joint Report of the Georgia State Senate and House Investigating Committees, 1964.

U. S. Bureau of the Census. *Agricultural Schedules,. DeKalb County, Georgia*, prepared by the Geography Division in cooperation with the Housing Division, Bureau of the Census, Washington, DC., 1850, 1860, and 1870.

U. S. Bureau of the Census. *Population Schedules,. DeKalb County, Georgia*, prepared by the Geography Division in cooperation with the Housing Division, Bureau of the Census, Washington, DC., 1830, 1840, 1850, 1860, and 1870.

U. S. Bureau of the Census. *Slave Schedules,. DeKalb County, Georgia*, prepared by the Geography Division in cooperation with the Housing Division, Bureau of the Census, Washington, DC., 1860.

BOOKS

Anonymous. *Custodians of Imperishable Glory*. Atlanta: Stone Mountain Confederate Monumental Association, 1925.

Anonymous. *Pioneer Citizens' History of Atlanta 1833-1902*. Atlanta: The Pioneer Citizens of Atlanta, 1902.

Bonner, James C. *A History of Georgia Agriculture 1732-1860*. Athens: University of Georgia Press, 1964.

Borglum, Mary and Casey, Robert. *Give The Man Room: The Story of Gutzon Borglum*. New York: Bobbs-Merrill Company, 1952.

Caughey, John Walton. *McGillivray of the Creeks*. Norman: University of Oklahoma Press, 1938.

Chalmers, David M. *Hooded Americanism: The History of the Ku Klux Klan*. New York: New Viewpoints, 1976.

Coleman, Kenneth. *The American Revolution in Georgia 1763-1789*. Athens: University of Georgia Press, 1958.

Coulter, E. Merton. *Georgia: A Short History*. 3rd edition. Chapel Hill: University of North Carolina Press, 1960.

Davies, A. Mervyn. *Solon Borglum: A Man Who Stands Alone*. Chester, Connecticut: Pequot Press, 1974.

Dickens, Roy S. *Cherokee Prehistory*. Knoxville: University of Tennessee Press, 1976.

Eldridge, Leila Venable Mason. *Stone Mountain*. Atlanta: Atlanta and DeKalb County Historical Societies, 1951.

Evans, Clement Anselm, ed. *Confederate Military History*. Atlanta: Confederate Publishing Company, 1899.

Felton, Rebecca Latimer. *Country Life In Georgia In the Days of My Youth*. Atlanta: Index Printing Company, 1919.

Flanders, Ralph. *Plantation Slavery In Georgia*. Cos Cob, CT: John E. Edwards Publishing, 1967.

Ford, Elizabeth Austin. *Stone Mountain*. Decatur, GA: Wommack Printing, 1959.

Garrett, Franklin M. *Atlanta and Environs*. 2 vols. New York: Lewis Historical Publishing Company, 1954.

Gay, Mary A. H. *Life In Dixie During the War*. Atlanta: *Atlanta Constitution* Job Office, 1892. Reprinted by DeKalb Historical Society, 1979.

Goulding, Rev. R. F. *Sal-O-Quah; or Boy-Life Among the Cherokees*. New York: Dodd, Mead & Co., 1870.

Harris, Neil. *Humbug: The Art of P.T. Barnum*. Boston: Little, Brown & Co., 1973.

Herrmann, Leo Anthony. *Geology of the Stone Mountain-Lithonia District*, Georgia State Division of Conservation, Department of Mines, Mining & Geology, 1954.

Hill, Mrs. J. F. *The History of Stone Mountain*. Np., 1916.

Hitchcock, Major Henry. *Marching With Sherman Through Georgia*. New Haven, CT: Yale University Press, 1927.

Hopson, C. A. "Exfoliation and Weathering At Stone Mountain," *Georgia Mineral Newsletter*, Georgia Geological Survey 11 (1958), 65-79.

Hudson, Charles. *The Southeastern Indians.* Knoxville: University of Tennessee Press, 1976.

Hudson, Charles. *The Juan Pardo Expeditions.* Washington, DC: Smithsonian Institution Press, 1990.

Hyder, William, and Colbert, R. W. "The Selling of the Stone Mountain Half Dollar, *The Numismatist.* Np., n.d. [Reprint edition in the Stone Mountain Collection, Atlanta Historical Center, Atlanta, Georgia.]

Johnson, Gerald W. *The Undefeated.* New York: Minton, Balch, and Company, 1927.

Kenimer, Harkness. *The History of Stone Mountain.* Atlanta: Kenimer Publishing Company, 1994.

Knight, Lucian Lamar. *Georgia's Landmarks, Memorials and Legends.* Vol. 2. Atlanta: Byrd Printing Company, 1916.

Lewis, David W. *Transactions of the Southern Central Agricultural Society, 1846-1851.* Macon: Np., 1852.

Lucas, Rev. Silas E. *The Fourth Land Lottery.* Easley, SC: Southern Historical Press, 1986.

Martin, Joel W. *Sacred Revolt: The Muskogees' Struggle for a New World.* Boston: Beacon Press, 1991.

Mixon, Kaye. *The Mountain of Controversy.* Stone Mountain, GA: Np., 1970.

Maynard, Poole, *How Stone Mountain Was Created*, Baltimore: Waverly Press, 1929.

Miles, Jim. *To The Sea.* Nashville: Rutledge Hill Press, 1989.

McMurray, Richard. "Early History of DeKalb County," *Georgia Magazine* 5 (August-September 1961), 18-22.

Neal, Willard. *Georgia's Stone Mountain.* Stone Mountain, GA: Stone Mountain Memorial Association, 1970.

Neal, Willard. *The Story of Stone Mountain.* Atlanta: American Lithograph Company, 1963.

New South Associates. *Historic Sites Survey, City of Stone Mountain.* Stone Mountain, GA: New South Associates, 1994.

Nichols, George Ward. *Story of the Great March.* New York: Harper & Brothers, 1865.

Patton, Kathryn. *The Story of A Village Church.* Stone Mountain, GA: First Baptist Church of Stone Mountain, 1989.

Patton, Kathryn. *A Sketchbook of Stone Mountain.* Stone Mountain, GA: Sue Kellogg Library, n.d.

Range, Willard. *A Century of Georgia Agriculture 1850-1950.* Athens: University of Georgia Press, 1954.

Rutherford, Mildred Lewis. *The History of the Stone Mountain Memorial.* Athens: Georgia Division, United Daughters of the Confederacy, 1923.

Rutherford, Mildred Lewis. *Miss Rutherford's Scrap Book.* Vol. 2. Athens: Georgia Division, United Daughters of the Confederacy, October 1924.

Schemmel, William. "Will Success Spoil Stone Mountain?" *Atlanta Magazine* (April 1970), 61-76.

Shaff, Howard and Audrey. *Six Wars At A Time: The Life and Times of Gutzon Borglum.* Sioux Falls, SD: Augustana College Center for Western Studies, 1985.

Shelton, Morris. *Georgia's Piece of the Rock.* Np., 1981.

Sholes, A. E. & Company, *Sholes Georgia State Gazetteer, 1879-80.* Atlanta: A. E. Sholes & Company, 1879.

Sherman, William T. *Memoirs of General William T. Sherman.* New York: Charles L. Webster & Co., 1891.

Sherwood, Adiel. *Gazetteer of Georgia, 1827.* Macon: S. Boykin, Griffin, Brawner, and Putnam, 1827. [Reprint: Atlanta: Cherokee Publishing Company, 1970.]

Sherwood, Adiel. *Gazetteer of Georgia, 1829.* Macon: S. Boykin, Griffin, Brawner, and Putnam, 1829. [Reprint: Atlanta: Cherokee Publishing Company, 1970.]

Sherwood, Adiel. *Gazetteer of Georgia, 1860.* Macon: S. Boykin, Griffin, Brawner, and Putnam, 1860. [Reprint: Atlanta: Cherokee Publishing Company, 1970.]

Smith, Marvin. *Archaeology of Aboriginal Culture Change in the Interior Southeast.* Gainesville: University of Florida Press, 1987.

Standard Directory Company. *Georgia Gazetteer, 1881.* Savannah: Savannah *Morning News,* 1881.

Standard Directory Company. *Georgia Gazetteer, 1886.* Savannah: Savannah *Morning News,* 1886.

Stiggins, George. *Creek Indian History.* Birmingham: Birmingham Library Press, 1989.

Vlach, John Michael. *Back of the Big House.* Chapel Hill: University of North Carolina Press, 1993.

Wilkes, Colonel Sam W. "The Georgia Railroad," *The City Builder* 10 (September 1926), 22-23.

Williams, Mark and Shapiro, Gary, eds. *Lamar Archaeology: Mississippian Chiefdoms in the Deep South.* Tuscaloosa: University of Alabama Press, 1990.

ARTICLES

Baker, Dr. W. B. "Some Interesting Plants on the Granite Outcrops of Georgia," *Georgia Mineral Newsletter* 9 (Spring 1956), 10-19

Brewster, Gaines. "Rocks to Riches or How Granite Has Benefited DeKalb." Paper presented at the DeKalb Historical Society, Decatur, Georgia, 28 February 1974.

Dickens, Roy S. "The Stone Mountain Salvage Project," *Journal of Alabama Archaeology* 11 (December 1965), 123-132.

Garrett, Franklin M. "The Early Days of Stone Mountain," *Georgia Magazine* (April-May 1970), 14-17.

Lewis, Ann E. "Have You Seen The Models?" *Georgia Magazine* 6 (December 1962-January 1963), 28-29.

Lewis, Robert. "Old Hickory Burned Trail Through Area, Too," *Lithonia Observer*, 12 July 1979.

Logue, John. "The Old Man And the Mountain," *Southern Living* 5 (May 1970), 70-73.

Mack, Elizabeth and Bradford, Robert. "The Stone Mountain Story," *Atlantan Magazine* 1 (April 1958), 7-10.

Worth, John E. "Late Spanish Military Expeditions in the Interior Southeast 1597-1628," in *The Forgotton Centuries: Indians and Europeans in the American South 1521-1704*. Edited by Charles Hudson and Carmen Tesser. Athens: University of Georgia Press, 1992.

Worth, John E. "Prelude to Abandonment: The Interior Provinces of Early Seventeenth-Century Georgia," *Early Georgia* 21 (1993), 25-58.

NEWSPAPERS

Atlanta Constitution.

Atlanta Journal.

DeKalb New Era.

Index

www.ingramcontent.com/pod-product-compliance
Lightning Source LLC
LaVergne TN
LVHW101321110826
845152LV00011B/24

* 9 7 8 0 8 6 5 5 4 5 4 7 2 *